Second Nature

Second Nature

Rethinking the Natural through Politics

Edited by

Crina Archer, Laura Ephraim,
and Lida Maxwell

FORDHAM UNIVERSITY PRESS
New York 2013

Ayten Gündoğdo's chapter was originally published in *Contemporary Political Theory* as "Potentialities of Human Rights: Agamben and the Narrative of Fated Necessity," Volume 11, Number 1, February 2012, pp. 2–22(21). Reproduced with permission of Palgrave Macmillan.

Library of Congress Cataloging-in-Publication Data

Second nature : rethinking the natural through politics / edited by Crina Archer, Laura Ephraim, and Lida Maxwell.
pages cm
Summary: "This volume examines the nature/politics relationship anew in the wake of recent critiques of the category of "nature." Its essays draw on contemporary and canonical thinkers to reflect on "second nature" as a site or paradigm of political contest and intervene into debates about environmentalism, human rights, and more"— Provided by publisher.
Includes bibliographical references and index.
ISBN 978-0-8232-5141-4 (hardback) —
ISBN 978-0-8232-5142-1 (paper)
1. Human ecology—Political aspects. 2. Nature—Political aspects. 3. Human ecology—Philosophy. 4. Environmentalism—Philosophy. 5. Philosophy of nature. I. Archer, Crina.
GF21.S4 2013
304.2—dc23
2012048070

Printed in the United States of America
15 14 13 5 4 3 2 1
First edition

CONTENTS

ACKNOWLEDGMENTS

This book has its origins in a graduate student conference and speaker series on "Second Nature: Rethinking the Natural through Politics," at Northwestern University in 2006–2007. Thanks to Soulymane Bachir Diagne, Peter Fenves, Sara Monoson, Keith Topper, and Linda Zerilli for their participation in and support of the conference; to Michael Warner and Jane Bennett for delivering memorable keynote addresses and Peter Euben, Bruno Latour, and Thomas Laqueur for their preconference talks; to the (then) graduate students at Northwestern who helped organize the conference, especially John Ackerman, Ashleigh Campi, Ross Carroll, Demetra Kasimis, Angela Maione, Jake Matatyaou, Laura Reagan, Chris Skeaff, and Doug Thompson; and also to all of the (then) graduate students who participated in the conference: Kiran Banerjee, Ashley Biser, Christopher Buck, Anita Chari, Keridiana Chez, Cigdem Cidam, Arthur Craig, Shirin Deylami, Stefan Dolgert, Lorenzo Fabbri, Tim Fisken, Loren Goldman, Ayten Gündoğdu, Jack Jackson, Mujeeb Khan, Amanda Kirk, Hagar Kotef, Christopher Lauer, Jennifer Lin, Alex Livingston, Eli Meyerhoff, Yves Winter, Mabel Wong, and Rafi Youatt. The Graduate School at Northwestern and (then) Dean Andrew Wachtel provided generous financial support for the conference, as did numerous Northwestern departments, programs, and institutes. Simon Greenwold and Maggie Wildman of the Graduate School also provided important assistance and administrative support.

For their contributions to making the book a reality, we wish to thank the anonymous readers whose insights helped sharpen and clarify the essays in this volume. Thomas Lay and Helen Tartar of Fordham University Press were supportive and helpful throughout the review and publication process. Melissa Meyer provided valuable research assistance. Friese Undine generously allowed us to use his painting for the conference program, and he has long inspired our thinking about nature and politics through both his artwork (available for viewing at www.frieseundine.com) and his friendship. We extend our thanks to Jim Denevan for granting permission to use the striking photograph of his temporary sand art on this book's cover.

We owe a special debt of gratitude to Bonnie Honig. From the earliest stages of planning the conference to preparing the book for publication, Bonnie has lent her support, encouragement, and keen intellect to the project. Her commitment helped make the conference and book a reality and enriched our thinking about "second nature."

Finally, and most important, we thank our partners. Japonica Brown-Saracino, James Owens, and Nathan Shepard have not only supported us with their love and patience throughout this process. They have also read (many) drafts, offered thoughts, and helped shape our thinking. Our lives, and the book, are the better for it.

Introduction: Politics on the Terrain of Second Nature

Crina Archer, Laura Ephraim, and Lida Maxwell

The late twentieth century and early twenty-first century have seen a sea change in political theorists' understanding of "nature." While much prior Western political thought invoked "nature" as a normative standard or ground for affirming or criticizing political arrangements, political theorists today seldom assume that nature can or should dictate politics. Influenced by poststructuralist, deconstructionist, feminist, and queer theory, political theorists, like their colleagues in related disciplines in the humanities and social sciences, have increasingly come to scrutinize dimensions of politics that long seemed fixed or determined by nature. They began to "denaturalize" everything from justice to law to gender to nature itself, revealing their conventional, cultural, politically constructed grounds.[1] Though the presumption of politics' conventional character was anticipated by some earlier political thinkers (such as Montesquieu, Vico, and Hume), today's loose consensus on the conventional character of political norms and institutions among many (although not all) political theorists—from Richard Rorty to John Rawls to Wendy Brown—is remarkable.[2] It reflects widespread recognition in the field that past claims to the naturalness of particular political arrangements had oppressive political consequences—particularly for minorities—and hindered emancipatory movements. As Stephen White recently characterized this prevailing mood of contemporary political theorists, "the sense of living in *late* modernity implies a greater awareness of the conventionality of much of what has been taken for certain in the modern West."[3] Indeed, most political theorists now seek to orient politics upon the terrain of *second* nature—be it habits, conventions, constitutions, praxis, or artifice—and to rid political claims of their former reliance upon natural givens.

Yet if the need to relinquish essentialist conceptions of nature is increasingly self-evident among political theorists, it is also increasingly obvious that political theory must find new ways to conceptualize nature in order to respond to the most pressing issues of our era. Political theorists who woke from the dream that nature could give stable grounds to politics emerged into a world of hybridity. In this hybrid world, it is both increasingly difficult to distinguish nature from politics and decreasingly clear that the effort to distinguish them is worthwhile. This hybrid world is enveloped by a climate warmed by industrial carbon emissions and populated with beings engineered from genetic material and computer technology—beings that defy categorization as either artificial or wild, human or nonhuman, political or natural. Are these hybrids harbingers of, or threats to, a more just and sustainable world? How should political theorists respond to dilemmas arising from events that blur, at a practical level, the distinction between natural givens and political arrangements that the denaturalizing turn accomplished in political theory?[4] At the least, our enmeshment in a deeply hybrid world seems to call for us to question whether a theoretical sensibility oriented by the indeterminacy or undecidability between nature and politics has resources to guide us through the ethical and political thickets that arise every day from the hybridity of nature and politics.

This introduction and the essays in this volume aim to do precisely that—to ask how and whether the denaturalizing turn remains relevant and offers meaningful political guideposts for a world where the denaturalizing of nature often appears as a dilemma for politics. While the contributors come to a range of positions on this issue, we will suggest by way of introduction to the volume that it would be a mistake either to abandon as anachronistic the denaturalizing turn's critique of essentialism or to rest content with familiar denaturalizing strategies of invoking "second nature" as a conceptual wedge separating natural givens from political constructions. In our view, the experience of nature's hybridity and lack of fixity can itself inform and help extend the core insight of the denaturalizing turn, namely, that nature is not a stable ground for politics. Indeed, nature does not "fix" (remedy or hold in place) politics because nature is always already a hybrid formation constituted through struggles that include (but are not exhausted by) the struggles of human political actors to dominate or emancipate one another and the world's nonhuman things. We thus propose to repurpose "second nature" as a term of art to encompass the enactment and more or less stable outcomes of such struggles in tandem with the struggles of animals, plants, and protozoa to survive, of electrons to bond or break apart molecules, and of wind to erode mountains, to name a few. We suggest that to respond to the deepened experience of hybridity in our age, political theorists would do well to consider the extent to which nature and politics were always already hybrid, overlapping categories, mutually shaped through contests among diverse forces both human and nonhuman, governed and spontaneous, constructed and organic. This turn to second nature insists upon the relevance of nature to politics but equally insists that political contest is always already an ingredient in the composition of the various natures confronted in political life.

Our repurposing of "second nature" is not the only attempt to find new critical purchase on the normative, practical dilemmas of hybridity—such as climate change, biotechnology, genetically modified foods, and human-machine interfaces—in the wake of the denaturalizing turn. In the next section, we consider several similar literatures, with a special focus on green political theory, and discuss why we see the "second nature" approach as more promising. While green political theory, like the approach we are proposing, takes for granted certain aspects of the denaturalizing critique of essentialism, we argue that this literature is ultimately pulled into nostalgia for an ideal of nature sans humanity, purified of contaminating political effects. Next, we discuss our "second nature" approach in more detail—both the tradition of thought out of which we see it emerging and the theoretical contribution it makes—and examine how "second nature," as we understand it, might offer us new traction on political issues defined by the undecidability between nature and politics. Finally, we provide an overview of the essays in the volume.

Alternative Responses to Hybridity: The Limitations of Stewardship and Sovereignty

Faced with hybrid phenomena such as climate change, genetic engineering, and machine life, some liberal theorists have made thoughtful attempts to recover some point of stable purchase that nature might still give us in an otherwise denaturalized paradigm. For example, Martha Nussbaum's work attempts to safeguard rationality as a normative aspect of our human "nature," one that is given prior to cultural production and thus could provide an unyielding point of fixity for politics.[5] But the desire to protect nature from the vicissitudes of culture and politics is not limited to theorists working within the tradition of liberalism. Some of the most important appeals to a "pure" nature beyond politics are made by green political theorists. Granted, many in green theory would reject liberal efforts to shore up the naturalness of human rationality as a form of anthropocentrism that puts nonhuman nature at risk. In this sense, green political theory is very much a participant in the denaturalizing turn. Yet some green theorists, such as those who contributed to the volume *Reinventing Nature*, have argued that efforts to expose the political constructedness of the natural environment take denaturalization too far, impeding environmentalists' calls for practices to return nature to something closer to its "original," unpolluted state.[6] At a moment when human interventions into the natural environment threaten to destroy life—human and otherwise—on the planet, green political theory challenges us to attend to the costs of decades of critique of the category of "the natural." Do these critiques hinder efforts to protect nature from destruction? Has the denaturalizing turn, for all of its important challenges to the anthropocentrism of naturalizing human rationality, unwittingly deprived us of the conceptual tools needed to understand and halt the detrimental effects of our existing practices on the natural environment? Do efforts to undo essentialism deny us the normative ideal of natural purity that environmental politics requires? Here, we attend to the questions raised by green theorists because we see their nostalgia for nature's traditional figuration as an essentially fixed and prepolitical category as an understandable but ultimately unsatisfying attempt both to marshal and move beyond the denaturalizing turn in the face of resurgent and troubling forms of hybridity.

It would be an exaggeration to suggest that the denaturalizing turn has been a preoccupation of most green theorists as they explore the political conditions for returning nature to something closer to its "original," unpolluted state—the contributors to *Reinventing Nature* are, in this sense, exceptional. Indeed, rather than offering explicit arguments in favor of a view of nature as nonpolitical, green theorists more often take for granted nature's original or ideal separation from politics as an uninterrogated principle or starting point for arguments about how to preserve nature. As William Chaloupka notes in a recent review, green theorists depend upon a "naturalistic ethic that fit[s] comfortably with the natural sciences" rather than the *politics* of appeals to nature.[7] In other words, green theorists often uncritically accept the view of nature as an objective, given domain that is best understood by those who use scientific methods to inoculate themselves against political appeals. What drops out of such scientized views of nature is the notion that political contest and natural reality could be mutually constitutive. Indeed, despite limited efforts to question green theory's naturalism in the mid-1990s[8] and more recent works that posit democratic politics and "radical pluralism" as integral to a naturalistic politics,[9] questions about the naturalness of nature have not reemerged in green political theory in a meaningful way.[10] To the contrary, recent work in green theory continues to take the goal of preserving "nature" as an unproblematized starting point for various theoretical projects. For understandable reasons, it has seemed untenable to advocates of natural preservation to cast nature as a hybrid production of human and nonhuman activities. If the natural environment is always already a *second* nature, then it becomes far less clear when and whether the effects of politics, culture, or economy on nature count as destruction or contamination.

While green theorists for many years stood outside the mainstream of democratic theory, some democratic theorists have recently argued that green theory, including the view of nature it assumes and espouses, offers important resources for democratic politics. Indeed, with the gradual greening of democratic and republican political theory, thinkers increasingly invoke the ideal of good natural stewardship as a normative principle for politics writ large. For example, Richard Dagger views green theory's valorization of a nature protected from human interference as an invigorating premise for theorizing democracy and civic engagement more generally. In "Stopping Sprawl for the Good of All," he argues that protecting natural spaces from sprawl is important because it protects the integrity of civic (urban) spaces and natural spaces that allow citizens to live a full life: "nature and the city both have their charms, and a good life is one that enables us to enjoy and appreciate both."[11] For Dagger, by "protect[ing] the natural environment against the encroachment of cities," we may also "enhance the *civic* environment itself."[12] Similarly, Terence Ball argues that democratic politics would be enhanced by embracing the protection of nature's interests as a normative requirement for representative democracy:

> The interests of non-deliberating entities—future people, animals, ecosystems—require protection. How these interests are to be given voice and protected and by whom is a matter for debate, deliberation and reflection by those who are capable of doing so. Protecting and accommodating those interests along with our own is best accomplished

> by the kind of transgenerational and trans-species representative democracy that I call biocracy.[13]

Just as we represent "the interests of those who cannot speak or vote"—as with "minors, severely retarded adults and others"—so we should understand democratic politics as a kind of "stewardship" where we elect people to "reflect on and articulate nature's interests before larger legislative bodies."[14] For Ball, the ethos of protectionism and stewardship invigorates democracy because it reminds citizens and representatives of their *accountability* for the full gamut of resources and interests that their policies, laws, and actions should protect. It also reminds citizens, Ball suggests, of the expansive impulse of democracy—that it must expand "those whose interests are included and whose 'voices' are heard and heeded."[15] Ball's biocracy thus resonates with John Dryzek's call for an "ecological democracy," in which communicative rationality would be extended to nonhuman entities by developing the human capacity to listen to nature's demands.[16] Dryzek, Dagger, and Ball represent a new kind of normative turn to nature in political theory: unlike natural law theorists, who saw nature as a foundation to secure the political good, they see nature as a fragile ward whose protection betters or enlivens politics. Extending green theory's idealization of "pure" nature, they use this ideal as the basis for a new standard of stewardship for representative democracy: the good polity, they suggest, is one in which nature's interests are given voice and represented, securing both nature and politics against corruption.

As Ball's neologism "biocracy" indicates, the greening of political theory does embrace a particular kind of hybridity. Like Bruno Latour's call for a "new constitution," in which human and nonhuman "actants" (a term he means to be less anthropocentric than "actors") would be represented by spokespeople, Ball's biocracy pictures politics as a domain in which humans and nonhumans are spoken for and have their interests represented side by side.[17] Yet the hybridity embraced by the stewardship model of democracy is limited if it presumes and seeks to protect an idealized, unspoiled nature, as Latour would be the first to point out. On the one hand, to have its own distinctive voice or interests, nature must be conceived as originally or ideally distinct from human interests and voices. On the other hand, it is proposed that nature's voice will demand its own preservation from human interference, restoring that original, ideal distinction. For Ball and Dryzek, the point of having nature speak is to promote a politics of sustainability that would protect nature against the undue interference that existing representative democracies all too often permit or encourage.

In this sense, the inclusion of nature's voice within politics works to call deeper forms of hybridity—particularly, human agency within the constitution of nature—to a halt.

The task of representing the interests of nonhuman nature in the political domain is meant to offer a corrective to the anthropocentrism that has long characterized Western political thought's engagements with nature. Within this tradition, it is typically presumed that the interests of human communities are quite distinct from—even opposed to—the interests of nature (which is cast as little more than a "resource" for human enjoyment).[18] As Ball acknowledges, once we move past this anthropocentric assumption and embrace the need to represent nature's interests within politics, it remains far from clear how or by whom nature should be given voice. But it is clear enough that nature cannot speak for itself, so that the responsibility to represent nature in all its purity must be assumed by human, political actors. Thus, while the stewardship model of democracy seeks to alleviate dilemmas about how to address the abasement of nature by humanity, it also and at the same time heightens a set of familiar anxieties about how nature can be known and described in all its objective givenness—that is, anxieties about who or what can speak for nature. What representative institutions or practices could serve to let nature's voice be heard clearly, without adulteration or misrepresentation?

This is, of course, the role traditionally ascribed to natural science, when science is seen as a domain of objective, dispassionate knowledge production. That view of science has been challenged by numerous studies of scientists' embeddedness in the very sociopolitical contexts that the scientific method promises to help them transcend—including pathbreaking studies by Bruno Latour earlier in his career.[19] Yet in his most recent work, even Latour turns to scientists as the best qualified "spokespeople" for nonhuman things.[20] Drawing in part on Latour, the political theorist Mark Brown has recently made the case that advisory panels staffed with scientific experts fulfill many of the "modes" of representation familiar from political representation and should play a heightened role in contemporary representative democracies.[21] The call to include nature's voice in politics thus seems to lend support to calls to amplify the voices of some humans—scientific experts, who are seen even by nuanced thinkers of science like Latour and Brown as best qualified to represent nature—over others. In other words, the stewardship model of democracy, for all of its principled opposition to anthropocentrism and support for expanding the voices that are heard in politics, seems also to accord new political importance to a particular subset of human spokespeople who are credentialed to speak for nature—an impulse toward expanding the authority of experts that seems at odds with Ball's, Dagger's, and Dryzek's commitments to reinvigorating green democratic politics.

Green theorists—and the widening field of democratic theorists who embrace stewardship of nature as a normative principle for democracy—surely depict nature as a sphere whose integrity is violated by human incursions because they hope it will help rally political action on behalf of environmental protection. Such efforts to solicit a public concerned with rescuing nature from its own unruly clutches could indeed be democratizing in politics and protective of the environment in some instances. But what are the costs to such formulations of nature as a kind of "maiden in distress" (or "mother in distress")?[22] For instance, given the quickening pace of humanity's technological imbrications with biological processes, might a political call for humans to *disentangle* themselves from nature risk creating a fantasy of political agency as something that can and *must* be separate from the natural world in order for it to be truly "civic" (in Dagger's terms) or emancipatory? Green theorists intend their claim to a "pure" nature that must be protected from human intervention by speaking (or being spoken for) in politics as an acknowledgment that nature should be more than a mute object of human knowledge or enjoyment—the conceit of anthropocentrism. But even as they advance a politics that includes nature as a coherent, guiding voice within politics, they valorize nature only when it speaks of its own original purity. They ultimately portray proper politics as opposed to, rather than potentially or actually enabled by, the deep hybridity of nature, culture, and politics.

In our view, the very ends of green politics demand that we acknowledge this deep hybridity. For example, as we will discuss further below, if even our supposed remaining "wilderness" is itself already changed and managed by human "protection" of it, might continuing to claim that wilderness as "pure" blind us to the importance of the human regulations and actions necessary to maintain it as "wilderness"?[23] Further, by casting "nature" as an essential and given realm of nonhuman entities in need of protection against human intervention, do green democratic theorists inadvertently privilege a politics of *experts* speaking for nature? And might this actually push citizens *away* from understanding their mutual implications with nature? The alternative we are suggesting is to promote a *politics* of nature, in which citizens are encouraged to view themselves as inhabiting a hybrid politico-natural world and where their agency and lives are enabled *and* troubled by their complex entanglements with nature.

Of course, there is good reason to be concerned that relinquishing the ideal of a prepolitical, unspoiled nature is to embrace an "anything goes" posture toward any and all proposals to bend nature to our purposes. There are many such proposals that deserve critical scrutiny. Industrial capitalists continue to find it profitable to pollute air, water, and soil. And optimistic futurists, today as in the past, promise to remedy everything from injustice to mortality by using technology to master nature.

The bioethicist Ronald Green, for example, argues that "deliberative interventions in our own and our children's genetic makeup—to both prevent disease and enhance human life" also promise to "foster our dreams of a more just society."[24] If we make the correct choices about how to pursue "babies by design" (the title of Green's book), he suggests, then genetic modification can create a more equal humanity, rather than a dystopia like the one envisioned by Margaret Atwood in *Oryx and Crake.* Seemingly unconcerned with issues like climate change or pollution, Green envisions a progressive expansion of the human ability to control nature: "We will certainly try to bring our biology under our control *as we have done with so much of nature.*"[25] Where Green finds hope in biotechnology, Ray Kurzweil looks to computer technology to bring nature progressively under our control and solve both medical and social problems. He projects a future in which humans will use the information technologies of their own invention to overcome the weaknesses of "our version 1.0 biological bodies," which are "frail and subject to a myriad of failure modes." Computerized medicine and implanted brain augmentations "will allow us to transcend these limitations of our biological bodies and brains"—a progressive merger between man and machine that will culminate in the eventual and, for Kurzweil, inevitable dawn of "The Singularity," in which humans achieve the fantasy of immortality by downloading their consciousnesses.[26] When Green and Kurzweil look at nature, they see anarchy and unpredictability—points of blockage to human will—that must be brought under human control if we are to exercise true freedom, interact as equals, and live well (perhaps forever).

For those who are discomfited by such valorizations of human control of nature—and the notion of liberty as self-mastery that they seem to take for granted—a countervalorization of nature as an unspoiled domain free from human interference may seem indispensable. Yet a theoretical stance that remains open to the original and continual hybridity of nature and politics—what we are calling the "second nature" approach—contains powerful resources for critiquing troubling efforts to master nature with technology. From such a standpoint, Green and Kurzweil seem poised to violate not nature's purity but its hybridity: they would make human technological forces the lone source of rule, calling to a halt the *contest* among plural forces that mutually constitute nature and politics both—including the force exerted by genes and cells in forging humans as the mortal, fallible creatures that we are. The second nature approach redescribes the forces that Green and Kurzweil see as blockages to the pure expression of human will as forces that contingently enable human freedom and equality. As Hannah Arendt reminds us, the idea of freedom *qua* mastery offers an unrealistic understanding of human affairs by portraying other humans as impediments to our sovereignty over ourselves and our surroundings rather than as people whose association and action in concert *enables* freedom. The fantasy that "man" and not "men" inhabit the earth, Arendt suggests, leads to violence, not freedom—that is, the violence of subordinating or doing actual violence to those people or objects that stand in the way of your will.

Arendt herself tends to cast nature as a blockage to political action: as a force of necessity that is contrary to human freedom. But, by using Arendt against herself, we might understand the "blockages" nature poses to our will not as debilitating obstacles to freedom and equality but as important reminders of the limitations of any individual human being and thus of our dependence on others and our material environment for freedom and equality. Rather than approaching science as Green and Kurzweil do—as a way better to *control* nature—we might learn more about science and its relationship to nature by asking after the political possibilities that science's relation to nature opens up or occludes. Might the unpredictability shared by the natural and political worlds serve to remind us of our natural/political hybridity and cast it as something not simply to dispose of but to cherish?

The "Second Nature" Paradigm

The limitations of the concept of nature as a ward in need of protection and political representation suggest that we might do well to seek out alternative understandings of nature as we confront dilemmas of environmental destruction and technological change. Rather than seeking to safeguard an aspect of "first nature" for normative orientation to the hybridity of nature and politics, this volume offers a theoretical framework that attends to how nature's meaning and authority is constituted in and through the mutual imbrications of nature and politics. Building on the denaturalizing turn's critique of essentialism, we begin by taking for granted that nature is always already a second nature. But we use the term "second nature" not to mark nature's actual or desired irrelevance to politics but as a redescription of the nature that matters enormously in politics, precisely because it is inherently and mutually imbricated with politics. The "second nature" framework has two primary components: (1) a *critical* picture of how appeals to either politics or nature over and against the other misrepresent the constitutive tie between the two, and (2) a *positive* picture of the important political capacities generated through the hybridity of nature and politics. Below, we discuss the second nature theoretical paradigm in more detail, eventually parsing these critical and positive aspects in turn.

Our understanding of nature as "second nature" draws on diverse sources for thinking the relationship between nature and politics and between nature and humanity. First, we draw upon alternative figurations of the relationship between nature and politics present in modern and early modern political thought. Unlike thinkers like Locke and Hobbes, who attribute a lawlike status to nature and ask that it both form and stand outside of politics, thinkers like Vico and Montesquieu portray nature and politics as mutually constituted and affirm the confluence of political activities with natural forces as the necessary condition for both law and projects to resist and transform it. For example, in the *Persian Letters*, Montesquieu suggests that in despotic governments, the "enslavement of the heart and mind" of citizens means that "nothing is heard but the voice of fear, which has only one language," but in free societies, we are confronted with the multiple voices of "nature, which expresses itself so diversely and appears in so many different forms."[27] In contrast to green theorists, who seek to represent and steward nature's univocal voice in politics through expertise, Montesquieu here suggests that free societies are characterized by a receptivity to plural voices of nature—uncapturable by a single discourse or set of actors—that shape and are shaped by our reception to them. Politics limits, opens up, and constitutes nature's diverse expressions. Similarly, in *The Spirit of the Laws*, Montesquieu suggests that we would learn most about societies not by attempting to find the "natural" standard that governs all of them but by studying the diverse *natures*—and principles of politics—present in diverse societies. As he puts it, we should understand "the government most in conformity with nature" to be "the one whose particular arrangement best relates to the disposition of the people for whom it is established."[28] While Montesquieu refers to "nature" here in the singular, it becomes clear in *The Spirit of the Laws* that the "nature" of any particular society is a fluctuating amalgam of relationships between climate, terrain, legislation, mores, social practices, and other variables. Nature for Montesquieu is always already *second* nature. While the normative import of Montesquieu's approach continues to be debated, one lesson is clear: any attempt to claim a "pure" nature separate from politics does an injustice to the changing, mutually shaped relationships between politics and nature that constitute the normative horizon of any society.

Giambattista Vico, too, endorses the constitutive role of nature in politics while troubling (more explicitly than Montesquieu) the social contract tradition's familiar narrative of nature as a given, objective domain capable of regulating the constructed, subjective domain of politics from outside. For Vico, nature as it is given (which for him meant given in God's creation) is *not* the nature that we encounter through our senses, come to know through science, or turn to for normative guidance for our political communities. Rather, he argues, we give ourselves the nature that matters in any and all human affairs through faculties and activities that rely upon even as they transform God-given nature. Our very senses remake whatever is given in nature into a sensible—because humanized—world, so that "we make the color of things by seeing, flavor by tasting, sound by hearing, and heat and cold by touching."[29] Vico considers the creativity of our faculties—especially the faculty of speech—to be the reason we can know nature at all. In other words, not objective detachment from given objects but active involvement in sensing and speaking to one another about nature is the condition of possibility for natural science.[30] Most importantly, as Vico presents it in his *New Science of Politics*, politics is founded and refounded in moments when human faculties and natural forces confront and transform each other. In his origin story, the first political communities were instituted when primitive men, frightened by massive thunderstorms, attributed their own qualities to the sky, as though it "meant to tell them something by the hiss of his bolts and the clap of his thunder."[31] Nature only becomes a source of command, in this story, through a confluence of climatological and political movements. For Vico, nature plays a necessary role in instituting politics, but only as a second nature, refashioned through an inaugural metaphor that likens the thundering sky to a shouting human.

The importance of second nature in these neglected strands of early modern political thought anticipates and resonates with Nietzsche's brief but provocative discussion of "second nature" in "On the Uses and Disadvantages of History for Life."[32] There, Nietzsche proposes that a critical relation to our past and present practices, if it is to further life, sometimes demands that we "combat our inborn heritage and implant in ourselves a new habit, a new instinct, a second nature, so that our first nature withers away."[33] We create for ourselves a "second nature," allowing our "customary inherited nature" to "atrophy." This, he admits, can be a disheartening and even "dangerous" task, since any creation of a second nature is initially much weaker than the first. But he offers the following "noteworthy consolation" to those who achieve victory against "first nature" and produce a new nature for themselves: "that of knowing that this first nature was once a second nature, and that every victorious second nature will become a first."[34] We read the curious relation Nietzsche poses between first and second natures not only as an exhortation to rethink nature as a site of contest between entrenched habit and new, emergent possibilities. It is also, we think, an exhortation to affirm contest as the condition of having nature as a life-sustaining force in politics at all.[35]

Taken together, Montesquieu's, Vico's, and Nietzsche's views of nature suggest that we view struggle over what "nature" is—for example, in dealing with political problems like climate change and genetically modified foods—as a constitutive part of how we are guided by nature. If we fail to affirm political contest as a part of nature's historical and contemporary constitution, turning to nature may well turn into the kind of oppressive exercise that proponents of the denaturalizing turn rightly castigate. Moreover, if we fail to acknowledge that natural materiality and vitality deeply condition politics, we risk excluding the category of nature from political discourse, rendering it difficult—even impossible—to gain traction on the dangers and possibilities of the new forms of hybridity that increasingly characterize our age.

Though Nietzsche does not view such struggles between first and second nature as characteristically political, we do. Retaining the language of nature while refusing its status as the original and foundational ground of politics, Nietzsche's concept of *second* nature implies that nature might sometimes be invoked to strengthen novel political creations, sometimes be rejected as a threat to new political forms, and sometimes be appealed to as a way of figuring the fixity of those inherited habits that we judge to be worth sustaining. Rethinking "nature" in this way, as something we give ourselves through struggle, suggests a rethinking of the view of politics derived from the social contract condition: namely, as the historical movement of human practices out of or away from their natural origins. Instead, we propose to conceive politics as contingent movements to naturalize and denaturalize a world that is, from the start, the site of politico-natural hybridity. Even when nature serves as a site of political fixity, it is a contingent fixity accomplished through political practices that sustain it (and may, ultimately, cease sustaining it). Rethinking nature in this way suggests that the struggles imminent to nature itself might be the most valuable aspect of nature. As Nietzsche suggests, the best vantage from which to understand the constructed character of political appeals to nature is to create a new nature, for in struggling to give ourselves a new nature we come to understand the struggles that previously installed old natures. Nature so conceived does not promise to solve difficult political contests as a point of unmovable fixity but to reflect, complicate, and reverberate with political struggles in ways that can help shift their terms and show them in a new light.

Contemporary poststructuralist thinkers have, like Nietzsche, questioned the idea of natural givens—for example, of a natural "sex"—and suggested that those supposed "givens" are actually normative ideals produced through regulation and discipline. Judith Butler, for example, famously argues that the idea of a natural "sex" is itself the product of performative gender practices and heteronormative regulation.[36] Butler's point is that any attempt to isolate a "natural" identity that precedes politics is inevitably built on exclusion. Consequently, emancipatory politics must reject identity (reliant on some concept of a "natural" given) as its ground and instead embrace contest *over* such identitarian closures as its "ungrounded ground."[37] Yet where Butler focuses on the emancipatory promise of *de*stabilizing the naturalness of sexed bodies, we also see emancipatory promise in appealing to nature's *own* instability, spontaneity, and flux to destabilize normalizing classifications of human bodies. For example, Anne Fausto-Sterling has drawn attention to the anatomical range of sex organs, which defy the sexual dimorphism that modern medicine surgically enforces (though her tendency to defer to anatomical "fact" as a trump to overrule social constructions arguably remains too beholden to a notion of nature as a source of normative stability, even as she uses such facts to destabilize dominant norms).[38] While particular iterations of "nature" may be oppressive, the ways in which both material bodies *and* human practices create, elaborate, and unsettle what counts as "natural" over time deserve theoretical attention in their own right. These human involvements in and interpellation into naturalizing, denaturalizing, and renaturalizing their own bodies and the world around them are politics; they are modes of stabilizing, destabilizing, and restabilizing political arrangements. By understanding nature as always already a site of instability that exists in tension and imbrications with politics, we can explore ways of contesting oppressive natural givens (such as the sex-gender system that has grounded patriarchal and heteronormative politics) in part by struggling to give ourselves a new nature—a *second* second nature, to replace the first (and to remind us that every first was once second). The second nature approach emphasizes the diversity and flux of nature and natural/political assemblages over and against the image of static and stabilizing "natural givens."

Second Nature as Critical Paradigm

Montesquieu, Vico, and Nietzsche portray the relationship between nature and politics as contestable *and* portray that contestation as itself the (sometimes unstable and sometimes *too* stable) "ground" from which we must address hybrid phenomena that seem troubling or promising. Building on these varied sources, we see "second nature" as, first, a *critical* paradigm through which to view troubling forms of hybridity between nature and politics. In contrast to green theorists' appeal to a nature as an ideally or originally pure, untrammeled domain, the "second nature" paradigm would emphasize the extent to which this ideal is actually *produced* by regulation, institutions, and practices. For example, the ideal of a "wilderness" that must be protected from human intervention is itself produced through legal regulations, the institutions of national parks, and practices of consumption that sustain a "market" for experiences of "pure nature." The point of revealing this ideal of "wilderness" as itself a product of regulation and consumption (among other things) is not to overthrow that ideal but rather to decenter it and to highlight the human practices that sustain it. In turn, highlighting the human role in constructing "wilderness" is done not to "unmask" wilderness as *un*natural but rather to remind us that sustaining such natural spaces is a deeply political project—a project that disavows and devalues its own roots when it casts the purity of the wild as prior to, and independent of, human interventions.

As we argued in the prior section, the second nature paradigm also offers a critical lens through which to view the progress narratives offered by advocates of using technology to master nature. Where an ideal of nature sans humanity portrays proper politics as distinct from, rather than enabled by, the human relationship with nature, an ideal of humanly controlled nature fails to acknowledge sufficiently how human relationships with nature often exceed, challenge, and transform human agency. To return to the example of genetic and reproductive technologies, Dorothy Roberts points out what is occluded by optimistic visions of the human freedom and equality promised by new reproductive technologies and the industry of "reprogenetics." Detailing how supposedly "natural" reproduction has always been and is becoming even more a market-driven, nature-politics hybrid, Roberts draws attention to the growing privatization of risk in childbearing. Through being interpolated into systems of genetic testing, women are increasingly cast as responsible for disabilities and birth defects. This privatization has important political implications as it not only allows society and the state to disavow responsibility for educating and caring for disabled citizens, but it may also amplify the state's claim to manage and surveil those (black, female, poor) citizens who are cast as least capable of managing genetic risk.[39] For Roberts, an effective and emancipatory political response to these reproductive inequities demands that we contest scientized claims to know "nature" on behalf of a democratization of decision making about new genetic technologies.

Beyond the sphere of reproductive technologies, we might also think of how the advancement of scientific attempts to understand and predict weather patterns—like hurricanes—might lead us to overestimate our ability to protect ourselves from devastating disasters like Hurricane Katrina. From the point of view of the second nature paradigm, the label "natural disaster" is a misnomer, insofar as it tries to set the consequences of natural forces apart from those of human activity. As many acknowledged in its aftermath, the disaster of Hurricane Katrina was itself a politico-natural hybrid caused by urban planners (and their failings), global warming (itself a hybrid phenomenon composed of weather patterns, failures of legal oversight, industrial processes, etc.), and the political disenfranchisement of poor, black communities, among other things. The hybridity of such disasters means that those who would isolate the "natural" forces involved in order to predict and control their effects, as many scientific experts and agencies would, actually misrecognize the phenomena they wish to understand. The second nature approach would thus endorse existing efforts to reconfigure disciplinary boundaries that unnecessarily isolate the natural sciences, the social sciences, and the humanities, in pursuit of appropriately synthetic understandings of famines, plagues, floods, and other destructive amalgamations of human and nonhuman forces.

Second Nature as Positive Paradigm

While the second nature paradigm offers a critical lens through which to view some approaches to politico-natural problems, it also offers a positive picture of the relationship between nature and politics that may serve as a useful point of reorientation for political theorists. Rather than portraying nature and politics as two domains that have become contingently or purposefully intertwined—either to our detriment or benefit—the second nature approach portrays these two domains as *constituted* through their mutual entanglement. More specifically, it portrays contestation over the relationship between nature and politics as constitutive of those domains—of their norms, their boundaries, and their sense of wholeness. This suggests that when addressing issues like reproductive technologies or climate change, we should attend to how our experiences of "nature" are implicated in political practices and how our political practices are implicated in the materiality, diversity, and vitality of nature.

The controversy raging over the Monsanto Company's introduction of Bt cotton seed—which has the gene for the bacterium *Bacillus thuringiensis* (Bt) inserted into its genetic code—to the Indian agricultural market provides a historical example of the distinct perspective offered by the second nature approach.[40] While advocates of Bt cotton argue that its disease- and pest-resistant genetic structure promises to emancipate small farmers from the unpredictability of insects and disease, leading to higher, more consistent crop yields, many local growers—and, increasingly, antiglobalization and green activists—protest the use of the seeds and raise concerns about their intended and unintended consequences. As the dominance of Bt cotton in rural cotton production has risen, local Indian farmers have expressed real concerns that their livelihoods are increasingly dependent upon, and controlled by, the Monsanto Company.

One way to approach the Monsanto debate would be to retrench the claim to "naturalness" on behalf of nonmanipulated seed stock, casting engineered seeds as a violation of natural processes by biotechnological intruders. The commitment to protecting nature's ostensibly given properties against the intervention of human technologies, applied to this case, could generate a call to preserve the traditional use of nonengineered cotton seed against Monsanto's invasive product. Yet such an invocation of "naturalness" focuses attention on Monsanto's damage to the ecological wholeness of rural India while neglecting to attend to the *political* harm effected by the introduction of Bt cotton. The insights of the "denaturalizing turn," on the other hand, might help us theorize the political stakes of Bt cotton—specifically, by allowing us to highlight that traditional cotton seed is not "natural" but is *also* a product of human activity, as it has been bred over centuries to produce cotton best suited to agricultural practices and consumer demand. From this point of view, the social and political damage that Monsanto's products and policies have wrought in rural communities—rather than the violation of cotton's essential nature—emerge as the central issue of concern with Bt cotton.[41] The turn from nature to politics sparked by a denaturalized approach to traditional cotton seed is highly productive in this case. However, a theoretical framework that depicts both Bt cotton and traditional seed as purely political is in jeopardy of occluding the hybridity of both plant life and the lives of farmers, as well as the kind of politico-natural worlds they symbolize and summon.

A second nature approach frames the Monsanto debates differently—not in terms of a conflict between nature and politics but in terms of contestation over the relationship between nature and politics as well as the proper interpreters of that relation. Indeed, one striking feature of Monsanto's seed technologies is their promise—albeit, often unfulfilled—to eradicate the unpredictability of nature itself, offering a fantasy of human control over natural risk. Yet the very diversity and unpredictability of nature that Monsanto seeks to obliterate are valorized by many local farmers as benefits of traditional seed. This valorization has found resonances in a burgeoning social movement of indigenous farmers and their supporters that frames resistance to Monsanto as an expression of a broader political commitment to diversity and flexible, nonsovereign political and environmental relations.[42] Traditional cotton seeds, already products of nature that blur the human/nature distinction, are cast as avatars of the traditional indigenous agricultural practices that are threatened by Monsanto. It is easy enough to hear indigenous defenses of traditional seeds as claims to first nature when first nature is the only kind of nature imaginable to us. Our paradigm gives us another way to hear these claims: as claims to a nature that is already second. Within the framework of a second nature approach, traditional seeds are not preferable because they are the given products of nature, unspoiled by human interventions; after all, these seeds are themselves the product of a series of contingent relationships between human beings and plant life over time. Rather, it is precisely this historical relationship between humans and plants that many indigenous communities have judged to be of higher political value than the purported benefits of Bt cotton. If we hear indigenous actors in this way—as claimants to a second nature that they themselves are part of forming, even as they are formed by it—we may be more alert to the *political* character of their objections to Bt seed.

Both Monsanto's supporters and its detractors deploy highly complex discourses that sometimes seek to fix human/nature relations—either by privileging a "pure" image of nature in need of protection from human intervention or by valorizing an inert and passive conception of nature as material available for human reengineering—and at other times are deeply invested in natural/human hybridity, as in the hybridity of Monsanto's Bt cotton itself or the quite different blurring of the artificial and natural represented by traditional seed. Yet neither an opposition between nature and politics nor a refusal to acknowledge the productivity of appeals to nature's diversity, unpredictability, and aversion to human mastery can fully attend to the complexity of this controversy.[43] Viewed through the lens of the second nature approach that we have begun to sketch here, the Bt cotton controversy emerges as a constellation of conflicting visions of politico-natural hybridity and opposed valuations of the significance of nature's plurality for human life. Though the second nature perspective, like the denaturalizing perspective that it extends, does not promise to provide univocal answers to the politico-natural problems of our times, we suggest that it can enable a new theoretical approach that gains a deeper purchase than the dominant views in the current literature.

To summarize, then, the "second nature" paradigm portrays the relationship between politics and nature as characterized by *flux* rather than fixity, by *contest* rather than incommensurable languages, by *degrees* of differentiation rather than by binary distinctions, by *historical* contingency rather than timeless differences. Beginning from a "second nature" paradigm that insists on the complexity and mutual imbrications of the relationship between nature and politics, political theorists may be better able to address difficult issues ahead that require precisely such a complex response. Yet the "second nature" paradigm, which casts neither nature nor politics as "pure" realms, also eschews the comforts of finding a pure point of critical purchase—a choice that brings with it risks as well as promise. How should we read and understand this combined risk and promise? The contributors to this volume all address and in different ways affirm this ambivalence as a condition of meaningful political theorizing about politico-natural problems. They do so through drawing on a variety of interlocutors—from Machiavelli to Arendt to Bergson—to theorize "second nature" as a point or paradigm of political contest that is both formed by and forms nature and politics.

The Essays

We begin the volume with an essay that comprehends both the political promise and danger in theories that cast nature as a production and site of human invention and contest. In "Necessity and Fortune: Machiavelli's Politics of Nature," Yves Winter suggests that Machiavelli's construction of nature as a teacher for human affairs aids human freedom and durability but also ultimately renders nature more available for human intervention and domination. Winter's Machiavelli draws our attention to the ways in which modern politics consists neither in practices of adhering to natural laws nor in practices of simply opposing nature with human artifice but rather in practices of originating plural natures, instituting and entrenching them, letting them atrophy, and supplanting them (and doing this over and over again). Yet in his reading of Machiavellian *fortuna*, Winter also emphasizes (as Nietzsche does more elliptically) that such practices are invariably ambivalent—perhaps positive for human freedom and durability while also enacting brutality toward the natural world. In a provocative reading of Machiavelli's conception of *fortuna* as a woman, Winter suggests that Machiavelli's crafting of nature as an instructor for human affairs ultimately renders nature more vulnerable to or available for human intervention: "the figure of *fortuna* as a force available for domination frames nature as a manageable sphere." By using metaphors to describe *fortuna* and *necessita* that depict them as figures available for human domination—for example, a woman or a river that may be dammed—Machiavelli does not simply tell us that *fortuna* is impetuous and rushing (like a river), but, rather, he may also "mark the intersection between the establishment of political power and the production of nature as a field of human intervention." Winter's analysis of Machiavelli thus sheds light on the interconnections between attempts at durability in contemporary political life and our continued domination and stripping of the natural world (spurred, for example, by our need for more and more oil) and pushes us to ask whether or how such durability might be imagined without continued plundering of natural resources that will ultimately be self-destructive and defeating.

Thomas Laqueur also presents nature as a site of both human construction and imitation in "Burning the Dead and the Ways of Nature," in which he examines the beginnings of the cremation movement in Britain in the late nineteenth century. Like Winter's Machiavelli, Laqueur's cremationists cast nature as the ultimate instructor for human social practices, and, thus, their claims to be nature's authoritative imitators functioned to shore up their technical power *over* nature. Challenging cultural attachments to the rites and rituals of burying the dead, the cremationists pushed for a technical disposal regime, by posing cremation as a more "natural" way of disposing of the dead—that is, "it mimicked nature." Yet Laqueur notes that this scientific, medicalized turn to nature was not simply a claim to imitate nature as such, for the cremationists' claim upon the dead "rested on the towering cultural authority of death: crudely put, if the dead belong to science, then so does much else." In other words, existing cultural practices gave enormous political weight to the cremationists' claim to naturalness, for practices of relating to the dead always occupy a central place in human civilization. In this sense, the claim of cremationists that science should have priority over cultural rites in managing dead bodies subsumes both nature and culture under the purview of science. By contrast with Winter's Machiavelli, who casts political actors as the privileged interpreters of nature, Laqueur's nineteenth-century cremationists cast scientists as its privileged expositors. But Winter and Laqueur alike suggest the ambivalent political consequences of casting human domination over nature as the necessary condition of human civilization (Laqueur) and of human freedom (Winter).

Intriguingly, Laqueur is not the only contributor to point us to the relationship between the dead and the living as a foundational site where nature is politically contested and agonistically imitated. Bonnie Honig's essay, "Corpses for Kilowatts? Mourning, Justice, Burial, and the Ends of Humanism," also takes its starting point from a technocratic challenge to traditional rites of death—specifically from contemporary plans in Durham, England, to "recycle" dead bodies into electric power. While the Durham plan may appear to signal an "end" to humanism in its challenge to human dignity, Honig argues that its attempt to assure "wasteless waste" is actually complicit in humanist ideals of sovereign efficiency. However, might alternative responses to death offer "ends" to humanism that are more politically promising and transformative? Through nuanced readings of two texts—the film *Sophie's Choice* and the play *Antigone*—Honig ultimately finds rites of mourning and justice to be inadequate responses to the rupture opened up by death, since they treat the dead body as a means to an end (proper mourning or justice), thus resuturing and not transforming the symbolic order. However, in *Antigone*, Honig finds an intimation of "forms of corporeal care" that may have allowed the actors in the drama, had they not been prohibited in the case of Polynices, to rework the symbolic order in which they were enmeshed. Such corporeal practices of service to the dead do not remove themselves entirely from capitalist economies of use and instrumentalization, as is attempted by Anne-Lise François's antihumanist ideal of "recessive action," one of Honig's touchstones in the essay. Even so, Honig suggests that the option of service to the dead—of "being of use"—may "disrupt the binding humanist binary of dignity versus use" and serve as an important site of agonistic political engagement. Giving the example of an AIDS activist who asked that his dead body be put on the steps of the FDA, Honig suggests that "those who provide service in the company of others become acquainted not just with mourning but also with pleasure as they undergo the sometimes transformative experience of action in concert." There is a natality even in mortality when the living serve the dead.

Where Laqueur and Honig focus on the ways that death poses a particularly fraught and potentially productive "natural" problem for politics, Ashley Biser discusses the politics of birth and reproduction in a world where reproductive technologies increasingly reveal and amplify the cultural-technological character of generating new life. In "The 'Unnatural Growth of the Natural,'" Biser responds to the concerns of thinkers such as Leon Kass, Francis Fukuyama, and Jürgen Habermas, who worry that "absent the ability to distinguish between the grown and the made . . . we cannot make the kinds of ethical and political judgments genetic technologies demand." Biser does not respond to this worry by attempting, as these thinkers do, to secure a concept of nature from which we might ethically judge new reproductive technologies, nor by arguing that a concern with nature is misplaced. Instead, drawing on Hannah Arendt's exhortation to think phenomena "without a banister," Biser argues that we should direct our critical attention to the phenomena and "stabilizing activities" that we have sought to describe with the nature/artifice distinction and ask whether or how new reproductive technologies may challenge or transform these activities. While Arendt is generally seen as a thinker who wants to shore up boundaries between spheres of nature and artifice, Biser suggests that an attention to these Arendtian "stabilizing activities" that the nature/artifice distinction has traditionally named—rather than an attention to stabilizing the nature/artifice distinction itself—allows political theorists to resist the "defensive posture" adopted by thinkers like Kass and Fukuyama and move instead into a posture of "resolved inquisitiveness" oriented to the worldly activities enabled and disabled by new reproductive technologies. Biser's alternative theoretical posture allows her to ask different kinds of questions about reproductive technologies—in particular, questions about how reprogenetics might affect the human plurality that Arendt sees as an essential attribute of the human condition. Where Laqueur's and Winter's essays emphasize the risk of understanding nature as a site of cultural, political, and scientific imitation and contest, Biser's essay suggests that attending to the specific practices that we mark with the term "nature" might hold promise for politically orienting ourselves to new natural/cultural phenomena like reprogenetics.

Ayten Gündoğdu also finds promise in the human articulation and contestation of nature for responding to politico-natural dilemmas—specifically, for responding to the ambivalence of human rights discourse and humanitarian intervention. In her essay, "Potentialities of Second Nature:

Agamben on Human Rights," Gündoğdu conducts a critical analysis of Giorgio Agamben's critique of human rights. Noting that human rights have become a kind of "second nature" in contemporary political life, as they presume man "in his natural condition to be the source and bearer of rights that he is born with" and that secure his membership in a sovereign nation-state, Gündoğdu sympathetically recounts Agamben's suggestion that this second nature actually has "inimical effects" and should be contested and uprooted rather than celebrated. While human rights are "usually conceived as normative setbacks to sovereign power," Agamben suggests that human rights discourse and humanitarianism also further expose human life to sovereign violence. Indeed, this is what Gündoğdu suggests is distinctive about Agamben's criticism of human rights relative to the criticisms of human rights by thinkers like Hannah Arendt and Wendy Brown—namely, Agamben's "attentiveness to the vulnerability of lives that are left at that borderline between biopolitics and thanatopolitics."

Yet while Gündoğdu is sympathetic to Agamben's argument, she questions his pronouncement that we must go "beyond human rights" in order to resist, rather than reinscribe, sovereign violence. Specifically, Gündoğdu critically examines Agamben's conception of "potentiality"—a conception that he finds in Aristotle and on which both he and Aristotle draw to contest a fatalistic position in which everything that is past is evacuated of its contingency—and suggests that Agamben should have himself deployed this understanding of potentiality in reference to human rights politics. If he had done so, he could have better respected the contingency of human rights' past invocation and thus better appreciated the "potentiality-not-to" in its future, that is, a potentiality not to be deployed as it has been in the past. Rather than siding with Agamben's "fatalistic assessments" of the "complex and contingent effects of the 'second nature' that we acquire with sovereignty and human rights," Gündoğdu argues that we and Agamben "need to be alert to how rights can be claimed in unanticipated ways, especially by those who are excluded from their constitutive terms ('man' and 'citizen') and rendered less than human." Gündoğdu thus portrays the humanization of nature in this instance—the notion of "human" rather than simply "natural rights"—as opening a space for political contestation and creativity, rather than simply instantiating Agamben's fatalistic narrative of the connection of human rights to sovereign violence.

Both Gündoğdu and Biser take an immanent approach to problems of nature in politics—that is, an approach that gives primary place to the human, worldly practices that constitute and enact the stabilizing forces and normative standards that guide political life. In "The Utopian Content of Reification: Adorno's Critical Social Theory of Nature," by contrast, Christopher Buck argues through a novel interpretation of Adorno that political theorists should be more open to the transcendent image of nature that emerges precisely on the terrain of second nature. Buck proposes that a "critical social theory of nature" requires a reconstruction of the immanent/transcendent relation. Finding resources for such a reconstruction in Theodor Adorno's critical reinterpretation of Marx's theory of exchange value, Buck argues for the "emancipatory potential" of a theory of nature that presses us to consider experiences of the material and nonhuman as encounters with the transcendent. In Buck's account of Adorno's theory of nature, we need not cast such encounters with the transcendent in terms of the eternal, fixed, and, thus, the prepolitical. Rather, Buck reads Adorno's claim that "nature 'does not yet exist'" as calling for an experience of the transcendent in nature that presses us to imagine alternative systems of valuation to that of capitalism.

In the final essay of this volume, Jane Bennett, like Buck, affirms the productivity for environmental politics of moving beyond the politics of demystification that seeks to expose the workings of ideology in the valuation of material objects. However, where Buck urges a reconceptualization of the transcendent, Bennett questions whether the discourse of nature—even of second nature, which she reads as privileging human actors as the ultimate source of the meaning of things—is capable of pressing us to attend to the "force of things." Bennett argues that a "politics of vital materialism"—which she both draws and ultimately distinguishes from nineteenth- and twentieth-century vitalism—may "pose a stronger challenge than 'nature' currently does to the destructive fantasies of mastery that infuse American consumption and production practices." It does so, on Bennett's account, because rather than attending to "biocultural assemblages" as products of human action and agency—as she sees second nature discourse as doing—a politics of vital materialism marks "the active presence, the amazing power, of nonhuman or not-quite-human things and forces." In facing up to how we may ultimately be unable to "give voice" to these nonhuman agentic assemblages and activities of assemblage, we may encounter precisely the "outside" that vital materialism seeks to mark—not an outside that commands or is commanded by us but that we encounter, respond to, and act with and sometimes against. Through attempting and pushing us to attempt with her this "impossible task," Bennett calls us to see that vital materiality is a site of our contestation, imitation, and effort but that it is not *only* this—it also resists our very attempts to understand it in these terms.

Yet with Bennett's challenge to the politics of "nature," we have come full circle to Winter's essay and the Machiavellian understanding of nature he draws out: namely, Machiavelli's argument that political actors should imitate nature's permanence and nonhumanness—permanence and nonhumanness, however, that Machiavelli constructs and that, in constructing, renders available for human intervention and domination. It is precisely this gesture that Bennett wants to avoid in her figure of materiality; she wants to invite human attention to, learning from, and interaction with vital materiality. However, we suggest that Bennett's and Winter's essays are best read as two moments in an important and emerging contest over the risks and promise of the interpretative framework that we have been calling "second nature." In this sense, Bennett's and Winter's essays remind us—as do the others—of the importance not only of attending to the productive political possibilities in recognizing and acting through the humanization of the natural but also of the dangers to the natural world, vital materiality, and human lives that come along with the fact of living in and through "second nature."

If we accept that nature can neither provide politics with its normative foundations nor serve as the realm that politics aims to overcome or master, how should we envision the relationship between the natural and the political? It is the tensions and disagreements, as well as the lines of overlap and connection, among the responses to this question provided by the volume's authors that point to the productivity of rethinking the natural through politics in terms of the paradigm of second nature. Rather than affirming or rejecting the political value of the natural, conceived as the realm of fixed and unchanging essences, the essays in this volume offer diverse and sometimes competing visions of politico-natural hybridity that acknowledge and extend the insights of the denaturalizing turn. Taken together, the essays suggest that the framework of second nature opens up an exciting site of political contest that speaks to contemporary problems facing us today in arenas as diverse as environmental policy, human rights activism, reproductive technology, and burial rites. We hope that this book can play an important role in provoking further response, debate, and reflection that might extend the second nature paradigm in new and unforeseen directions.

CHAPTER 1

Necessity and Fortune: Machiavelli's Politics of Nature

Yves Winter

In the famous letter to Vettori, dated December 10, 1513, where Machiavelli announces the completion of his "*opusculo*" about principalities, he describes it as a study of the "art of the state" (*arte dello stato;* CW, 929–930).[1] Since chapter 19 of *The Prince* juxtaposes *arte* and *natura*, a careful reader may well conjecture that Machiavelli considers the art of the state—or politics—to be unnatural (76). The contrast between nature and politics is further mobilized in the opening chapters of the work, where Machiavelli opposes the "natural" prince to the "new" prince (6–7). The natural prince, Machiavelli tells his reader, inherits power through the bloodline. Unless something unusual occurs, he will always be able to preserve his state; unlike the new prince, he need not have recourse to the art of the state, since nature has bountifully provided for him. The art of the state is thus in some sense a substitute for nature. It stands in and replaces the continuity, lineage, and ancestry Machiavelli associates with the term "nature." If nature stands for the permanence and stability of old political structures and imaginaries, the art of the state is the art of undoing the old, of unraveling the natural, and of severing the present from the past. Accordingly, politics is not only a stand-in for nature but also its opposite:

antinature. It would seem, then, that Machiavelli draws on the classical Greek dichotomies *physis/nomos* and *physis/technē* to contrast the realm of nature to that of human artifice and convention.

However, as soon as the conceptual difference between politics and nature is set up, Machiavelli unravels it, by stating that the new prince, whose violence we thought was unnatural, acts in accordance with "another natural and ordinary necessity" and that his desire to acquire is considered a "very natural and ordinary thing" (P III, 8; 14). The recourse to nature thus ratifies not only the hereditary order but also the disturbance and challenge to that very order. As is typical for the early modern period, nature stands both for continuity and for change, for the old as well as for the new. Nature and politics, in other words, do not represent entirely separate spheres. Nature is not the base on which politics emerges as a superstructure; nor should we think of politics as a domain that is entirely artificial and therefore unnatural. What seemed to be a contradiction between nature and politics is thus really a tension *within* nature. The distinction between statecraft and nature is a difference internal to nature, more specifically, one that characterizes the nature of the human.

Human Nature as Second Nature

Notwithstanding the dubious philosophical premises, it remains a widespread practice among students of political theory to classify political thinkers according to their philosophical anthropologies, as if an author's political ideas could be derived from his or her views on "human nature." In the case of Machiavelli, this formula typically yields the claim that his realism is a consequence of his view of human nature as evil or corrupted.[2] But as various readers have noted, there is an *unnatural* element in Machiavelli's account of human nature: the concept of *ambizione*. The wellspring for human conflict, quest for power, and discontent, it is what sets the human animal apart from other animals.[3] If this is so, then human nature is profoundly contradictory. Not only does it include both the natural and its opposite, the unnatural, but more importantly, if *ambizione* is what distinguishes the human among other animals, then the definitional attribute of being human is the capacity to be or become unnatural. What defines humanity is the becoming unnatural of nature, and "man"—in the fully gendered sense this term always has for Machiavelli—is the denaturing animal, that animal whose nature it is to undo nature. If the nature of man is to become other than nature, to become an other to nature, and if the source and impetus of this becoming-unnatural is lodged in this animal's nature, then human nature is never original—it is always in some sense "second nature," a point implied by Machiavelli in a key chapter of the third book of the *Discourses*, where he effectively identifies human nature with convention or custom (III.43). Situated right at the end, in the last section of the third book, chapter 43 is placed amid a small number of select chapters that, substituting for a conclusion, condense some of the central points of the *Discourses*. In a propositional form quite typical for the *Discourses*, it is titled: "That Men Who Are Born in One Province Observe Almost the Same Nature for All Times." The fact that, as Mansfield and Tarcov point out, this is the only chapter in the *Discourses* where the word "nature" appears in the title may or may not be significant.[4] What is beyond doubt is that the topos of "second nature" fundamentally structures Machiavelli's view and understanding of the human. The claim advanced is that "a nation keep[s] the same customs for a long time" and that such customs, virtuous or not, do not change frequently. The nature that people born in one province "observe" is thus not a nature at all but a habit.

Habits or customs replace nature; they are "second" in the sense of succeeding and resulting from nature, "second" in the sense of not being original. As Machiavelli explains, the constancy of a custom in a given place results from the underlying stability of the human passions. Worldly things, he writes, "are the work of men, who have and always had the same passions, and they must of necessity result in the same effect" (D III.43, 302). Any further variation between geographic locales is explained by reference to different modes of life and education. How these differences should arise, given that all customs are direct effects of the unchanging passions, Machiavelli does not tell us. We do know, however, that a diversity of customs emerges and that even though these conventions are distinct from the shared nature that gave rise to them, Machiavelli insists on calling them "nature." The name "nature" thus functions as a misnomer for what is not natural; it produces an appearance of nature, dressing the unnatural in nature's attire. Moreover, it functions as a *metonymy*, substituting an effect for a cause. The constancy and regularity implied by the term "nature" is the consequence of the repetition and iteration entailed in customs and habits, not its cause. Convention trades place with nature; it is a belated instantiation of nature, a nature that is second because it is "the work of men."

The characterization of habit as "nature" indicates that what we tend to regard as an original and unmediated given is in fact the product of a mediation. This is a critical insight Machiavelli presents, even though he does not quite have the language to conceptualize the process by which this mediation is produced and, more importantly, how it is *naturalized*. Yet Machiavelli insists that human customs are not only second, in the sense of deriving from nature; they appear as "the same nature for all times" (ibid.). The recourse to an origin is thus not simply supplanted by an offshoot: the synthetic substitute must present itself *as nature*. As we shall see, the *appearance* of nature is what serves Machiavelli as a political resource. To leverage nature in politics is to invoke the gloss of the natural.

In *The Prince* and the *Discourses*, the term "nature" appears in five different senses. Nature describes the universal essence of a thing in contrast to its accidents. Thus Machiavelli speaks of the nature of men, of peoples, or of princes.[5] In this context, nature generally designates a fixed, unchanging essence. What is often regarded as Machiavelli's philosophical anthropology—his pessimistic account of human nature, most vividly expressed in his literary work—falls in this category.[6] However, nature also designates the characteristics of a *specific* individual or people (*natura particularis*) as distinct from the generic and *universal* nature of a being (*natura universalis*).[7] "As nature has given each man an individual face, so she has given him an individual disposition and an individual imagination" (CW, 896–897). This is the idea that human nature exists only as a particular, that each individual has his or her own nature that influences their behavior. On the face of it, this appears to be incompatible with the idea of a universal nature shared by all men, princes, or peoples. Whereas these first two meanings of nature specifically concern humans and human collectivities, the remaining categories refer to the sphere of nonhuman nature, which Machiavelli tries hard to keep separate. The third sense of nature is what we have encountered above in the ambiguous relation between *arte* and *natura*, namely the nonhuman *cause* and *origin* of things. Under this heading, nature is distinguished from art and convention.[8] Fourth, nature stands for *regularity*, for the normal and ordinary course of things.[9] The frequently occurring phrase "natural and ordinary" alludes to this meaning of nature, which is tied to the idea of a cyclical recurrence and applies not only to nonhuman regularities but also to customs and conventions that remain stable over time (D III.43, 302). The fifth meaning refers to an *order* that structures the conditions for human action and transcends them, an order that "forces you" to do something, such that you do it "by nature and not by choice" (D III.9, 239). This is the sense of nature to which Machiavelli points when he writes that "we are unable to oppose that to which nature inclines us" (D III.9, 240).

The complexity of this typology provides a clue that the concept of nature is a condensation point for a series of theoretical problems in early modern political thought. "Nature" is the site at which political, historico-philosophical, anthropological, and methodological questions intersect. What stands out in Machiavelli's taxonomy of nature is the division between human and nonhuman nature. To one side of the division lies the idea of a human nature as a basic source of motivations and forces that drive action. To the other side is the theme of a nonhuman order that structures the conditions for action, a set of regularities that constitutes the circumstances and forms within which humans act. We already know that human nature is ridden by a fundamental tension between the putative originality of nature and the movement of its own becoming. As we learned from the chapter of the *Discourses* examined above, what we call human nature is at least in part convention and custom. In keeping with this idea, Machiavelli suggests at various places that men can take on a new nature, that they change their nature or "color" it.[10] The premise of nature's fixity is thus compromised. Indeed, the only element of this characterization of human nature one might call permanent and unchanging is the name "nature." This, incidentally, is why Machiavelli writes that the founder who establishes a political order must "presuppose" human nature to be evil (D I.3, 15). A philosophical anthropology must be *presupposed* because it cannot be *known*. Human nature has no constitutive content. It functions as a necessary axiom. If human nature is empty and a purely formal construct, from where does Machiavelli's politics draw its content? If the human is the Promethean animal whose nature it is to become unnatural yet who is nonetheless condemned to mimic nature and continually to refer to it, then how are we to interpret Machiavelli's rhetoric of nature?

The Cycle as Quintessential Figure of Nature and History

A second look at chapter 43 of the third book of the *Discourses* reveals that this turns out to be the place where Machiavelli lays out some of the central methodological premises that guide his study and that further illuminate his concept of nature. The *Discourses*—Machiavelli's book about republics—draws primarily on historical material, taking as its explicit object the first ten books of Titus Livy's history of Rome. Rome is the model, particularly the early Rome, from the city's origins to the establishment of its hegemony over the Italian peninsula but prior to the Punic Wars that heralded the construction of an overseas empire. Yet even though the history of the Roman republic is all over the *Discourses*, Machiavelli's interest is not primarily historical. Rather, the objective is to examine the causes of the Roman republic's rise to glory: the conditions, institutions, dynamics, problems, and obstacles that shaped Rome's ascendancy. Historical knowledge is significant not for its own sake but as a resource to understand the present. Thus, Machiavelli calls history the "teacher of our actions" (*la maestra delle azioni nostre*), evoking the Ciceronian topos of *historia magistra vitae.*[11] History is a storehouse of examples that can serve as the basis for inferring general propositions or theorems. The immediate aim is not cognition, not an appreciation or grasp of history on its own terms, but the formulation of hypotheses for the present. Cicero, who considered history in the context of rhetoric, argued that knowledge of the past is a condition for persuasive public speech. Like the Machiavellian political actor, a good orator aspires to intervene in particular political conditions and for these purposes takes recourse to history as a collection of patterns and correspondences.[12]

Implicit in the analysis of history as a model is the expectation that there is a *uniformity* that links the past to the future. If one cannot expect the future to be in some way analogous to the past, history cannot serve as a teacher for the present.[13] And indeed, Machiavelli contends that in order to predict the future, one must look to the past, "for all worldly things have their own counterpart in ancient times" (D III.43, 302). Historical experience—"ancient times"—provides the schema of expectations for the future. Earlier in the *Discourses*, Machiavelli articulates this premise in terms of a *cyclical* model, which treats historical regularity as a subset of the cyclical course of nature:

> Whoever considers present and ancient things easily knows that in all cities and in all peoples there are the same desires and the same humors, and there always have been. So it is an easy thing for whoever examines past things diligently to foresee future things in every republic and to take the remedies for them that were used by the ancients . . . . (D I.39, 83–84)

It is possible to forecast the future because "in all cities and in all peoples there are the same desires and the same humors, and there always have been." What imparts regularity to historical time is the axiom of a fixed and unchanging nature. The guarantee that the future will be analogous to the past is provided by the assumption of a stable nature across time and space. Worldly things, Machiavelli tells us in the *Florentine Histories*, "are not allowed by nature to stand still. As soon as they reach their ultimate perfection, having no further to rise, they must descend" (V.1, 185). Once worldly things "have descended and through their disorders arrived at the ultimate depth, since they cannot descend further, of necessity they must rise. Thus they are always descending from good to bad and rising from bad to good" (FH, V.1, 185). An eternal cycle, a succession of ups and downs, constitutes the historical movement. Politically, this is reflected in the cyclical succession of forms of government, which Polybius in the sixth book of his *Histories* called *anacyclosis*.[14] Distinguishing between three good forms of government and three bad ones, Polybius suggests that moral corruption leads to political decay and converts a good constitution into its bad counterpart. His theory of *anacyclosis* is an attempt to think political change from the perspective of immanent historical necessity. And it is in this revolving cycle, Machiavelli recapitulates, "that all republics are governed and govern themselves" (D I.2, 13).

The theory of historical repetition is modeled on natural cycles: on the rotation of the planets, the natural seasons, on the succession of birth, growth, decay, and death. According to *The Golden Ass*: "You see the stars and the sky, you see the moon, you see the other planets go wandering, now high, now low, without any rest; sometimes you see the sky cloudy, sometimes shining and clear, and likewise nothing on earth remains in the same condition always" (CW, 758). To the extent that historical movements—including the patterns of historical regularity, sequence, and recurrence—emulate natural cycles, we might think of history as part of nature, if not exactly as a "second nature." Unlike the Enlightenment, which will rigorously differentiate between the orders of nature and that of history, Machiavelli draws no strict line between the two. In this sense, "second nature" is perhaps a misnomer for what Machiavelli means by history. A better way to put it would be to say that nature and history share certain structural characteristics: they are both in constant movement, perpetually becoming other than themselves, yet they also always return to the same places, to their beginnings.[15]

If Machiavelli's politics cannot be derived from the anthropological premises that are often attributed to him, does the idea of nature as a cyclical pattern that undergirds historical movement offer us a better grip on his political thinking? Has Machiavelli merely replaced the idea of a substantive human nature with that of a natural history? And if so, doesn't the pattern of historical cycles and recurrences confine political action to a straitjacket comparable in rigidity to the limits foisted upon it by the discourse of "human nature"? Or, put differently, if history revolves in cycles and things are continuously either descending or ascending (FH, V.1, 185), then how can human action be effective? What are the conditions for political action to intervene successfully in a world structured by cyclical recurrence?

It is clear that even though history may move in cycles, Machiavelli by no means resigns himself to the idea of an inescapable fate. Indeed, his very project is a call for action and responsibility.[16] This is what Machiavelli has to say about the idea of surrendering oneself to a transcendent force:

> To believe that without effort on your part God fights for you while you are idle and on your knees, has ruined many kingdoms and many states. . . . There should be no one, with so small a brain, that he will believe, if his house is falling, that God will save it without any other prop, because he will die beneath that ruin. (CW, 764)

Neither the natural order nor divine providence nor, least of all, the end of history will intervene to advance human affairs. The responsibility for the world must be carried on human shoulders if one does not want to be crushed by the ruins of time. To interpret the theory of historical repetition as the fateful and eternal recurrence of the same thus misses the point. The historical analogy is Machiavelli's pedagogical model. By interpreting the present in the light of the past, the political actor is asked to infer a general rule. This is what Machiavelli intimates when he calls history "*la maestra delle azioni nostre*" and writes that "all worldly things in every time have their own counterpart in ancient times." To orient one's action by the experience of the past is to gain purchase on historical necessity, not to surrender to it.

By labeling history *la maestra delle azioni nostre*, the "teacher of our actions," Machiavelli edges history close to *necessità*, which is also repeatedly referred to as a teacher. The convergence signals that "necessity" is (among other things) Machiavelli's term of art to account for the cyclical, regular, and repetitive dimension of human affairs. Lest Machiavelli's philosophy of history be assimilated to a rigid, deterministic schema, the concept of *fortuna* serves to fragment the order of necessity and to capture the sometimes erratic volatility. As we will see, necessity and fortune are Machiavelli's two main metaphors for nonhuman nature, figures that are deployed as didactic devices, as models for how to stage and project forces in the political field.

Necessity as Limit and Category of Action

As a functional replacement for the role divine providence played in early Italian humanism, the concept of *necessità* is one of Machiavelli's original contributions to the field of philosophy of history. It has been called a "paradigm shift" in historiography and political theory, for it is the first time that political events are interpreted within a framework of pure facticity.[17] Machiavelli juxtaposes necessity to freedom, suggesting that "men are led by necessity to do what it was not their intention to do."[18] Frequently surfacing in the context of adversity, poverty, and ecological disasters like floods, plagues, and famines, *necessità* at first sight appears to designate the limits of human action, the perimeter beyond which human "*arte*" and "*industria*" are ineffective. In this context, necessity appears as an overbearing power that Machiavelli at one point even likens to "*violenza*" (D I.38, 83). It is a synonym for heteronomy, for what is given and set and not available to human intervention and transformation. Confronting necessity, the *arte dello stato* is powerless; thus the political actor must approach this limit in a different way.

Yet necessity designates not only the limit of human freedom. Machiavelli transforms *necessità* into both a category of the understanding and of action. As a category of the understanding, necessity allows Machiavelli to think order and regularity in a world of constant movement: "Since all things of men are in motion and cannot stay steady, they must either rise or fall; and to many things that reason does not bring you, necessity brings you" (D I.6, 23). In other words, necessity provides a measure of coherence to a world in flux, an immanent rationality that structures human affairs. Necessity "puts the world in order again."[19] Offering a hermeneutic for thinking order, necessity is frequently referred to as a teacher, implying that it can be known or, at the very least, that its historical traces bear a significant pedagogical value. "Certainly," Machiavelli declares through the voice of one of his heroes, a plebeian revolutionary, "when nothing else teaches us, necessity does" (FH, III.13, 122).[20] To take necessity as a teacher has a double meaning. On the one hand, it signifies that one must learn to think in terms of necessity. But on the other hand, it also means that one must learn how to *deploy* necessity, to convert it from a category of unfreedom into a concept of action.

As a category of action, necessity becomes a strategy of political subjection. To take necessity as a teacher involves *imitating* necessity and thereby subjecting others to it. Necessity is an important instrument of rule: "men work either by necessity or by choice," and since one does not control others' choices but can manage necessity, it is a more reliable strategy to produce order and stability (D I.1, 8). Machiavelli even describes necessity as a condition for political virtue.[21] It serves as an incubator for art and industry, checking the human tendency to idle.[22] As a set of obstacles, necessity provides a constant impetus for human creativity, ingenuity, and initiative. Necessity must therefore be mobilized for political purposes, and when natural necessity is lacking, the *fabrication* of necessity is an effective political strategy.

Indeed, the manufacture of necessity becomes Machiavelli's model of theorizing law and legal institutions. In the very first chapter of the *Discourses*, as if to mark the importance of this insight, Machiavelli discusses how one can produce political necessity as a supplement to the necessities nature has provided. The task of the law, he writes, is to impose "such necessities" as are not supplied by the given conditions (D I.1, 8–9). As Wendy Brown points out, this notion of law differs radically from the liberal tradition. For Machiavelli, the law does not represent the liberation from nature by civilized society but the "replication within society" of the "struggle with nature."[23] Legal and institutional arrangements are conceptualized not as the subjugation of nature but as an imitation, the task of which is to establish artificial conditions of necessity. In short, the law itself functions as a "second nature," and the problem of politics is to produce conditions akin to nature, to introduce laws that have the same power, that are as binding as the laws of nature. Necessity, Machiavelli writes, quoting Livy, is "the last and greatest weapon" (D III.12, 247–249); it both limns the limits of human action and serves as a paradigm according to which the social world should be ordered.

From an anthropological perspective, the imitation of nature becomes necessary because of human limitations and the fundamental dissonance between man and nature—or better: between human and nonhuman nature. As we have seen, Machiavelli's conception of human nature is itself split between an unnatural nature, constituted at least in part by convention, and a necessary appeal to nature. This tension is replicated as a discordance between human and nonhuman nature. Machiavelli shares the common opinion among Renaissance authors that human dispositions are not entirely adequate for the encounter with natural forces. *The Golden Ass* vibrantly conveys the topos of "man as a stepchild of nature," originally drawn from Pliny.[24] There, the discrepancy between man and nature manifests itself in terms of the deficiencies of the human senses and the dysfunctional condition in which humans enter the world. The lack of fit between the human animal and nonhuman nature is a symptom of the peculiarly unnatural dimension of human nature and the tension this produces: "Only man is devoid of all protection; he has neither hide nor spine nor feather nor fleece nor bristles nor scales to make him a shield," Machiavelli exclaims.[25] Other Renaissance humanists, such as Campanella, who appealed to the same theme, saw in the capacity of reason the redeeming feature of the human condition.[26] However, for Machiavelli, reason cannot compensate for human deficiencies. Whereas authors like Ficino and Pico della Mirandola emphasized human potential, linking it to a moral theory, Machiavelli—speaking as a boar in *The Golden Ass*—acidly remarks that even with regard to the four cardinal virtues of prudence, fortitude, justice, and temperance, nonhuman animals come out on top.[27] *Necessità* is the supplement that offsets the dissonance between human aspirations and limitations.

Necessity's Counterpart: Fortuna

Balancing necessity's deterministic connotations is its counterpart: chance, or what Machiavelli calls *fortuna*. Like *necessità*, *fortuna* is a figure for a force of nature that exceeds human control. The distinction between necessity and fortune is one that can be traced back to Greek and Roman mythology, which had two distinct goddesses personifying destiny: *ananke* (or *necessitas*), the mother of the *moirae*, signifying unalterable necessity and fate, and *tyche* or *fortuna*, standing for luck, chance, and accidents. Thus Aristotle distinguishes chance [*tyche*] from what happens "of necessity and always" or at least "for the most part."[28] The Romans worshipped *fortuna* in the shape of a veiled or blind goddess, signaling that the mythic forces ascribed to her elude visibility.[29] By the Middle Ages, the distinction between necessity and fortune was largely lost, and the two were collapsed in the same figure. In Rome, the goddess of fortune was represented with the symbols of the cornucopia, the rudder, and the wheel. In the Middle Ages, the cornucopia and the rudder gave way to the wheel of fortune—popularized by Boethius—that turns in only two directions, either up or down. The shift from a blind goddess to the image of a fixed spinning wheel indicates the altered character of fortune, from fickleness to inescapability, "bringing men, not riches or famine, nor their ultimate destiny . . . but an ascendant or a descendant movement in relation to other men."[30] It is against this background that Machiavelli reintroduces the distinction between necessity and fortune, prying them apart and reverting to the Roman imagery. He depicts fortune anthropomorphized, a "female power—mysterious, seductive, vengeful, cunning, associated with the impenetrable and unpredictable ways of nature."[31]

Machiavelli's *fortuna* often represents the irruption of an uncontrollable force into human affairs. She is a "cruel goddess" with "fierce eyes" who "rules with fury" and whose "reign is always violent"; an "aged witch [with] two faces," she "turns states and kingdoms upside down as she pleases" and "times events as suits her."[32] As Strauss notes, *fortuna* "takes the place of all gods" and becomes the generic figure for nonintentional "accidents."[33] Fortune tends to lack the regularity and uniformity of necessity; she sometimes appears as the pure event, unpredictable and volatile. Neither countable nor accountable, she exceeds every effort at calculation.

Yet it would be wrong to understand *fortuna* only as an external accident that may befall you—*fortuna* also stands for the mismatch between actions and historical conditions. In this sense, *fortuna* is not an external agency but "a function of the relative fit" between human action and the conditions of action.[34] To escape fortune one must understand one's time or even shape it.[35] This is the dimension of *fortuna* Machiavelli underscores when he writes that good and bad fortune is caused by "the matching of the mode of one's proceeding with the times." If one always wants to have good fortune, "one must vary with the times" (D III.9, 239).[36] We can infer that *fortuna* designates not the materialization of a transcendent force modeled after the divine. Rather, *fortuna* only has contextual meaning; it is tied to a particular constellation of forces.[37]

Necessità and *fortuna* are Machiavelli's terms of art to describe a backdrop of conditions beyond human control. Even though these shifting figures of nature are all somewhat ambiguous and, as Pitkin argues, "close to interchangeable," some distinctions can still be made.[38] Usually, necessity designates what is given, unalterable, regular, and stable, whereas fortune stands for the unpredictable, variable, and erratic (D I.11, 35; FH IV.33, 184). Machiavelli uses necessity to illuminate certain aspects of warfare (how to force a response or how to avoid being constrained in a particular way), whereas he never refers to fortune in a comparable sense. The contrast is perhaps starkest in the *Capitoli* on Fortune, where Machiavelli depicts *fortuna* as a mad whirlwind, shifting, moving, and volatile, whereas necessity is said to put "the world in order again" (CW, 747). The regularity and reliability Machiavelli associates with necessity partly compensates for its more violent side, whereas fortune lacks that redemptive power and is typically represented as a danger and threat.

The explicit appeal to necessity as an instructional device and the catachrestic reference to it as a "weapon" indicate that this reified category is not a mythic force but a pedagogical contraption. The same can be said for fortune. These concepts facilitate the categorization of events, relations, and temporalities; they offer a schema for the phenomenological experience of natural forces. What are the political consequences of this typology of forces? How do these figures structure the space of political action? If "all our actions imitate nature" (D II.3, 134), then these would seem to be crucial questions. And indeed, as we will see, there is a political dimension to this typology of forces. In accordance with the distinction between necessity and fortune, Machiavelli prescribes two different modes of managing them. For this purpose, it will be important to pay special attention to the variation of rhetorical figures Machiavelli deploys in his discussion of these forces. The next two sections reconstruct how fortune and necessity operate within the space of representation and how Machiavelli leverages tropes and mythic imagery to mobilize nature as a resource in the theater of politics.

Two Strategies to Control Necessity and Fortune

Managing Necessity: The best way to deal with necessity is to *anticipate* it by doing what necessity would force one to do. This is why Machiavelli commends him who "always proceeds as nature forces you," adding that he has a more "prosperous fortune" (D III.9, 239; cf. also P X, 38). By willing necessity, one can preempt being forced against one's will and thus gain power. Translated into the language of a geometry of forces, the force that aligns itself with existing vectors leverages their momentum. As an example, Machiavelli presents the decision of the Roman Senate to allow, as an exception, its subject peoples, the Latins and the Hernici, to arm and defend themselves against an attack while Rome was unable to assist them militarily because of an outbreak of the plague. While it contravened Roman policy to let subject peoples fight their own wars, the Senate knew that the Latins would "by necessity" do so anyway and preferred that the inevitable not be seen as a violation of its authority (D I.38, 82).[39] By willing and acting in accordance with necessity, the Senate maintains its authority and ratifies its status as the relevant political body that decides about peace and war. In a similar vein, the *Art of War* instructs: "I want you to take this general rule: the greatest remedy that is used against a plan of the enemy is to do voluntarily what he plans that you do by force. For by doing it voluntarily, you do it with order and to your advantage and his disadvantage. If you did it having been forced, it would be your ruin" (AW, IV, 93–94). The anticipation of necessity preempts the harm and injury that necessity might inflict. It converts necessity from a force that subjects us into an object of regulation.

Beyond the obvious tactical advantage one accrues by keeping the initiative and momentum on one's side, there is also a less tangible dimension to the principle put forward by Machiavelli. As emerges clearly in the case of the Latins and the Hernici, at stake is not whether these subject peoples draft their own armies (they will do so anyway) but the present and future authority of the Roman Senate. By feigning control over the subjects' actions in the face of utter feebleness, the Senate fabricates a façade of power. In Victoria Kahn's words, "the realm of representation can be used to distance oneself from, and thereby in some sense control the realm of necessity."[40] The representational field of politics introduces the possibility for humans to exploit the domain of appearances in order to gain a real measure of autonomy. Through the practice of mimesis as well as the production of illusions, an interval is created, and a certain control over the forces of nature can be achieved. The representational space of politics gains purchase on the overbearing natural power by projecting a fictitious competency to manage nature.[41]

It is here that we see the consequences of Machiavelli's determination of politics as a field of representation. Recall the counsel in the infamous chapter 18 of *The Prince*, that what matters in politics are not real virtues or vices but the ones that are *projected* in the realm of appearances (P XVIII, 70). The production of images, simulations, and replicas reveals itself to be constitutive of the formation of power and authority. The appearance, which is neither original nor authentic and thus, in another sense of the word, secondary—though perhaps not identical with "second nature"—turns out to be substantially more than a "mere" image. Or rather: it demonstrates that there is nothing behind the image, no essence or substance to which the appearance could be compared and against which it could be judged as lacking something. In ontological terms, politics is an aesthetic regime of images and appearances that are characterized not by a lack of reality or a deficiency but by a surplus of signification, where signs reflect back on each other, as in a house of mirrors.[42]

Managing Fortune: The management of fortune, by contrast, is more complex, not least because the extent of her actual power is unclear. Machiavelli calls *fortuna* "the arbiter of *all* human things," but elsewhere she is "the arbiter of *half* of our actions," leaving "the other half, or close to it, for us to govern" (CW, 553; P XXV, 98, my emphasis). We will have to return to the question of fortune's reach below. Meanwhile, we observe that coping with fortune demands *direct and immediate intervention.* Unlike necessity, which is to be preempted or anticipated, fortune must be vanquished by "greater virtù" if her violent reign is to be ended (CW 745; trans. modified). Machiavelli presents the strategies of dominating and domesticating fortune in two famous allegories that appear in the penultimate chapter of *The Prince*—the violent river and fortune as a woman. On the one hand, Machiavelli likens fortune to

> one of these violent rivers [*fiumi rovinosi*], which, when they become enraged, flood the plains, ruin the trees and the buildings, lift earth from this part, drop in another; each person flees before them, everyone yields to their impetus [*all'impeto loro*] without being able to hinder them in any regard. [But] it is not as if men . . . could not provide for them with dikes and dams so that when they rise later, either they go by a canal or their impetus [*l'impeto loro*] is neither so wanton nor so damaging. It happens similarly with fortune, which demonstrates her power where virtue has not been ordered so as to resist her and therefore turns her impetus [*sua impeti*] where she knows that dams and dikes have not been made to contain her. (P XXV, 98)

On the other hand:

> it is better to be impetuous [*impetuoso*] than cautious, because fortune is a woman; and it is necessary, if one wants to hold her down, to beat her and strike her down. And one sees that she lets herself be won more by the impetuous than by those who proceed coldly. And so always, like a woman, she is the friend of the young, because they are less cautious, more ferocious, and command her with more audacity. (P XXV, 101)

These passages figure fortune in two images: the allegory of a "violent" or ruinous river assimilates fortune to a natural force that can turn into disaster; the traditional metaphor of fortune as a woman, which Machiavelli modifies by introducing elements of (hetero)sexual conquest and violence, frames the control over fortune—and thus the politics of nature—as a question of manliness within the phallic imagery of power.[43] As a river, fortune is restrained by dikes and dams, structures that are intended to contain a future eruption. Anthropomorphized as a woman, fortune must be coercively conquered or even raped in order to make her submissive. The conquest of fortune is staged as a complicated tableau with interwoven strands of coercion, seduction, desire, and violence. It is through the passions that fortune can be compelled, for she smiles upon audacity and favors the brave (or even ferocious). Each of these two morphologies thus implies a different management strategy: the trope of the river demands a strategy of prevention and containment; the metaphor of the woman indicates a strategy of seduction, compulsion, and violence.

Just as we thought that we had grasped the distinction between necessity and fortune as a taxonomy for the phenomenological experience of natural forces, Machiavelli unravels it. By making use of two apparently incompatible metaphors for fortune (river/woman), he appears to divide fortune and muddle his categories. Are the two metaphors substitutable, or do they complement each other? Do we have to decide between them? If building dikes and dams is a cautious strategy, then it would seem that Machiavelli explicitly rejects it when he declares that fortune favors the ferocious and audacious. This is what Pitkin suggests when she argues that Machiavelli develops the trope of the river and then proceeds "to a reexamination or partial rejection of his own metaphor."[44] Agreeing with Pitkin that the two tropes are incompatible, Robert Orr proposes a different solution: he temporalizes the human relation to *fortuna* and divides it into multiple phases. Thus, the preparations for the flood correspond to the first stage of fortuna's "visit," while the immediate confrontation is the response option when fortune is directly upon you.[45] While Pitkin's and Orr's interpretations are provocative, they both presuppose a categorical distinction between the techno-scientific management strategy and the strategy of force. But what if this assumption does not hold? What if the interference in the regular course of nature is not as innocent as Pitkin and Orr imagine?

Figures of Fortune as Reversible Tropes

The imagery of fortune, as a river framed by dikes and dams, evokes Heidegger's depiction of the Rhine in "The Question Concerning Technology." While this essay does not mention Machiavelli, I would like to turn to it briefly because it can illuminate our tropological conundrum. Heidegger argues that technology is a truth procedure: it discloses and unconceals things, bringing them into the world, what Heidegger calls revealing [*entbergen*]. If all kinds of technology share this aspect of conveying things and letting them emerge into view, modern technology is specific because, unlike the Greek *technē*, it no longer functions within a natural harmony; instead, it brings things forth by challenging nature. Modern technology constitutes nature as a resource, as a store and source of reserves that can be unlocked and exposed. Thereby, it transforms the thingness of nature into objectivity, into a calculable and orderable field of intervention. Heidegger explains this process by invoking the example of the Rhine, which has been converted, he argues, from a fierce river into an object of planners and engineers who consider it a store of energy and resources.[46]

The question concerning technology is thus the question of how humans relate to nature or, in Heideggerian diction, how being is unconcealed and revealed. The danger of modern technology is that it tends to frame the world as a stock of resources that can be ordered, secured, and appropriated. Ultimately, this will turn not only nonhuman nature into stockpiles of objects but will also do the same to the human. While Heidegger does not consider this a political issue and turns to art, not to politics, as a remedy, what his nostalgia articulates is the transformation of a political ontology. For our purposes, this raises the question of whether Machiavelli's problematic of fortune may mark the intersection between the establishment of political power and the production of nature as a field of human intervention.

Turning back to Machiavelli's metaphors, we might ask not only how the natural imagery serves as a way to explicate the disruptive character of fortune but also how the figure of fortune as a force available for domination frames nature as a manageable sphere.[47] A closer look at the two metaphors for fortune—river and woman—reveals that there is in fact semantic overlap. The river floods the plains, Machiavelli writes, when it becomes "enraged." The surging water is described in anthropomorphic terms, as though the floods resulted from a passionate mood swing in the river's emotional economy. Within the allegorical representation of fortune as a river, the force of the river is figured as a catachresis: the inundation is depicted as a result of human passion rather than as that of hydrological forces. It would thus appear that the imagery of a natural disaster for the irruption of fortune is thus *reversible.*

Analogously to the mysterious force of fortune, which cannot be fully controlled by human action and must therefore appear allegorized as a river, so the force of nature must appear personified in order to be contained and channeled. Consequently, we cannot assume that the prophylactic strategies of dealing with fortune qua river are innocuous. Rather, the image of fortune as a river turns out to be simultaneously an allegory of the river as fortune. Turned this way, it is not only the river that stands in for fortune but also fortune (in the shape of a woman) that stands in for the river, by way of a catachresis, and synecdochally, even for nature. It is not only fortune that demands a figurative rendition (woman/river) but nature itself. Nature, here appearing in the garb of the river, only becomes an object of intervention through the image of the struggle with the gendered figure of fortune. Just as coping with unexpected forces becomes intelligible only when represented figuratively as building dikes and dams, so the anthropomorphic image of the ferocious struggle with woman-as-fortune serves as a heuristic device to make the techno-scientific rendition of nature thinkable. To put it in Heideggerian terms, the technological revealing of nature as an object of rationalization and administration by engineers and planners is marked by the rendition of the human relation to the river in terms of a gendered political syntax—the struggle with fortune. There are representational requirements for nature to become an object of functional calculation and instrumentalization, and the convergence of these tropes is emblematic for the representational practices with which such a transformation is associated.

The second trope, then, does not metaphorize fortune anew as a replacement for the figure of the river, but it operates as a rhetorical figure of a second order, introducing a further tropic level. If the river provides a natural analogue for fortune, the woman functions as a political metaphor not only for fortune but also for nature. The human intervention in the natural order, by constructing embankments to channel the river, is thus metaphorized as a gendered form of conquest and rape. The imagery of sexual violence blended with the dialectic of desire mediates the view of nature as a supply of resources available to human consumption and intervention. Gender and gendered forms of violence turn out to be the prisms through which this objectification of nature is figured. And violence serves as the symbolic outlet to construct the domination of humans over nature. The figures of violence are the grid through which Machiavelli thinks not only political domination in the narrow sense of the word but also technical domination over nature.

Conclusion

The instability between nature and politics in Machiavelli's text points to a tension that is internal to nature. If the nature of the human is the becoming other than itself, and if the recourse to a fiction of nature remains politically significant within the field of appearances, then the nature that is projected into the political space is necessarily "second." Machiavelli's man is that animal whose nature it is to be historical, to have no fixed nature, yet who must constantly refer to nature, the animal who is condemned to mimic and replicate nature. The nature that the human is summoned to imitate is figured in terms of two concepts: necessity and fortune. As teachers, necessity and fortune are not just overbearing powers that confront the human but also didactic devices: they model what it means to stage natural forces in the arena of politics and project them into the realm of appearances. If the capacity to project images is part of what constitutes political power, this move represents an effort to fashion political and natural worlds such that particular structures and events appear as given or as changeable, as constraining or enabling, and as available or unavailable for political-technical intervention. At issue, then, is the symbolic order that generates the relation between the natural and political world, the order of appearances that determines what counts as an object of regulation and what is the threshold of a world that transcends such control.

If fortune governs "all human things" (*tutte le cose umane*) but only "half of our actions" (*metà delle azioni nostre*), then we must assume that the other half of our actions, those that we decide by our "free will" (P XXV, 98), are not part of "all human things." If they are not part of "all human things," such *azioni* must belong to the realm of nonhuman nature. They must transcend the limitations that set humans off from the rest of nature. Effective political action, Machiavelli seems to say, must not be marked or recognizable as human; it must, paradoxically, be a form of *azioni nostre* without being part of *tutte le cose umane*. The nonhuman becomes the explicit horizon of a form of action that is not determined by fortune. It is unclear what kinds of actions might be excluded from *tutte le cose umane*, but in chapter 18 of *The Prince*, Machiavelli famously distinguishes between two types of combat, "one with laws, the other with force" (69). The former is appropriate for humans, the latter for beasts. If a prince, as Machiavelli insists, "needs to know both natures," the human and the beastly, does the recourse to *forza* pave the way for the political actor to bypass the human condition of being a stepchild of nature? Is violence the nonhuman kind of action that escapes the determination by fortune because it is both an imitation of nature and antinature?

It is surely no accident that Machiavelli uses the same word—*impeto* and *impetuoso*—to refer both to the ways of fortune and to the necessary attribute of a political actor who aims to control her. Indeed, impetuosity and its various derivatives turn out to be crucial terms here, occurring ten times in the penultimate chapter of *The Prince*. The iteration implies a formal correspondence between fortune's mode of action and its human counterpart. Insofar as both generate an impetus, human action and fortune are on some level substitutable. The *impeto* of such action emerges from the (re)production of nature in the political field. The iteration and imitation orchestrate nature in the name of political purposes. If effective action has to shed its attribute of belonging to *tutte le cose umane*, we may speculate whether the vanishing point of Machiavelli's theory of action isn't the site where action and necessity converge. At this point, action models *necessità*, for it aims to structure and congeal the circumstances and forms within which other forces on the political terrain operate. It marks the point of indistinction, where the distance between necessity, fortune, and human action is collapsed. The upshot is that even as Machiavelli begins to think the becoming-unnatural of politics, political action remains modeled on a natural causality; it is asked to mirror not the weeping foundling without a place in the natural order but the force of this very order itself.

CHAPTER 2

Burning the Dead and the Ways of Nature

Thomas Laqueur

In 1907, a brilliant twenty-six-year-old French sociologist and student of Emile Durkheim—Robert Hertz—published a hugely influential paper that made clear that there were two kinds of dead: one in nature, the other in culture.[1] (He himself died in the trenches of the Great War eight years later.) On the one hand, there are the dead as bodies: flesh, soon to putrefy, that has lost whatever made it alive and is now subject to decay like any other organic matter. These dead—corpses—have little history. Bystanders in an early thirteenth-century panel by Duccio held their noses in the presence of an enshrouded but already decaying Lazarus, just as we would in similar circumstances; in an early Christian ivory pyx, they turn away.

On the other hand, there are the dead as social facts, as creatures who need to be eased out of this world and settled safely into the next. How this needs to be done—through funereal rites, proper mourning, and other kinds of postmortem attention—is deeply, paradigmatically, indeed foundationally, part of culture. It is not, like natural death, something that happens more or less in an instant; it takes time—in difficult circumstances a very long time—for the dead really to be gone. They may not go easily to their fate and instead lurk dangerously among the living. These were the grotesque, monstrous, undead Norse *aptrangar*—the "one who walks after death"; the central European Nosferatu; the Chinese dead who walk in droves to appropriate burial places; the mournful "shadow" of Odysseus's mother who slips from his arms and explains that he cannot hold her because a "ghost, like a dream flutters off and is gone" (11:221). These dead are different from us, whatever else they might be, but they are also not quite dead either. Janos Kadar, the last communist leader of Hungary, feared the return—and refused to the speak the name—of the executed and improperly laid to rest Imre Nagy, the prime minister of the 1956 revolutionary government, with the same fervent fear a South Sea Islander might have in speaking a necronym.[2]

Robert Hertz's distinction entered anthropological theory a century ago, but the profoundly cultural nature of how we treat the naturally dead, as if they were not quite dead, was evident already to Herodotus, who puts this wisdom in the mouth of the Persian king. On the one hand, there is the belief that one's own death customs are irreducibly right and ethically inescapable, as if grounded in nature; on the other hand, there is the realization that other people with radically different views hold theirs equally dear and equally natural:

> . . . in the course of his reign he summoned those of the Hellenes who were present in his land, and asked them for what price they would consent to eat up their fathers when they died; and they answered that for no price would they do so. After this Dareios summoned those Indians who are called Callatians, who eat their parents, and asked them in presence of the Hellenes, who understood what they said by help of an interpreter, for what payment they would consent to consume with fire the bodies of their fathers when they died; and they cried out aloud and bade him keep silence from such words. Thus then these things are established by usage, and I think that Pindar spoke rightly in his verse, when he said that "of all things law is king."[3]

In other words, how one disposed of the dead was at the same time foundational—"it is not likely that any but a madman would make a jest of such things"—and customary, a matter of law. And so the matter stood for thousands of years.

In the late nineteenth century, however, a group of doctors, hygienists, chemists, and progressive thinkers more generally argued a very different position: one particular way of disposing of dead bodies was natural. It mimicked nature. By claiming that the dead existed primarily in the realm of matter that needed to be managed by the techniques of metallurgy, economics, and public health, they were at the same time creating new relationships between the living and the dead and thus new possibilities for civilization. The dead as part of nature lent their power to a modernist cultural program.

Decay—the way of all flesh, indeed all organic matter—was but oxidation, and burning was but oxidation speeded up. One might speak about the aesthetic and cultural virtues of cremation—this was the brief of neoclassical commentaries and practices from George Lessing in the eighteenth century through the Homeric reenactment of Shelley's funeral pyre on the shores of the Mediterranean through the learned praise of Jakob Grimm thirty years later. But this was not the essence of discussions after 1870. The idea that "fresh earth is the best disinfectant is itself a delusion" was said by the lecturer George Wotherspoon to a London audience that had heard earlier the distinguished psychologist Henry Maudsley on the lessons of materialism and the pioneer statistician and freethinker Karl Pearson on matter and the soul. Ask Nature "what is the great purifier," he suggests, "and her very echoes will answer Fire." There was always more at stake than hygiene, even in the most materialist literature. Purity is never just natural. But that said, so direct a query to nature on a matter that had seemed so securely cultural represents a radical turn.[4]

The ground shifted under the dead. Being dead was unthinkable once one tried to think about it, the advocates of cremation argued, and the sooner the evidence of decay and corruption—the disgusting inevitable consequences of being dead—could be eliminated, the better all around. And especially the better from the perspective of life, from the perspective of hygiene, of "the art of preserving health."[5] The simple fact with which Henry Thompson, the distinguished surgeon and one of the most prominent European advocates for cremation, began his 1874 tract speaks worlds; all the rest is commentary. At death, he insists, the body is "instantly consigned to the action of physical and chemical agencies alone," however much we might want to talk about "the unknown and incomparable vital thing that is life."[6]

In fact, the dead body teems with life, but not its own. "Rest! Not for an instant," continues Thompson. Never was there such activity. Thousands of changes have begun. "Forces innumerable have attacked the dead." "The rapidity of the vulture" is nothing compared to the rapidity with which the forces of synthesis that constituted life are reversed. Nature "has another end in view": decomposition. She "acts herself to work in disposing dead animal matter" by resolving it into carbon dioxide, water, ammonia, and various minerals. A German university professor and material philosopher had announced twenty years earlier that these minerals—phosphorous in particular—were crucial to mental development and that hence only cremation, which returned them to circulation, would assure that the living were as smart as they could be. But it was Sir Henry Thompson, the earliest and most important voice in Anglo-American discussions of cremation, who put the matter in a broader perspective: it is still necessary, he wrote, after fifteen years of agitation to "explain the sanitary laws which must inevitably render cremation, or some method of disposing of the dead other than burial, *inevitable.*"[7] "Inevitable" meant "dictated by nature." The dead were organic matter, and what to do with them therefore was essentially an empirical, factual question. Chemists and physiologists and their ilk had the answers.

Of course, recourse to nature as the moral authority for action was not a late nineteenth-century novelty. The nature/culture distinction, notoriously unstable as we know it to be, was itself always predicated on the sense that the first of these terms represented, in some fashion, a sort of unchangeable adamantine reality that we humans ignore at our peril.[8] But the critical and ironic novelty here is that those who were advocating cremation as dictated by nature were explicitly denying a millennia-old rule of custom in putting the dead to rest, and in so doing they were themselves making a claim that rested on the towering cultural authority of death: crudely put, if the dead belong to science, then so does much else. I shall return to this point at the end of this chapter. For now, I want only to show how the foundations for this position were fixed in one national context, starting with Thompson's foundational text.

Buried dead bodies, Thompson writes, caused untold amounts of misery and disease. Thousands of lives are "cut short by the poison of decay," he continues, supporting his claim with some fifteen pages of evidence, ranging from hoary eighteenth-century stories to the latest experiments of Louis Pasteur on the dangers to livestock of burying animals who had died of anthrax. Twenty-two additional pages, based on the previous fifteen years of research, give added weight to these views in the expanded 1889 edition: 73,747 out of the 537,276 people who died in Britain in 1886, for example, succumbed to so-called zymotic disease, diseases caused by "ferment," including smallpox, measles, scarlet fever, diphtheria, whooping cough, typhus, enteric fever, simple fever, dysentery, and cholera. All of these newly dead could be blamed on the decaying dead who preceded them. Research, in short, had proven that "putrefaction affecting organic matter disseminates the germs of fatal disease" and that, through the very act of internment itself, we "literally sow broadcast [*sic*] throughout the land innumerable seeds of pestilence" that lie dormant until, at some future time, they "fructify in premature death and ruined health for thousands."[9]

Cremation stops the process before it can begin; there is no way around this. In itself, Thompson's way of arguing is not new. The public health danger of dead bodies in ancient churchyards was an Enlightenment medical set piece and found new articulations among nineteenth-century sanitary reformers. By the time cremation became a matter of debate in the 1870s, the dead in their new burial places had already come, to a great extent, under the intellectual and administrative purview of public health specialists. The contest between cemeteries and churchyards had been ostensibly fought, if not won, on hygienic grounds. Old ways of burial were no longer viable, it had been argued since the eighteenth century, because of the danger to the living of pathogenic effluvia, suffocating gases, and poisonous fouled water. It was the Board of Health in Great Britain that inspected town after town to judge whether their disposal practices met new health standards, and it found that they generally did not. Everywhere in Europe bodies had come to be the professional concern of the same people who worried about cholera, smoke, milk, and water.

In that sense, the dead ought to have been used to being treated as dirt, but not as just dirt. Custom still ruled in the new cemeteries; bodies came to be buried more hygienically than before, but still, they *were* put in the ground, as they had been since the Romans turned to inhumation. After the 1870s, however, the dead—along with the refuse of abattoirs and the rubbish of the streets and the waste of sand toilets—would be joined together in a new technical discussion to an unprecedented extent. Of course, they never left culture behind entirely; they almost always remained more than mere matter, and crematoria and columbaria still bore the marks of history. But never before had the crucial cultural question of how to put the dead to rest become so much a part of the question of nature, one part of the technical problem of disposal.

Sanitary engineers, doctors, and public health experts adapted the furnaces of metallurgy for their own purposes. It became axiomatic even outside technical fields that the sooner society rid itself of this odiferous garbage the better. Since decay in the grave is but slow burning, as a sympathetic clergyman wrote, fire is just speeding up the same process in which bodies are rendered "into their compound atoms," dispersed, and "re-contributed to the vast material world, to an ever living and changing Cosmos, from which they were originally borrowed." (Being devoured by wild beasts or being lost at sea was faster, too.) What had once been the horrible fate of placeless dissolution would become a culturally resonant gloss on what happens when a dead body is ingested or cremated. But the new reality was that dead bodies were being claimed by sanitary engineers who thought along such paths.[10]

William Eassie, who became secretary of the newly formed Cremation Society upon its founding in 1874, made his name first in the Crimea, where he supervised the building of the Erenkoy Hospital. Back home, he was well known as the author of what became the standard handbook for building healthy houses, a work dealing in a detailed, technical way with proper drainage, ventilation, and "kindred subjects." But he thought of himself as engaged in a far grander world-historical project: "at length, the sanitary day is dawning." Mankind will at last be "restrained from committing suicide by setting at defiance all the laws of Health." The preservation of public health, he argued, was crucial if we—we British—are "to hold our own in the rapid race for pre-eminence amongst the nations of the earth." "Science is to triumph;" "facts not fancies must be our guides." Finally, rotten back drains, the infiltration of sewage into wells, and disused drains would get their due. "Permanent sanitary temples," like the one built in Leeds in 1871, would, he hoped, soon serve as shining examples.[11]

In fact, only the prefaces of his books offered such high-flown thoughts. He devoted the rest to the details of getting rid of waste—mostly of the bodily sort—and its smells: water closets should not be placed in cramped quarters; they, and sinks too, must have proper traps that he describes in detail; the state of urinals is the best index to the sanitary condition of an establishment; earth closets are fine as long as "all possible smell" is avoided. Avoid ammonical dust—suggestive of the smell of composting bodies—when choosing chemicals for wetting streets, he counsels. From here it is a small step to cremation and its history. From the earliest times forward, people have burned bodies, Eassie argues, on sanitary grounds, to "protect the living from the effects of corruption."[12] Now we know in detail why. Foreign doctors have done basic research about carbonic acid levels in graveyards; we know that only recently graves have poisoned wells in Finchley.

His colleague from the Crimea, Edmund Parkes, to whom he looks for authority, had set up the terms of the problem clearly: basically, the dead are in the same category as excrement. A section of Parkes's much reprinted *Manual of Practical Hygiene* on "ordinary London sewage" explains that it produces one to 1.5 cubic inches of gas per hour per gallon: asphyxiating gases—carbonic acid, sulphurated hydrogen, sulfide of ammonia, and a residue category of "putrid organic vapors." Sewage also contains "multitudes" of "dead decaying matters," "infusoria," and "fungi."[13] Likewise with bodies. A section on air in churchyards follows one on sewage: again, we find the claim that 2.5 million cubic feet of carbonic acid are produced by 52,000 dead bodies in London; again "fungi and germ infusoria abound."[14]

Parkes, who founded a much-publicized temple to health in Leeds in the early 1870s, had no systematic ideas before 1874 about what to do with all this human sewage. He warns about the accumulation of bodies that one finds in the great cemeteries of Anatolia; he explains that bodies are eventually oxidized into simpler components—gases and volatile salts that go back into the soil. The question he addresses is how to accommodate these substances. Deep burial has advantages in terms of keeping pollution away from the living even if it is a slow way to recycle, charcoal helps with smell but is expensive, and burning costs more than burial at sea, which is cheap and allows the body to "go at once to support other forms of life."[15] Eassie makes use of all this by adapting to a specific purpose the general observations of an acknowledged master of hygiene.

By 1883 Parkes had discovered the cremationists who had already discovered him. (He had also discovered Sir Francis Seymour Haden's earth-to-earth wicker coffin, which he thought had possibilities because it hastened decomposition and was sanitary if it was buried deeply enough.) The new editions of his book add a long and approving section of what the Germans and French had learned about disposing bodies in their 1870–1871 war. Simply digging up superficially buried bodies and burning them by covering them with pitch and straw—one ton per fifteen to twenty bodies—met with mixed results; some thought that only the surface of the dead soldiers were burned by this technique. But there was a plan that worked in Metz in 1870. A pit seventeen feet deep was dug, a row of bodies was placed side by side, a second was placed across them, and so on, with powder placed between rows. In a pit filled to within six feet of the surface, 8,400 of the dead could be swiftly incinerated.

No one proposed anything so drastic for civilian life, and, when the time came in 1914 to consider once again what to do with the dead of war, mass cremation was the antithesis of the solution developed in Metz. Even Parkes must have understood that what he was describing was less than appealing. There was a nicer way to achieve the same results: Mr. Eassie, he tells his readers, has recently proposed an "ambulatory cremation furnace," which would "unquestionably be of immense advantage from a hygienic point of view."[16]

But the central point remained: the dead were, before all else, refuse and had to be treated as such. They were an acute problem for a military sanitary engineer in time of war but also a chronic one for civilians in ordinary times. There were, one lecturer warned, some four million stone of putrefying flesh produced in Great Britain per year; precisely 28,791 stone in Hull alone, if one calculated eight stone per average body. Burying this mass merely preserved "scaly germ covered bodies instead of destroying them." Refuse is refuse. "No sound arguments can be urged" against the cremation of dead animals and garbage, argued an American proponent of cremation with reference to his British colleagues. Eassie had shown how important it was to burn dead horses in the Crimea; an article in the *British Medical Journal* had shown how animal bodies cut up into chunks could be burned in the furnaces of gas works. In short, "science has shown that cremation merely produces quickly what putrefaction takes a long time to accomplish."[17]

Furnace technology was almost as important in making the dead mere matter as was hygiene. Henry Thompson bequeathed a genealogy of incineration to his successors that was resolutely and self-consciously shallow. In the beginning were the Italians—not Romans or Renaissance humanists, but professors of medicine one and all, who were the first to experiment with burning human and animal bodies during the late 1860s. He—Thompson—first got interested in the subject when he saw Exhibit #4149 at the 1873 Great Exhibition in Vienna, in which one Prof. Brunetti presented his apparatus and its products—miscellaneous piles of ashes neatly contained in labeled glass cubes along with a model of his furnace. Never before had burnt corpses been at the center of what we would now call a poster presentation at a scientific meeting. Brunetti's results were impressive, but his methods were primitive: it took 3.5 hours and 150 pounds of wood in a primitive furnace to convert an adult human to 1.7 kilograms of delicate white ash. Cremation was still in its R&D stages.

Thompson moved it nearer to full production. No sooner was he back from Vienna, early in 1874, than he obtained an emaciated, forty-seven-pound body—it could only have belonged to a pauper, but he does not tell readers how he came by it—and reduced it to 1.75 pounds of ash in the furnace of one of Britain's leading machine works: Maudsley, Sons, and Fields, famous for having built the engines and propelling equipment for Brunel's "Great Western." Twenty-five minutes from start to finish. A robust, 140-pound pauper took only minutes to be converted to four pounds of ash. No odor. "Nothing can be more purer tested by sight or smell than they are"; a "portion of refuse" had been turned into a refined substate.

In an interview that he gave to Edmund Yates, the muckraking journalist and writer of sensational novels, Thompson offered to show his interlocutor a "curiosity": two glass cubes no more than five inches on a side, one containing the remains of a twelve-stone (168-pound) body, the other an eighteen-stone (234-pound) one, which, he proudly announced, were entirely mineral in content and small in volume; "there is nothing offensive about either specimen." The larger of the two must have been a pig that he cremated in Birmingham at the invitation of his friend William Siemens, the German steel furnace magnate and inventor; the other, he says, was cremated at "Maudsleys below the bridge," but its original weight does not correspond to either of the bodies in the initial experiments he described in print. Perhaps it was the result of further trials.[18]

The details of body burning, although of the greatest interest to the early advocates of cremation, need not detain us here. The point for now is simply that technology and not ritual was the new way to make the dead clean, moving them along and out of the way. Thompson himself thought that Siemens's regenerating furnace did this best. It reheated the products of combustion from one chamber in a second one and then channeled the hot gases back to the original chamber for further combustion. The process had all sorts of advantages for fuel economy and revolutionized steel production: by the 1890s the Siemens process had outstripped Bessemer's in tonnage manufactured. It likewise made possible the incineration of bodies by allowing them to be thoroughly consumed without fouling the air.

Particulate was a problem for those who wanted to think of the dead as waste. Thompson himself, as vice president of the British Sanitary Institute, took up as one of his last crusades the elimination of "the abominations which are loading the air with unknown mischief": the lighter particles and scraps of garbage that escaped from the wicker baskets used by London's dustmen to transfer each house's "dust" to a collecting cart. The closed collectable bin that is still used today was his contribution to metropolitan cleanliness. Burning bodies could be even more polluting than collecting rubbish the old-fashioned way. Several councilors of the Imperial Board of Health in Vienna, for example, had suggested that cremation was not as clean as advocates claimed: one brought to the attention of his colleagues reports from India that the air was poisoned for miles around after a suttee. The matter was referred to committee. (The Indian comparison was immediately relevant because William Eassie, the sanitary engineer who was also secretary of the Cremation Society, had described how a poor person could be burned in Poona "with all necessary respect" and at "low cost." A twenty-year-old paper by an English doctor working in India, which claimed that simply building a high chimney for each burning ghat would do the trick, was apparently not widely read.)[19]

Thompson and his colleagues were on the case. As he recalled years later to a journalist, he had reduced a 227-pound animal body to under five pounds of ash in fifty-five minutes with not a particle of smoke: only "heated hydrocarbons in gaseous form" and hot air escaped.[20] Walter Smith, speaking to the Salford Gas Department Mutual Improvement Society—there may have been professional self-interest here—described a mortuary plant that was perhaps less sophisticated than Siemens's furnace but whose seventeen gas-fueled banks of six retorts each could burn a day's worth of dead bodies from metropolitan Manchester in just five hours. Gases would go up the chimney with no more prejudice to the environment than one factory chimney.

Other more farfetched, schemes were mooted. Even if the Siemens's furnace was the top of the line for now, new technologies were on the horizon: the body might be shrouded in sheets of asbestos, with large copper plates placed at head and feet. It would be like a "filament in an incandescent lamp" that, when a current was passed through it, "would be instantly carbonized."[21] The image does not quite work: filaments are meant to glow and not burn up. In any case, no one ever tried so madcap a scheme; the newly founded Cremation Society settled on a furnace for its new facility at Woking designed by an Italian anatomist named Paolo Gorini. The critical point, however, is that making the dead clean, which had been the work of ritual and culture, was now thought to be a job for technology and environmental engineering.

If one took this step, then the dead also became, more explicitly than ever before, a part of political economy—in fact, the management of resources more generally—and were subject to its laws. (Readers of *Our Mutual Friend* and of Catherine Gallagher's writings about it will not be surprised at this extension of a mid-nineteenth-century theme.)[22] The defunct human, like manure and other organic remains, are part of nature's capital, Thompson argued, and "capital is intended to bear good interest." Burying bodies is thus like burying money or anything else valuable and preventing it from being fruitful; cremating them makes them available for reinvestment. Consider, he suggests, that there are 80,430 deaths in greater London each year. These could yield 206,282 pounds of ash—six to eight times more valuable than an equal weight of dried but still extant bones—plus another 5,584,000 pounds of gaseous food for plants that would otherwise not be available for fifty to one hundred years. Multiply these numbers by nine, and one gets an astounding figure for what the whole country's dead would yield. (He uses a low number because London's death rate is higher than the national average; its population is more like ten percent of the whole population.)

Thompson was not the first to think so concretely about bodies as agrarian capital. Louis-Sébastien Mercier, the French Revolutionary playwright, father of science fiction, and passionate follower of Jean-Jacques Rousseau, opposed cremation for a number of aesthetic and political reasons: the pyres were hateful, flames cadaverous, and the private sepulchers made possible by having one's dead grandfather and uncle in urns that could be put in the cupboard were "an affront to the calm and repose of society." But he added an argument that Thompson would have understood even if it pointed in a different direction. Corpses do not belong to us but to the earth from which their elements came. Fire, he says, robs the soil of what it "has a right to expect for the reproduction of vegetable life and the building up of chalky soils" because most of the cremated body goes up in smoke. And cremation wastes whole forests for fuels.[23]

For seventy years, little would be heard of this talk of environmental economy, and when it reappeared it was in support of cremation. Gas would replace wood, and a very different sort of calculation showed how economical cremation really was. Indeed, burial wasted resources, Thompson shows, if calculations take national income into account. Britain imported £409,590 worth of animal bones as the raw material for fertilizer in 1866, £600,029 in 1869, and £753,185 in 1877 because the nation was "hoarding" its own bones six feet underground. Add to this the cost of freight for imported bones and the cost of funerals and burials, £10 on average multiplied by the eighty thousand dead in London alone, and the economic madness of current burial practices become clear. (The boundaries of what could be spoken had shifted dramatically since 1845–1856. Then, the revelation that paupers were beating animal bones—and, it was hinted, bones from the local churchyard—into fertilizer meal at the Andover Workhouse caused a scandal for eliding the boundaries between the worthless poor and valuable skeletal remains.)

There were still limits to how far proponents might want to take the ecological argument. William Eassie admitted that the case for cremation had suffered from an early proposal that the dead might be used to produce illuminating gas.[24] But even if it was not clear how, technologically or within the limits of what society would tolerate, bodies could be effectively recycled, it was clear that this was the goal. As another writer hopefully forecast, "some higher use may possibly be made of our bodies by enabling them to increase the food and wealth of others" once they were of no more use to us. (The same writer looked forward to the day when "dust to dust, ashes to ashes, will no longer be words without meaning.")[25]

But in the meantime, it was thought, the negative impact of corpses should at least be mitigated. One could economize on space, for example. Buried bodies took up a lot of space. A cremated body fit into a cube six inches on a side, as Eassie pointed out; Thompson's experimental subjects had fit into a five-inch cube. With such a radical reduction in volume, a million corpses—a year's worth of mortality—placed in a million urns would take up no more than one acre; a square mile of earth could contain the dead of six hundred years.[26] More utopian calculations in the late nineteenth century harkened back to the most grandiose funerary fantasies of the eighteenth century—the neo-Egyptian cenotaph of Etienne Louis Boullée or the "monument to brave citizens who died for the nation" of Jean-Jacques Lequeu, for example, although there is no evidence that these were in the minds of the new cremationists.

Suppose, the argument goes, that we were to convert the ashes, especially of poor people, into cubic-foot-size cubes. Then we could build a pyramid of these—the "one indestructible form of architecture"—with a base of 9,801 square feet. Going fifty feet high, with four sides, we would get a 166,650-cubic-foot structure that contained precisely that number of bodies. Multiply by four and we get 666,600 corpses in four pyramids that could easily fit onto a one-acre plot, doing the work of twenty acres of cemetery. Alternatively, bury the urns in twenty-foot-deep graves, and fifteen acres would have room for 13,680,000 remains with room to spare for an another fifty thousand more prosperous bodies in exposed urns set in niches around a wall and five thousand more in vaults: in total, 912,000 bodies per acre excluding the rich and prominent.[27] And consider the alternative. The costs in land alone of providing a place for bodies could be enormous: Manchester had just spent £100,000 for a new cemetery; lands taken away from agricultural and recreational use would cost the metropolis £270,000. Half a million dead required seven thousand new acres of cemeteries a year, and so forth.

The point of citing all of these calculations about land use as well as those about hygiene and furnace technology is to show how in one national context—and here the story is politically and religiously but not structurally different from elsewhere—the dead came to be thought about in crucial ways as part of the realm of nature. Put differently, new technologies, new kinds of urban planning, and new ways of thinking about the economy of flesh and bones were meant to strip away two millennia's worth of history and sentiment that bound the dead to culture. Calls for cremation constituted a radical, almost lunatic, modernism grounded in matter.

But of course, culture does not go away. Cremation exemplifies the general claim I made at the beginning of this chapter: that the dead—or, to be both more and less precise, what we do with them and how we imagine the meaning of our practices with respect to them—are foundational in making and defining civilization.

The dead and the condition for their existence—death—is especially important in what I called civilization making because, to begin with, a consciousness of death and the emergence of taboos and practices to contain it stand, rather like incest in Claude Lévi-Strauss's view, at the instant of the creation of culture, neither before or after its advent but constitutive of its coming into being. Indeed, the notion that death is constitutive of civilization is itself foundational for another constitutive, civilization-making activity: the effort to understand the origins of one's civilization. Whether or not true in some objective sense, this notion has been taken to be true since antiquity. Perhaps only language and kinship offer any competition.

From this fact, I draw a second sense of death as civilization making: practices of putting the dead to rest—disposing of, mourning, and remembering them—are foundational. Giambattista Vico, one of the greatest of the eighteenth-century proponents of speculative historical anthropology, thought that burial of the dead was one of the three "universal institutions of humanity" that produced and continued to sustain civil society.[28] The other two "universal institutions" are matrimony and religion, but they too come back quickly to the dead because the living stand between the dead ancestors and their own progeny: it is the primal *lex*—the law of genealogy—that creates the family or the clan as an institution, that connects the unborn and the dead and projects it into historical time. Necrotopology is thus both a general sign of human activity and a way of doing specific cultural work. It is the family or the clan who are responsible for the proper care of the dead. Death and religion are so fantastically elaborated that their intimacy was already a self-evident commonplace in antiquity. Necrotopology is thus both a general sign of human activity and a way of doing specific cultural work. Vico gets much of this from Cicero, who gets it from earlier sources. Where one sees mounds of earth marking the places of the dead, there one sees the work of civilization.

From the observation of Vico follows a third sense of the civilization-making work of the dead: treatment of the dead is normative, a characteristic of the level and quality of civilization, at least from the perspective of its adherents. At the border of savagery and civilization, propriety and barbarity, lie the dead. This cultural border and its normative function were what, in the fifth century B.C.E., Herodotus had already understood.

There is a fourth sense of the work of the dead in civilization making: they have been—or rather, they have been taken to be—representative of essential, defining characteristics of a civilization. The dead have always made excellent synecdoches. Thus, as Nicole Loraux has argued, Pericles' funeral address—like the annual orations for the dead of war more generally—was a reenactment of the polity, a representation of the people to themselves.[29] Garry Wills understands Lincoln's address at Gettysburg—itself a direct descendant of the Athenian form—in this light as an almost magical recreation of a polity over the bodies of the dead, as an epochal reinterpretation of a nation through mourning and remembering its dead soldiers.[30]

Finally, there is the sense in which death—the fact that it exists, that we mourn loss, that it has seemed so inscrutable, that it constitutes so radical a change in the body and in the relationship between the body and what has animated it, and so on through a score of other facts—represents some ultimate truth about the human condition. The work of the dead is to proclaim such ultimate truth. This is the sense in which Socrates says that the true end of philosophy is to prepare for death; it is the sense in which Heidegger develops a philosophy out of the relationship between Dasein and death.

If there is a single general point to this chapter, it is a paraphrase of the point that Lévi-Strauss made about animals: the dead are "good to think with." I would go further. They are essential to producing what we and those who came before us have understood to be human, and they will continue to be so, I think, for those who come after us. Of course, they do not speak univocally. Even the burning of the dead has had many different registers. At one extreme are the ovens of Auschwitz, made by the same company—Topf of Essen—that furnished the crematoria of socially progressive towns like Hamburg, where cremation went hand in hand with liberalism. In the contexts of the camps, bodies as mere matter reached a cultural degree zero. But the cremated dead also returned to columbaria, to nature itself as they were scattered over the seas and the mountains, and even to the inside of churches, from which they had been banned almost everywhere by the middle of the nineteenth century. Clearly, social death as a matter of culture did not disappear; Hertz's distinctions hold. But all that said, the very fact that bodies could be for so long and so seriously regarded as the province of the technicians of nature says something: that the foundations of an almost two-millennia-old civilization based on Christian death rituals that had inhumation in the sacred space at its center was seriously under attack.

CHAPTER 3

Corpses for Kilowatts?: Mourning, Justice, Burial, and the Ends of Humanism

Bonnie Honig

I grieve that grief can teach me nothing, nor
carry me one step into real nature

—EMERSON, "Experience"

What is wrong with this?[1] "In Durham, England, corpses will soon be used to generate electricity. A crematorium is installing turbines in its burners that will convert waste heat from the combustion of each corpse into as much as 150 kilowatt-hours of juice—enough to power 1,500 televisions for an hour."[2] The idea "makes cremation much greener by utilizing its by-products," explains the cremation engineer Steve Looker, referring to the pollutants that would no longer be emitted by crematoria were they to be captured for recycling as energy. He is not wrong. Yet there is surely something not quite green, as it were, going on here.

Green has become the new word for nature friendly, but it is distinctly different from what is called environmentalism. The environmental movement seeks to topple human consumption from its perch as the reigning value of modern society. Environmentalists call for us to respect and preserve the environment, to understand ourselves as part of a fragile and resilient ecology and not as sovereign masters over it nor consumers of it. The new world of "greening" seems, certainly in Durham, to have been taken over by the very thing environmentalists oppose: sovereign efficiency.[3] In the new green world of efficiency, it is a crime to waste (your) potential.[4] Not only is all waste composted and recycled; everything is potential waste, even humans.

Humanists will see in the Durham plan the end of humanism, one of whose constitutive commitments is the proper burial of the dead. But plans like Durham's are not humanism's only end. While some convert corpses into kilowatts for consumption in the name of efficiency, others argue against efficiency but also seek, further, to decenter the human on behalf of a more worldly, organic politics that is less violent, less intrusive, less insistently productive. This orientation to the world can lead in at least two directions. On the one side are those who are adamantly antisovereignty and antiefficiency. Anne-Lise François's *Open Secrets* is a good example. The book promotes the idea of "recessive action" or "affirmative reticence," both, in François's view, significant features of novels and lyric in which, as she puts it, "nothing happens." François singles out Emily Dickinson's poems for admiration because they make "hope redundant and collapse the opening up of prospects into its opposite, the inability to do more than stay close to the earth and the little it has yielded."[5] At several points in this chapter, I will assess how certain issues can be seen anew from the perspective of this ideal of recessive action, while also underlining the limits of this ideal from the perspective of an agonistic politics.[6]

On the second side are those who privilege not the nonhappening but the nonhuman happening. Rather than chasten agency, thinkers in this camp see it everywhere and contest the supposed human monopoly over it. Thus, drawing on the vitalism of Bergson, Deleuze, and others, Jane Bennett contests humanism's ontology of the human exception by putting the human on a continuum with bacteria, plants, and animals. As Bennett makes clear, the human exception grounds the human claim to sovereignty over nature, a claim that arguably ends, all too ironically, with corpse-fired televisions for human viewing.[7]

My point of departure in this chapter will be the first option, that of chastened agency. The model of reticence explored by François in Dickinson and elsewhere shares some features with other accounts that promote self-chastening as central to politics. For example, Richard Flathman, moved not by environmental politics but by more classically liberal commitments, develops a model of chastened agency that postulates a more sovereign subject than that of Anne-Lise François.[8] Where François's ideal develops as a *critique* of modernity, Flathman's is deeply *indebted* to modernity and to the forms of individuation, freedom, and withdrawal it makes possible. In contrast to both, however, and recurring in particular to François's work, I highlight the insufficiencies of withdrawal and chastening as responses to the political demands of our moment. More to the point, I will propose that in these chastenings there is a certain *problematic* chasteness, a purism that sees moral satisfaction in withdrawal and foregoes the political satisfactions of more volatile options that risk implication in the practices they oppose. Judith Butler's recent calls to mourn the violence of sovereignty rather than to quest after sovereignty's power provides another example of this tendency or temptation in contemporary left theory.[9] By contrast, I argue that instead of steering clear of sovereignty and rather than rejecting instrumentalism, agonistic democrats would do well to seek these out, risking their reperformance in orthogonal ways on behalf of new forms of politics that privilege not withdrawal but the experience of service and the risk of exposure.[10]

From an agonistic perspective, impure and action-oriented, we may ask again: What is wrong with the Durham plan? Isn't it just doing what nature has always done? When we bury bodies, they become, in the words of Shakespeare's Mercutio, "worms' meat" and fertilize the earth. Is that so different from converting their waste heat, emitted in the process of cremation, into energy? Perhaps the Durham proposal incites a certain horror because it confronts us with an economy that puts even the dead to work. Perhaps what unsettles, that is, are the lengths to which we see we can go in an effort to satisfy the insatiable demands for wasteless waste—the infinite production and consumption of energy. An ethics and politics of recycling that began as a respectful acknowledgment of human finitude turns out to be infinite in its energetic conversion of everything into energy and into resources for energy production. Extending Marxist critiques of the infinite (an)economic demands of capitalism, we can see in the Durham plan a demand for the ceaseless production of surplus value, even post mortem, so that even the Night(s) of the Living Dead may be well lit.[11]

What is most shocking in the Durham plan, however, is surely not just its exposure of late capitalism's ceaseless demand for human productivity (that is hardly news) but also its complicity with its supposed antagonist—environmentalism—whose commitment to recycling becomes all too easily a not too different kind of demand for ceaseless (but now also wasteless—but this is only more efficient) (re)productivity. The ruptures of capitalism are sutured back together by the supplement of environmentalism, and the Lacanian Real, momentarily sensed in the moment of their conflict, is once again obscured. As anthropologists will tell us and as Hegel knew, death is one of those ruptural moments in a community's life that call for meaning-making rituals. These cover over mortality's revelations of the Real, in which the daily work of meaning making and its insufficiencies—

but also its alternatives!—may be glimpsed. For agonistic democrats, such encounters with, or glimpses of the Real may provide an opportunity to make something (else) of them.[12]

Thus, lighting on the secret complicity between capitalism and green politics, or on the absorption of the latter by the former, is crucial for agonism because it prevents us from concluding that the Durham plan is shocking simply because it converts subjects possessed of dignity into objects for use, which is how we could put the problem by enlisting Kant's language and distinctions. This would be the simple humanist objection (and also the religious one, at least as far as Judaic, Christian, and Islamic values are concerned), and it has force, but it also limits our thinking. It insists on the possibility of pure practices of dignity unimplicated in use, and it objects to all instrumentalizations of the human in death, even though all such instrumentalizations are not the same. For example, there is a distinct difference between the Durham crematorium and the AIDS activist who, protesting U.S. federal government disinterest in a public health emergency that wiped out nearly two generations of gay men, declares, "When I die of AIDS, do not bury my body: leave it on the steps of the FDA." For this activist, the proper burial that promises dignity in death constitutively supports an unjust social order, folding him into its ground. Such sentimental absorption, its postmortem enlistment of the dead on behalf of a heteronormative humanism seems best opposed by nonburial, but nonburial seems to instrumentalize the corpse. We may ease the grip of the binary between good dignity and bad instrumentalization, however, by seeing here an invitation to experience and perhaps extend a public encounter with the Real that might force some rearticulation of the terms of an unjust social existence.[13] From this angle of vision we may see that if, as Jean Comaroff argues, the respectful treatment of the dead by the living is part of a needful practice that connects present to future, then improper burial may at times be needed to connect present to a better future.[14]

If we assume, with Jacques Derrida, the inevitability of a certain cannibalization of the dead, without, however, obviating the distinctions among the different sorts, then we are pressed into adjudicating the differences among them, rather than seeking, as Anne-Lise François seems to, a way out altogether. Thus, rather than treat Emily Dickinson's poetry as an incitement not to "reinvest the dead in a cultural or psychic economy," to borrow François's phrasing,[15] we may find in Dickinson and others an invitation to pluralize our economies of mortality, reinvesting in them and redirecting them so as better to force such rearticulations and advance some reinvestments over others. In the absence of pluralization, the fantasy of withdrawal in which François arguably indulges may seem real, and it may leave us unable or unwilling to distinguish the instrumentalizations of the AIDS activist from those of the Durham plan.

With these issues in mind, I turn to two texts that seek dignity for the dead but keep getting caught up in the economies of use and waste that Kantians reject. Both texts lurch between mourning and justice as rites of response, but these rites are not adequate responses to the ruptures they seek to repair. In both texts there is some suggestion of a third, perhaps better or supplementary option: labor or service. This is not the sort of labor whose consuming power Hannah Arendt fears, or at least it is not reducible to that. It is the labor of burial or after-death care. It may be performed with a variety of motives and in many ways. There is nothing necessarily pure about it. For example, when Antigone, whose commitment to her brother Polynices is rarely disputed by critics, seems to devote herself to her dead brother over her living sister, we may see a not unproblematic and quite unagonistic preference for the sibling who does not talk back over the one who does. Still, in such service, never pure and always complicated, something transformative may occur.

Sophocles' *Antigone* is one of two texts to which I turn. The other is the film *Sophie's Choice*, in which Dickinson's poetry plays a key role and in which burial is not an option. Written over two thousand years apart, both explore the tragic outcome of the divergent pulls of mourning and justice in the aftermath of genocide or civil war.[16] Read together, something else becomes apparent: in both, a conflict between mourning and justice is explored by way of characters deprived of the opportunity to bury the dead. Might the apparent incommensurability between mourning and justice be in some way connected to that deprivation? Might service to the dead body—the work of burial—provide a way to work through loss? Might our contemporary talk of working through be, in fact, a symbolic residue of an earlier practice and even express a certain longing for it?

The conflict between mourning and justice is explored also by Thomas Laqueur, who notes the different role of the body in each—in one as a focus of mourning, in the other as a corpus delecti, the dead body of evidence that enables the identification and prosecution of wrongdoers and war criminals. The body postulated by mourning seems insulated from use (though even there, as Derrida points out, it is difficult to insulate the service of eulogy from more instrumental forms of self-service).[17] The body postulated by justice, the corpus delecti, is instrumental to justice and is caught up in politics in a way that humanists claim lamentation is not.[18] In other work, I have shown how lamentation practices are, contra Laqueur, no less—and possibly more—political than justice, noting the not unproblematic but still powerful role of mourning in activist and dissident movements from Iran to Argentina to the United States.[19] Here, though, I want to ask after the complex complicities of the supposed opposites, mourning versus justice, and identify what is marginalized by their opposition: practices of care for the dead. Thus, I close with a discussion of Laqueur's essay, showing how the conflict he depicts between two modes of relation to the dead is itself productive. Focused on their conflict, exaggerating its features, Laqueur resecures the distinction between dignity and use postulated by the pairing—mourning and justice—but also attenuated by it: Both mourning and justice, after all, position the dead body as a means to their ends—as the corpus delecti of justice or as mourning's balm of closure. Both thus rule out other meanings the dead body might have, and both distract attention from its potential meaning(lessness) and from our own politics and practices of investment in and service to it.[20]

Sophie's Choice

> Pardon my sanity in a world insane
>
> —EMILY DICKINSON, in a letter to a friend during the Civil War

In the film *Sophie's Choice*, Sophie, a Polish Catholic woman, somehow ends up in Auschwitz and suffers unspeakable horrors. Before Auschwitz, Sophie was a secretary to her law professor father, who demeaned and dominated her, a fate to which she reconsigns herself when she marries one of her father's disciples. That she married her father is further suggested in the film by her wedding photo, perched on a shelf behind her prewar typewriter: in it, Sophie stands in her wedding gown between two men, and it is unclear which is her father and which her husband. Both men are killed by the Nazis, but Sophie survives and after the war, in the United States, Sophie tethers herself to the unpredictable rhythms of life with a schizophrenic, Nathan Landau (Kevin Kline), who by turns worships and torments her. In her hailstorm of a life, there is only one moment when Sophie seems to experience an autonomous pleasure. Soon after arriving in the United States, seated in an English class for immigrants, Sophie is moved by a poem recited by her instructor. He shares it to show his struggling students that the English language is not just torturously difficult for those who want to *use* it for communication but also possessed of great beauty, for those who want to *delight* in it.

> Because I could not stop for Death,
> He kindly stopped for me;
> the carriage held just ourselves
> and Immortality.

Sophie asks a classmate for the name of the poet and jots it down. Then she takes herself to the New York Public Library and seeks out the book.

"Excuse me, sir. Could you tell me what . . . Where would be that listing in catalog file . . . for . . . nineteenth-century American poet . . . Emile Dickens, please?" she asks the librarian in accented, broken English. "In the catalog room on the left," the librarian gestures roughly, exhibiting unmistakable disdain for her. "But you won't find any such listing," he adds, as she turns in the direction just indicated. "Oh, I won't find that listing? Why won't I . . . find it?" she asks, her arched brow and her repetition registering an awareness of his disdain and the wherewithal to return his mockery, somehow. "Charles Dickens is an English writer," he sniffs. "There's no American poet by the name of Dickens." "I'm sorry. No," she insists, her eyes again on the scrap of paper where she has jotted down the name: "that is, I'm sure, American poet. Emile Dickens." The librarian explodes, fairly hissing at her, his bigotry or mere impatience palpable in the impropriety of his response (a librarian shouting in the library?): "Listen! I told you! There's no such person. Do you want me to draw you a picture?" And then, as she stutters to calm him and tries to leave his presence: "I'm telling you, you hear me?!" Perhaps retraumatized by this reappearance of her father—a disdainful, demeaning, sarcastic, bullying man—Sophie faints and then throws up as her head is cradled in the hands of a handsome stranger who comes to her rescue. It is Nathan, who takes her home, nurses her back to health, and romances her with the poetry of Emily Dickinson, a volume of whose work he gives to Sophie as a gift on the night of their first meeting.

Dickinson's attractiveness to Sophie is never explained, but her poetry provides a leitmotif for the film. If Anne-Lise François is right in her reading of Dickinson, then Sophie, who has experienced the hyperinstrumentalism of survival in wartime, where everything is and must be useful or subject to exchange (her body, her shoes, her children), may sense in Dickinson a cessation of that ceaseless calculation by which the war and postwar American consumerism are both (however differently) governed. It may even be that Sophie and Nathan both find in Dickinson some relief from the ceaselessness of the demands embraced by each: for mourning, for justice.

The mishap in the library is occasioned by the unimaginability to Sophie and to the librarian of a woman poet. It is not Dickens, after all, but rather—as Nathan rightly discerns—Dickinson that Sophie seeks; not Emile but Emily. This scene of comic-gothic error in the library is filmed as Dickens would be or, indeed, has been filmed. Like the judge in the 1968 film version of Dickens's *Oliver Twist*, the librarian in *Sophie's Choice* is propped up on a large desk that communicates and enhances his (self-)importance. He is an impatient, pettily powerful male, less brutish than Mr. Bumble but echoing him nonetheless, and he is powerful only in relation to Sophie, an Oliver-like, hapless, weak-bodied orphan, lost and running a fever in a cruel world but soon to be saved by the kindness of a stranger. Sophie's kind stranger, Nathan, is no Mr. Brownlow, but then Sophie is no Oliver. Hers is a death-driven world, not merely an indifferent or cruel one. Her world is Dickinsonian rather than Dickensian or, better, it is both. Perhaps that is the point of the film's staging of the confusion of the two names. Their merger unites the indifference and cruelty of Dickens's suffering world with the thanatoerotic remove of Dickinson's and links Dickens's quest for a justice in which each gets his due with what others, if not François, have taken to be Dickinson's quest for proper mourning, in which death is not unwelcome and nature provides its elegies.[21] In the merger as it is enacted here, the redemptions of Dickens and the light grace of Dickinson are lost. There will be no happy ending of just deserts, and Death will not come for Nathan and Sophie; they will take it for themselves. Both Nathan's and Sophie's quests, for Dickensian justice and Dickinsonian mourning, for a good life and a good death, will be for naught.[22] The recessive action that François herself endorses and locates in Dickinson, the ideal non-doing of chastened agency, is not developed here, though it is discernible in one of the doomed couple's pleasures—literature—and it is associated in particular with the film's third main character: Stingo.[23]

Whatever else it is, the story of Sophie and Nathan is also about literature and literariness, the locus of François's ideal of reticence. Sophie and Nathan meet in the library. On their first night together, Sophie reads to Nathan, at his request, from a Polish translation of Thomas Wolfe's *Look Homeward, Angel*, and he reads to her from a book of poems by Dickinson. The teller of their story, the film's narrator, Stingo, is an aspiring writer from the South who, like Wolfe, migrated North to write his first novel. In these three main characters, we have the three main functions of the elegist, as François describes them: The elegist's task, she says, "entails a specific set of motivations and obligations—memorializing the deceased, exorcising the guilt of survival, proving through his rhetorical power the living's claim over the dead."[24] Nathan seeks to memorialize the deceased who cannot be memorialized since they are nameless, faceless; Sophie seeks to exorcise the guilt of survival; and Stingo proves through his rhetorical power, as narrator, as author, and, finally, as elegist, the living's claim over the dead. François sees Dickinson as offering something else entirely, when she "leaves undefined the occasions and premises of her texts."[25] This alternative of self-chastening subjectivity sensitizes us to the manic doing that all three of this film's characters share, but when François endorses the undoing powers of release by contrast with the three kinds of elegiac practice, she sets aside the possibility of their agonistic recombination.[26] Withdrawal is privileged over service, insulation preferred to risk.

Stingo tries to be a caretaker to Sophie and Nathan, but they need more care than he can provide. He enters their manic world hoping for friendship and more. He leaves their world after delivering their eulogy, altered but sufficiently intact to tell their story. At the outset, he is bedazzled by their seemingly worldly ways and by their seemingly flattering views of him. Nathan welcomes Stingo to their rooming house, sending him Whitman's *Leaves of Grass*, with a card: "from one of Brooklyn's earliest bards to Brooklyn's newest one" (evoking Emerson to Whitman, "I greet you at the beginning of a great career").[27] Stingo is moved into authorship by Nathan (who disparages and adores him by turns) and Sophie (who mothers and later sleeps with him before returning finally to Nathan). "I wanted to be and hoped or dreamed to be a writer," he says in his narrator's voice at the film's beginning. "But my spirit had remained locked . . . unacquainted with love and a stranger to death." These problems will be solved for Stingo by Sophie and Nathan.

The story Stingo had intended to write is about a twelve-year-old boy whose mother dies. (The story is his own, he admits at one point. His mother died "because I did not love her enough," he tells Sophie in a late-night confidence. This confession gives the lie to his earlier claim in his narrator voice that he was "a stranger to death." Perhaps he was not acquainted with *enough* death to inspire writing. If so, Sophie will solve that problem for him, too.) Stingo's planned story of a motherless child (which the film audience never hears, although reams of paper are typed nightly by Stingo), is replaced by "Sophie's Choice," the story of a childless mother, Sophie, whose two children died in Auschwitz. Subtly, the film suggests, the motherless child, Stingo, is America, willfully innocent, naïve, and free of its past. Sophie, the childless mother, is Europe, possessed of a past or, rather, possessed by the past: she is too haunted by it to have a future.

The problem to which literature is here called to respond is that of horror or maybe merely of history. But it is stymied. The film's author cannot write, or he writes too much. Nathan and Sophie find some comfort in Dickinson, Wolfe, and others but no salvation. In post–World War II Brooklyn, Sophie, the European Catholic Holocaust survivor, and Nathan, the bipolar American Jew, cannot move past the war, Sophie because she suffered irreversible trauma in Auschwitz and Nathan because he is, as Sophie says, "obsessed with the Nazis." The walls of Nathan's room are papered with pictures of Nazis not yet brought to justice. Nathan tortures Sophie with cruel interrogations about what she did to survive the war, given that so many Jewish victims died. "Explain something to me," he says miming her Polish accent, "the reason maybe of why you are here . . . walking the streets . . . wearing this enticing perfumery . . . while at Auschwitz, the ghosts of the millions of the dead . . . still seek an answer." Sophie does not respond. She moans. The quest for justice in the face of the Holocaust cannot be satisfied. And Nathan is not wrong when he asks, "[did] the same anti-Semitism . . . for which Poland has gained such a worldwide recognition . . . did this similar anti-Semitism guide your own destiny, help you along . . . protect you in a manner of speaking, so you became one of the miniscule . . . handful of people who lived . . . while the millions died?"[28]

Nathan cannot stop talking about the Nazis. But Sophie, like many survivors, cannot bring herself to speak of them at all. Bit by bit over the course of the film, her story comes out, in different iterations, half-truth by half-truth. The details do not matter here. What does matter is that both characters are haunted, one by her proximity to the violence, the other by the guilt (the guilt of American Jews) that comes from having been distant from it. Each suffers survivor guilt, expressed in him through madness, in her through melancholia, driving him to seek justice, her to seek mourning.

And each loves Emily Dickinson. The poem Nathan reads to Sophie on their first night together is a burial poem that might also have been (almost) a wedding song:[29]

Ample make this bed
Make this bed with awe;
In it wait till judgment break
Excellent and fair.

Be its mattress straight
Be its pillow round;

> Let no sunrise' yellow noise
> Interrupt this ground

At the end of the film, when Sophie and Nathan have committed suicide, Stingo will stand at their bedside, gazing at their bodies coupled in death, and his eyes will fall on the Dickinson volume on a nearby tabletop. He will open the book and read the same poem as their eulogy: "Ample make this bed . . ." But he turns to go, leaving the police to complete their investigation and leaving it to others to dispose of the bodies. Called to serve the dead, he is a man of words, not actions. If Anne-Lise François is right to connect literature and recessive action, then Stingo here marks that connection and alerts us to the limits of François's ideal.[30]

Stingo leaves the Brooklyn rooming house, and as he walks across the Brooklyn Bridge (referencing Whitman again: "Crossing Brooklyn Ferry") with the sun rising above him, his narrator's voice says:

> And so ended my journey of discovery . . . in a place as strange as Brooklyn. I let go the rage and sorrow for Sophie and Nathan and for the many others who were but a few . . . of the butchered and betrayed and martyred children of the Earth. When I could finally see again . . . I saw the first rays of daylight reflected in the murky river. This was not judgment day, only morning. Morning: excellent and fair.[31]

It may seem that "morning" here returns us to Anne-Lise François's Dickinson, the poet of light, unintrusive nonmeaning. But this last line of the film actually directs us to another Dickinson, or two, by rewriting Dickinson: Her more active call for "*Judgment* . . . excellent and fair" is deferred for another day and is replaced without comment by "*morning* [or mourning, since it is a homonym and the film viewer cannot know], excellent and fair." Thus the film enlists Dickinson not to escape (as François would have us do) but rather to restage the contretemps between mourning and justice. Stingo walks toward a new day, propelled by a complicated palimpsest of Dickinsonian morning/mourning/justice.

Taken as *mourning*, the line suggests Stingo is able to cross the bridge into a new future because he is now acquainted with but not broken by experiences of love and death. He is capable of moving beyond rage and sorrow to do the work of Dickinsonian mourning. Through the eulogy of the poem and the telling of the story of Nathan and Sophie, Stingo, an emerging writer, works through the issues that trapped these bearers of justice and mourning in their insane, impossible, death-driven romance. (Indeed, one critic refers to the novel as Stingo's bildungsroman.)[32]

Taken as *morning*, by contrast, the line suggests that the unbearable lightness of recessive action is a more problematic political withdrawalism. In the latter, Stingo represents a New World naïveté, possibly willful. He lets go. He just moves on, leaving the past and its ruins behind. He has a future, though its apparently unencumbered nature may suggest it is mere fantasy.[33] This reading is supported by the film's intimation, throughout, that Stingo is foreign to this place and its drama. He refers at the film's opening and closing to these events as his "voyage of discovery in a place as strange as Brooklyn." To Stingo, Nathan and Sophie are exotics. He has never known people like this before. He—like Wolfe—is from the South. There is a bucolic home to which he can retreat (he is heir to a farm "south of Virginia" on which he might live), an option unavailable to Sophie and Nathan, who are stuck in their historicity. That Stingo is not stuck in his, or does not see himself that way, is made clear when Nathan taunts Stingo, suggesting that because he is a child of the South, he knows something of racial violence or lynching. Stingo takes umbrage at the suggestion. He thinks himself entirely innocent of the charge. His is an American innocence, which is to say that by some force or chance he is positioned (or positions himself) as unimplicated in the racial history of his home, while Sophie is utterly implicated even in America in Europe's racist past that still destroys her. Playing on the pun of mo(u)rning, we may ask whether there isn't willful (that is, American) naïveté in the belief that it is possible to elide or overcome the difficulties surveyed here (the conflict between justice and mourning, between Dickens and Dickinson) by way of literature (on François's account) or perhaps even, as one critic of Whitman today points out, by way of national song.[34]

But the film's reference to a Whitmanesque openness to a new day is—no less than its traffic in Dickinson—a repetition with a difference, in this instance a dismal difference: here the first rays of daylight are reflected not in the "gladness of the river and the bright flow" by which Whitman in his own poem is "refreshed" but rather in a "murky river."[35] That murkiness is nature's new deficit and it suggests that Stingo may not be quite fully refreshed by the mo(u)rning visited on him. Might this be because Stingo's service in death is limited? Unlike Sophie and Nathan, he can visit the dead, witness their deaths, and eulogize them. But his service is also constrained or limited in that it is only literary not corporeal, worded not laborious. His speech act gives words to the Real, resuturing the symbolic order, not (re)working it.

Sophocles' Antigone

The butchered, betrayed, and martyred listed but not distinguished by Stingo in the closing lines of *Sophie's Choice* are in *Antigone* personified by three characters: Polynices (butchered in that he is left to decompose like an animal), Eteocles (who betrays and is betrayed by his brother), and Antigone, who will die a martyr for her cause. The question of how to relate to these various deaths is central to a drama that critics have seen as staging a singular and timeless conflict between mourning and justice.[36]

In Sophocles' play, Nathan's stuck, raging, impotent commitment to justice (or something analogous to it) is represented by Creon, and Sophie's infinite melancholic mourning (or something analogous to it) is represented by Antigone, though the latter pair are importantly different from each other.[37] Antigone calls for her brother's death to be avenged and curses those responsible; Sophie, perhaps because she feels responsible for her children's fate, does no such thing.[38] Creon's principle of giving each his due as a matter of political and civic responsibility conflicts with Antigone's principle of lamenting the loss of a life in order to usher the dead along to the next life, where the question of just deserts—a separate issue—will be decided by gods, not men. But, by centering the action around the question of (non)burial, the drama points beyond the conflict so often taken to be at its center. It points beyond justice versus mourning to a practice that subtends them both: service to the dead, forms of corporeal care that surpass the tender eulogizing of Stingo and highlight the continuities between such elegy and the recessive action to which it is opposed by François. For Stingo, the craft of writing—he tells the stories of Nathan and Sophie—takes the place of the work of burial.

But nothing can take the place of burial in Sophocles' *Antigone.* The play begins in the aftermath of near civil war.[39] The conflict occurs in the wake of the rule of Oedipus, who ruled Thebes wisely and well but who also, with his acts of parricide and incest (unintended, unknowing, but still *his* acts), polluted the polity and brought it to near ruin.[40] Oedipus's reign ends with his wife's/mother's suicide and his own exile. Left behind are the four children of his incestuous marriage to Jocasta: Eteocles, Polynices, Antigone, and Ismene. The sons, Eteocles and Polynices, both claim the throne after their father leaves. Some versions of the story suggest they agree to rule by turns. Eteocles takes power first, but when the time comes to pass the throne to Polynices, Eteocles refuses to do so. Polynices raises an army at Argos and besieges Thebes to claim what is his. The brothers battle, and each dies by the other's hand.

The play opens with Antigone telling her sister Ismene awful news: their brother Eteocles has been buried with full military honors by Thebes' new leader, their uncle Creon. But Polynices, their other brother, it has been decreed by Creon, is "to be left," as Antigone puts it, "unwept, unburied, a lovely treasure for birds that scan the field and feast to their heart's content."[41] Creon, Antigone rightly perceives, has "graced one with all the rites and disgraced the other." In so doing, Creon means to do justice. Although the chorus welcomes Creon as "the new man for the new day,"[42] Creon does not begin anew. Instead, he begins by orienting Thebes toward the past in order to position it for a better future. The city cannot turn a blind eye to the fact that one brother besieged the city ("he thirsted to drink his kinsmen's blood and sell the rest to slavery," says Creon of Polynices)[43] while the other sought to defend it. One brother is a friend of Thebes, a patriot, the other an enemy, a traitor.[44] To do justice, to give each brother his due, is also to stabilize the polis, to prevent the brothers' rift from giving rise to ongoing sectarian conflicts between the brothers' followers. Thus, Creon promotes one as an honored son and denigrates the other as a traitor.

To pick either of the play's main characters as hero is to dilute the play's tragic quality. Tragedy, after all, is the form in which there is no right thing to do because whichever course is chosen, another, equally compelling, is left undone.[45] Besides, things are not so clear when it comes to heroes and villains in this play. Taking into account the brothers' destabilization of Thebes and the recent troubles under Oedipus, the reader may well begin the play with a certain appreciation for Creon's alertness to the politics of friendship and enmity. Rather than being blind to the importance of mourning and burial, Creon is highly aware of their political implications. That is why he enlists them for political purposes. He wants mourning to serve the cause of justice and justice to provide Thebes with stability. This is what leads him to prohibit the mourning and burial of Polynices, who, after all, went too far. Polynices pursued justice too far (it *was* his turn) and slipped into enmity.

In the end, Creon will pursue justice too far as well. He is not unlike Polynices. Creon too is immoderate.[46] Creon seeks justice without measure (an irony, since justice for the Greeks is about measure: giving each his due). Creon slides therefore from being a potentially worthy captain of the "ship of state" into being an irresponsible navigator who will run it aground.[47] That Creon and Polynices share this same flaw is suggested by the fact that they suffer the same or similar fates. The play opens with Polynices, who, deprived of burial rites, is unable to move from this world to the next, and it closes with Creon longing for death but stuck among the living, also unable to move from this world to the next. Just as Creon sought to prohibit anyone from clustering at Polynices' altar, so Creon finds at the play's end that no one is left to cluster at his. Alone and bereft at the end of the play, Creon receives his just deserts. There is irony in this, too, since just deserts is what Creon and Polynices both told themselves they stood for.

Most commentators comment upon the worth of Antigone's cause—the dead must be buried, the gods of the underworld must not be denied, the oral law must be respected; at the very least, she is said to help illustrate the idea that, as the blind seer Tiresias says later in the play, there must be a balance between human (Creon) and divine (Antigone) law (though Creon claims the gods too, for his side, and Antigone, as the daughter and sister of previous kings, is also identified to some extent with human law).[48] That the play calls for balance is clearly at least partly right, but this message does not argue only against Creon. Disaster would have followed as well had Antigone had *her* way, had mourning triumphed over justice. Mourning Polynices would fulfill an obligation, but to grace him with such rites would have left justice (giving each his due) undone. And this is no small matter. Leaving justice undone was the omission of which Oedipus was accused, after all. It is only when Thebes is visited by a plague, after many years of Oedipus's rule, that Oedipus is finally led to open an inquiry into the death of Laius, the king whom Oedipus succeeded. Laius's murderer had never been found, had not even been actively sought, and had never been brought to justice. The Thebans had mourned their king, but they had not ever done him justice, and, for this failure, Thebes is punished. It is as a result of the ensuing inquiry that Oedipus discovers a series of awful truths: the stranger he killed on the road to Thebes was in fact King Laius. Laius was Oedipus's true father. And Jocasta, the widowed queen whom Oedipus married upon his arrival in Thebes (the prize given to him for liberating Thebes from the terror of the Sphinx by solving her riddle), was none other than his own mother.

In sum, the play insists on the simultaneous necessity of justice and mourning and on the necessity of their conflict. But the conflict occurs in the context of treason and as a result of a ruler's subsequent determination to instrumentalize a traitor's dead body to teach the lesson of loyalty and the consequences of betrayal. If we focus on the family's unacknowledged claim to mourn, we simply reinstate again the conflict between mourning and justice. Alternatively, we may, with the guidance of *Sophie's Choice*, note that the family in *Antigone* is deprived not just of mourning but of the opportunity to look after the dead. This causes the outrage, noted by Antigone and by the seer Tiresias, of birds and dogs feasting on Polynices as carrion, his corpse a source of pollution and a danger to the public health.[49] But his exposure is also a different sort of offence, depriving others of the work of burial, leaving them without an occasion of service.

Service and Reconciliation: The Word and Work of Burial

> In mourning it is the world which has become poor and empty; in melancholia it is the ego itself.
>
> —SIGMUND FREUD, "Mourning and Melancholia"

For some readers, Antigone's inflexible commitment to her cause is a shortcoming, but it is clearly also the source of her great power. Perhaps, however, we should read her inflexibility not as cause but rather as effect. What so many take to be a sign of backbone or principle—Antigone's inflexibility—may be an effect of her inability, given Creon's prohibition, to care for Polynices properly, ritually. What the *Antigone* may point us to, in other words, is not only the importance of mourning and justice but also their insufficiency. It may point us beyond that pairing to the labor of after-death care. Sophie mourns the loss of her children, but Antigone mourns not the loss of her brother but, more specifically, her inability to care for him after death. Burial is named as the second of the pair of acts forbidden by Creon: Antigone says, early in the play, that it has been decreed that Polynices must be left "unwept, unburied." Unwept, unburied is the condition as well of Sophie's children.

Alongside the decree of justice and the edict against mourning, next to truth and reconciliation, rights and loss, lie those rites and rituals by way of which we *inter* the dead. The word *inter* comes from Middle English, meaning to put into the ground—*in terra.* For Hegel, however, the function of burial is not just to inter but also to inter-rupt the processes whereby the interred dead might become merely part of the mere organicism of nature. We, the living, put ourselves in the way, to interrupt the mere decomposition of death. With the word and deed of ritual, we insert ourselves into nature's processes and claim even the dead for the human community. Insofar as the emphasis here is on human doing and not being, agency and not recessive action, it may seem, from François's perspective, that all this doing merely foreshadows rather than forestalls our century's appropriation of corpses for kilowatts. From this perspective, we might think that this latest energy recycling is not importantly different from earlier iterations in which the dead's mystical energy was put to good use, as it was, for example, in the hero cults of the ancient world and as it is now in national death practices that enlist the dead for postmortem patriotism.[50] But here we meet the limit of François's alternative, it seems to me, for it both sees all such actions as continuous and demands an alternative untouched by them.

By contrast, we may find alternatives *in* them. Notably, when we humans (specifically it is the sister who, of the various members of the family unit, is uniquely obligated in Hegel's ideal state to bury the brother) bury the dead, we (though Hegel does not note it) take on the role of the gods in Homeric Greece, who were said to have warded off the decomposition and disfigurement of Greek heroes by way of active intervention.[51] As Jean-Pierre Vernant explains, drawing on three episodes reported in the *Iliad* and elsewhere,

> In all three cases, the scenario is about the same. The gods miraculously save the hero from the shame of abuse that—by disfiguring, denaturing his body until it is no longer recognizable as his own, or even as a human body, or even as a body at all—would reduce him to a state of nonbeing. To preserve him as he was, the gods perform the human rituals of cleansing and beautification but use divine unguents [they need to! A miracle is needed: Achilles' abuse of the body of Hector, for example, is so extreme that the body is unrecognizable as a body, much less as Hector's]: these elixirs of immortality preserve "intact," despite all the abuse, that youth and beauty which can only fade on the body of a living man [because, as this statement implies but does not aver, not only death but also life itself involves decomposition]. Death in battle fixes forever on the hero's form [his youth and beauty], just as a stele remains erect forever to mark a tomb.[52]

This kind of physical care is what Antigone seeks to do, but she cannot do it alone. Creon's decree abuses the body of Polynices, passively, through exposure, while Homer's Achilles abused the body of Hector actively, but the result is almost the same: both require a (super)human intervention. Antigone cannot provide it, however; she cannot lift the body of her brother without her sister's help. When Ismene refuses, Antigone is limited to what she can do on her own: pour libations, scatter dust, sing laments, call for vengeance. But it is not enough, and even these of her efforts are in any case repeatedly undone by Creon's underlings. As others have noted with respect to Hegel, the sister is not adequately empowered to perform the tasks assigned to her.

To underline the importance of service is not to proclaim its purity. The service we provide to the dead when we oblige their right to have rites is always also self-serving; Aristotle's three registers of friendship—virtue, pleasure, and use—exist here in contaminated contiguity. This should be unsurprising: Derrida pointed out their complicated commingling in his *Politics of Friendship*. But there is something to be learned from that contamination in this particular context: we may find here an incitement to refigure "use" from the lowest to the highest register, thus contesting capitalism's degradation of use, its collapse of all service into labor, and its degradation of labor. This opportunity is made manifest when Beth Knox, the founder of a nonprofit resource center for after-death care alternatives, says that "During a time of mourning, especially after a sudden, unexpected death, people want to feel useful." Knox does not give a reading of that desire to *do* something. It may connote survivors' cathexis to agency, even manifesting a touch of the mania that often results from an awareness of mortality when proper mourning has not (yet?) done its promised work. But the desire to be of use may also connote the impulse to serve, to be of service, even to act in concert, perhaps in some contaminative contiguity. Yet "all too often," as Knox explains, the impulse lacks an opportunity to be realized: "the expression of condolence—'Is there anything I can do?'—has no response. In this country, where 99 percent of all deaths are handled by funeral directors, there's rarely anything of substance for friends and family *to* do. But . . . giving people a task—picking up the death certificate, buying more dry ice, building the coffin or digging the grave—provides *a physical way to work through grief*."[53] Service to the dead provides survivors with the work needed to work through the death. This gives a literal and insightful cast to the current favored expression for grieving: *working through*.

The work of burial is an object of political struggle in the United States and Europe, as activists contest the takeover of death rites by funeral homes and state institutions. They publicize the little known permissibility in most states of burying the dead on private property and keeping the body at home before burial. They seek to educate "the family to act as funeral director—legal in almost all states in the United States," though few people seem to know this. Home burial is nowadays associated more with secret murders than with after-death care.[54] Much of the recent politicization is no more or less than consumer activism, and so this work on behalf of the work of burial, it must be said, is not necessarily a site of political hope. Thus far, the goal is simply to offer more "choices" and financial savings to those caught in the monopolies of the death industry. But we can discern in the arguments of the activists something more promising: a sense of the worth of burial and the practice of care for the dead. Tending to the body, once the work of the gods, is, as the *Antigone* may suggest, a way to work through, by *working* through (with physical labor), the loss of the other and the otherness of loss. At a moment at which the ego has become uninvested in the world, recessive action is no ideal. More to the point, such a moment might be politically activating: those who provide service in the company of others become acquainted not just with mourning but also with pleasure as they undergo the sometimes transformative experience of action in concert. This is different and less sentimental from humanist calls to experience sharedness in the fact of finitude, and we can outline the difference by parsing two approaches to Walt Whitman's seeming humanist effort in this direction: his poem "Reconciliation."

In "Reconciliation," Walt Whitman describes one man kissing another, deceased, across enemy lines.

> Word over all, beautiful as the sky!
> Beautiful that war, and all its deeds of carnage, must in time be utterly
> lost;
> That the hands of the sisters Death and Night, incessantly softly
> wash again, and ever again, this soil'd world:
> . . . For my enemy is dead—a man divine as myself is dead;
> I look where he lies, white-faced and still, in the coffin—I draw near;
> I bend down, and touch lightly with my lips the white face in the coffin.[55]

The poem is often read as a humanist call to join together across lines of friendship and enmity in the aftermath of the Civil War, the other war that provides the context for *Sophie's Choice*. It is to this conflict that we are directed by the film's references to Dickinson and Whitman, the former horrified by the conflict and withdrawn from it, the latter engaged by it into a period of hospital service and seeking in his *Memorandum* and in his poetry some redemptive reconciliation in the aftermath of violence. But there is yet more to Whitman's poem than its invocation of the sharedness of mortality. There is also the power of the word and, further, the moving and (especially in our own context of insulation) shocking experience of encounter with the dead other in his casket.

Further still, however, there is also in the poem a gesture to death care and the service of solicitude with which Whitman himself had become familiar as he tended in hospitals in Virginia and Washington to those wounded in the Civil War. Referring to Death and Night as sisters, Whitman calls to mind those women who nursed the wounded, whom Whitman tended, too.[56] These sisters are Hegel's sisters too, engaged in the ceaseless lamentation to which the philosopher assigned them, while assigning no one to *their* care. But these sisters are not those of Sophocles. Engaged in the soft washing of the world, they show no hint of the vengeful violence called for by Antigone in lament. In this way, they are too pure, perhaps. But they are not only pure. They risk impurity when they take on the ceaseless soft washing that surely violates the ideal of recessive action and overcomes the temptation to withdraw from the world when its violence is visited upon us.

Conclusion

Being of use in some way, pressing ourselves into service with others in contaminated contiguity to them, is an apt democratic response to the decentering impact of death, which opens up the Real of uselessness in a way that disturbs and exceeds the Kantian idea of dignity. Kantian dignity is tied to "use" as its opposite in a way that indicates the horror of an instrumentalizing usefulness but also the deeper horror of being useless.[57] François's argument seems to me to be informed by the Kantian aspiration to break out of such instrumentality on behalf of the human and its dignity. But what gets lost is a different idea of use, those forms of service that are both dignified practice and (often) democratic. This idea is not present in most humanist work on death. Instead, often, humanists dignify the dead by insisting on their (secular) sacredness or by emphasizing precisely the functional values to which, in Kant, dignity is entirely opposed. We can see the paradox at work in Thomas Laqueur's "The Dead Body and Human Rights," in which the historian tracks two functions of the dead body (he was not then, in that essay, attending to the third function—call it the Durham option). Laqueur seeks, as I have done here, to underline the importance of the corporeal encounter with death, but he veers away from the scene of encounter with its solicitation to service. Instead, in order to absorb the dead into a symbolic or cultural politics, he tells "the story of how each dead body became a corpus delecti leading to prosecution or some sort of political action and the story of how each body becomes the site of mourning, remembering, remaking of self and community."[58]

These two stories are stories of justice and mourning, respectively. The former seeks out "medico-juridical truth, which grounds legal or political action." The latter seeks out "truth for the purposes of remembering [or] communal therapy." Thus Laqueur cleanses each of the traces of the other, overstating their differences in a rather Hegelian way, investing mourning with merely ethical and psychological significance and casting only justice as political, though we know of many instances of radicalization via mourning (many of which invoke Antigone herself as an inspiration, perhaps most famously the Madres of the Plaza), and though democratic activists know that in the call for justice to be administered by courts and experts there is often a certain worrisome displacement of politics and diminution of political accountability. Still, for Laqueur, the two are discrete and in tension, and he deepens that tension, pressing it to the point of incommensurability: "It is not clear that the named bodies of the dead will serve us as both a corpus delecti . . . and as the balm of closure."[59] Indeed, "the rhetoric of memory is manifestly different from the rhetoric of justice; the question is whether the one might serve as a substitute, an excuse, for not pursuing the other."

Faced with this conflict between mourning and justice, Laqueur searches for a bridge between them, and he finds it in a humanism of finitude, or what I call elsewhere a mortalist humanism: the "bridge between the two functions of the dead body" is "that these are not the bodies of beasts; they did not 'die like dogs' outside of law and culture" (recall here Whitman's "A man divine as myself is dead"). But, as Laqueur immediately realizes, this humanist bridge will not support him, for the people in question here precisely did die like dogs. That is the very problem to which Laqueur's essay, which focuses on murders, massacres, and genocides, is itself addressed. So Laqueur corrects himself: "Or rather, they did 'die like dogs' despite the fact that they were human . . . ." This corrected claim is more accurate, but it cannot provide the sought-after bridge. Instead it plunges us right back into the divide Laqueur sought to escape, as becomes clear when he adds: "which is why it is so important subsequently to determine their identities and their histories," so that "the named bodies of the dead" can serve as either "a corpus delecti" or "as the balm of closure." But not both. Justice and mourning are again at odds: "The will to prosecute may well be blunted by whatever peace remembering brings."[60] Neither justice nor mourning alone can offer the dead and those who survive them all they need and deserve, and, indeed, each may thwart the other. Having cleansed mourning of the calls for vengeance it often features, Laqueur turns mourning almost into recessive action and leaves all the action to a juridical justice assigned to scientists, judges, and lawyers. Noting the unavoidable conflict between them, a conflict that is now also one of laypeople versus experts or professionals, Laqueur does not offer a solution.

Laqueur's emphasis on the incommensurability of mourning and justice gives the impression that these exhaust the range of options, and this obscures that third site of connection between the living and the dead: burial, or tending to the body. Where mourning and justice focus attention on those who survive, burial puts the focus on the dead, the rites by way of which survivors tend to them, their willingness to risk exposure to them. A focus on burial switches the question from "how can the dead serve us?"—by enabling justice (corpus delecti) or allowing for mourning—to "how can we serve the dead?" What might happen to our politics if we make such service our focus? Here, being useful or making ourselves useful is paradoxically the better counter to the instrumentalizing degradations of use than any invocation of dignity. Instead of rejecting the economy of use, we turn it to political advantage by pressing ourselves into service. In this inhere various forms of undignified and indignant dignity, such as that displayed by the AIDS activist who puts his body on the line for the sake of a world not yet born. Service, not restricted to but exemplified here by the role of the living in serving the dead, may disrupt the binding humanist binary of dignity versus use. It asks us to take the risk of use and to make ourselves useful. Where Anne-Lise François wants to make "hope redundant and collapse the opening up of prospects into its opposite, the inability to do more than stay close to the earth and the little it has yielded,"[61] agonists hope against hope for something more and locate it in the messy interstices of our ordinary lives. The withdrawal and disengagement of recessive action are among the options available to us, but they are not enthroned by agonists into criteria by which all forms of (in)action should be judged. The work of politics is too pressing for that.

CHAPTER 4

The "Unnatural Growth of the Natural": Reconsidering Nature and Artifice in the Context of Biotechnology

Ashley Biser

What is so unsettling is the fact that the dividing line between the nature we *are* and the organic equipment we *give* ourselves is being blurred.

—JÜRGEN HABERMAS, *The Future of Human Nature*

The "Unnatural Growth of the Natural"

There is a deep-seated anxiety that attends the blurring of this distinction between nature and artifice. For Jürgen Habermas, in his *The Future of Human Nature*, it is merely "unsettling." Leon Kass argues that this ambiguity should "offend," "repel," and "repulse" us "because we intuit and feel, immediately and without argument, the violation of things that we rightfully hold dear."[1] In *Our Posthuman Future*, Francis Fukuyama suggests that the loss of this distinction between the natural and the human-made "threatens" our humanity and pushes us toward "a 'posthuman' stage of history."[2]

For each of these thinkers, biotechnology, in the form of genetic engineering, challenges the distinction between nature and artifice.[3] The fact that human beings have the capacity to create life and pattern it according to our own design confounds our ability to distinguish between the "grown" and the "made." But the sense of anxiety these texts exude cannot be traced to a simple fear of the "unnatural." Although each begins with the question of how genetic technologies affect the nature of humanity, they shift quickly to articulating another far more interesting dilemma. For these thinkers, the problem with blurring the distinction between nature and artifice is that it calls into question our ability to think ethically. For Habermas, the issue is how the "biotechnological dedifferentiation of the habitual distinction between the 'grown' and the 'made' . . . changes our ethical self-understanding as members of the species."[4] For Kass, "a world whose once-given natural boundaries are blurred by technological change" becomes synonymous with one "whose moral boundaries are seemingly up for grabs."[5] Fukuyama makes the connection to ethical thinking most explicitly when he says that "nature itself, and in particular human nature, has a special role in defining for us what is right and wrong, just and unjust, important and unimportant."[6] For each of these thinkers, blurring the line between nature and artifice eliminates one of the key bearings by which we navigate our world. Absent the ability to distinguish between the grown and the made, they argue that we cannot make the kinds of ethical and political judgments genetic technologies demand.

Because these thinkers connect the distinction between nature and artifice to the ability to think ethically, they respond to this "biotechnological dedifferentiation" in a defensive manner. Leaving aside Habermas's response for the moment, Fukuyama and Kass assuage their anxiety by attempting to rebuild the wall separating nature from artifice. Empirically, they try to shore up this barrier by calling for an outright ban on certain technologies. Theoretically, they work to reestablish conceptual distinctions between nature and artifice. Fukuyama seeks to reinvigorate the tradition of natural law by offering a definitive conception of human nature informed by recent research in neuroscience and genetics.[7] Kass asks his readers to attend to their gut feelings of "repugnance" when confronted with technologies like cloning in order to erect sharp boundaries between the natural and unnatural.

This framing of the debate surrounding genetic technologies as a threat to the distinction between nature and artifice is typical of discussions of reprogenetics.[8] I focus here on the perceived threat posed by genetic technologies—particularly those that fall under the rubric of reprogenetics, such as prenatal testing and preimplantation genetic diagnosis.[9] I argue that fetishizing the *concepts* of nature and artifice and worrying about the loss of their distinctness actually impedes meaningful discussions about the political implications of these technologies. Rather than attempting to reinscribe this distinction onto an empirical reality to which it no longer corresponds (if it ever did),[10] I suggest that we need to take up the Arendtian challenge to think reprogenetics "without a banister."[11]

The Grown and the Made

For Kass, Fukuyama, and Habermas, the threat posed by reprogenetics rests on the sense that these technologies allow parents ever greater control over the genetic makeup of their offspring. Prenatal testing lets doctors diagnose in utero conditions like Huntington's, Tay-Sachs, cystic fibrosis, and dwarfism; based on this information, parents can then choose whether to continue a pregnancy. Preimplantation genetic diagnosis (PGD) allows couples undergoing in vitro fertilization to decide, based on a similar battery of tests, which embryos to transfer. Although all three thinkers find both prenatal testing and PGD worrisome, it is the specter of *future* developments in reprogenetics that haunts them. Though as yet unfeasible, gene therapy and reproductive cloning exemplify more extreme forms of genetic manipulation, and these thinkers worry that they will bring "more and more of what we are 'by nature' . . . within the reach of biotechnological intervention."[12] In order to recognize potential threats, each takes up a futuristic perspective in their discussions of reprogenetics—what Habermas terms the "perspective of a future present."[13] This move to speak in terms of hypothetical situations and what "might" and "could" happen effectively evokes a sense of heightened urgency while simultaneously implying that ethical thinking can still be "rescued."

In this section, I trace the specific ways in which these three thinkers connect the conceptual distinction between nature and artifice to ethical thinking. For Kass and Fukuyama, the translation to right and wrong is relatively simple. Habermas's translation is far more complex and deserving of attention. In particular, his discussion of the communicative relationships forged by reprogenetics merits further discussion and will be taken up later in this chapter. Despite their varying political and theoretical commitments, however, all three thinkers end up with a call to protect some approximation of human nature from the incursion of biotechnology—thereby putting the theorist in a defensive position with regard to future developments in reprogenetics. Instead of remaining open to the possibilities of reprogenetics, these thinkers begin from a premise that necessarily casts reprogenetics as a threat—something to be guarded against. Proceeding from this assumption of danger, their theorizing becomes an activity of preservation rather than exploration.

For Kass and Fukuyama, the concepts of nature and artifice map sloppily onto a whole series of conceptual dualisms they see as necessary guides for ethical thinking. Nature and artifice are used interchangeably with the natural/unnatural, natural/artificial, natural/cultural, natural/conventional dualisms that so many contemporary theorists seek to contest. Despite the fact that each thinker makes use of a variety of different terms, I will use nature/artifice to refer to the dualism they set up between that over which human beings seem to have little control (nature) and that which is the product of intentional design (artifice).

Kass, more obviously influenced by his religious background, frames his discussion in terms of the "begotten" and the "made."[14] In one of his most famous essays, "The Wisdom of Repugnance," he goes to great trouble to differentiate the natural from the conventional. "It is wrong," he argues, "to treat such naturally rooted social practices [particularly heterosexual marriage] as mere cultural constructs."[15] This deep desire to connect traditional marriage and family-rearing practices to nature reflects his belief that what is natural is permissible and valuable, whereas what is unnatural should be questioned. The distinction between the natural and the non- thus operates to elevate and justify "natural" social practices above those that Kass can label the result of convention.[16] What is important to note about Kass's way of understanding the distinction between nature and artifice is that it requires a clear-cut demarcation between the two concepts. The barrier separating them serves to protect nature from human interference and puts human life decisively on the side of the natural. Eliding the difference between nature and tradition, Kass conceives of nature as an important source of knowledge and stability in the realm of human affairs.

For Fukuyama, the translation from nature and artifice into right and wrong is (only slightly) more complicated. Fukuyama argues that we simply need to *know* humans' intrinsic capabilities in order to develop a conception of human dignity. Absent a "stable human nature," Fukuyama is convinced that we have no way of talking about "ultimate human goods or ends." And without a conception of these goods and ends, Fukuyama argues that human rights cannot be defined or protected. Although he admits to a "huge variance" in this nature, he insists that human beings are not "infinitely plastic."[17] In a paradoxical twist, he suggests that recent research into the genetic bases of behavior can actually help theorists better understand what this nature might look like.[18] But any attempt to *change* this nature through engineering—social or genetic—is unconscionable to him. His basic argument is that absent an understanding of what human beings *are*, we cannot say what should or should not be done to them.[19] Like Kass, Fukuyama sees nature—in this case human nature—as in desperate need of protection. Although his understanding of what constitutes this nature is perhaps broader than Kass's, Fukuyama, too, requires that nature be something stable and separate to which theorists can have recourse when they want to determine what is permissible.

For Habermas, the path from nature and artifice to right and wrong is far more circuitous.[20] In the context of his ongoing attempts to differentiate strategic from communicative action, the concept of instrumentality is more salient than the nature/artifice dualism. For him, the decisive line that needs to be drawn is between therapeutic and enhancement technologies. Whereas the former are oriented toward enabling personal autonomy, the latter are seen by Habermas as an affront to the self-determination of future generations. Because enhancement technologies fundamentally alter the opportunities open to future children, Habermas sees them as a form of "alien determination" that creates an asymmetrical relationship between child and parent.[21] For him, conceptual distinctions like that between nature and artifice (or the grown and the made, as he terms it) form the "taken-for-granted background" upon which all ethical self-understandings are based. It is because we understand ourselves as "born" rather than "made" that Habermas argues that we can "critically appropriate" our life histories.[22] The concern registered in his text is that these background conditions might so drastically change that "we may no longer see ourselves as ethically free and moral beings guided by norms and reasons."[23]

In his focus on the asymmetrical relationships created by the use of reprogenetics technologies, Habermas adeptly sidesteps many of the pitfalls inherent in Kass's and Fukuyama's accounts and provides a welcome reprieve from more conservative discussions of bioethics. Despite the somewhat misleading title of his essay, Habermas is not primarily worried about "unnatural" relationships and makes few claims about a stable human nature.[24] Instead, he convincingly argues that the instrumentalization of human life occasioned by reprogenetics should concern us.[25] Rather than seeing ourselves as autonomous beings capable of political action and ethical decision making, Habermas states that "we cannot rule it out that knowledge of one's own hereditary features as programmed may prove to restrict the choice of an individual's way of life."[26]

In this sense, Habermas's undertaking seems to require no ontological claims about what humans *are;* instead, he attempts to lay out a conception of "deontological virtue" by articulating "an ethical self-understanding of the species which is crucial for our capacity to see ourselves as the authors of our own life histories, and to recognize one another as autonomous persons."[27] However, the extent to which Habermas's project avoids the pitfalls of a conception of human nature is debatable, as he himself recognizes.[28] While rare, his worries about the "transgression" of boundaries and the "penetration" of nature nonetheless construct nature as a separate sphere—one capable of being invaded.[29] Although his concept is far more plastic than either Fukuyama's or Kass's, an implicit understanding of human nature lies behind Habermas's distinction between therapeutic and enhancement technologies, and he remains tethered to the dichotomous thinking such dualisms encourage. Absent knowledge of what we are, it would seem impossible to recognize what constitutes enhancement. Although he posits no direct line between the natural and the right, he nonetheless argues that we need the "stabilizing context of an ethics of the species . . . to endure if morality itself is not to start slipping."[30] In this way, the formulation of ethical arguments becomes once again bound (albeit in a far more nuanced manner) to the nature/artifice dualism.

Because each of these thinkers views nature as threatened by advances in reprogenetics, each calls upon the state to enact strict guidelines for the use of certain technologies and to outlaw some altogether. Given the importance each ascribes the nature/artifice distinction, this call for regulation can be understood as the empirical component of their theoretical attempts to shore up a conceptual distinction that seems to safeguard ethical thinking. So long as certain reprogenetic techniques are deemed unlawful, the fissure occasioned by genetic research remains manageable.

However, basing this call for regulation on a fissure in the wall separating nature from artifice puts the theorist in a peculiar position—attempting to rebuild what appears to be a barrier that has already been breached.[31] With each passing year, the particular technologies that concern thinkers like Kass, Fukuyama, and Habermas become simultaneously more commonplace and impervious to control—making arguments critical of them more difficult to articulate.[32] In what follows, I argue that such a defensive posture is an unproductive one for the political theorist. It puts those who are skeptical of reprogenetics in the uncomfortable company of conservative political movements or else in the awkward position of attempting to draw almost arbitrary distinctions between those technologies that are permissible and those that or not. Instead, I turn to Hannah Arendt's work to suggest that there might be a way beyond this impasse. Through a close textual reading of her (admittedly idiosyncratic) understanding of nature, I complicate the assumption that nature can serve as a stable background upon which to base our theorizing and develop an alternative interpretation of the relationship between Arendt's conceptual categories. What happens, I ask, if we approach the task of thinking reprogenetics not out of a concern for the conceptual categories of nature and artifice but with an eye toward the political implications of their various entanglements?

Thinking Reprogenetics without a Banister

Building off of Arendt's critique of totalitarianism, I suggest that although traditional concepts like nature and artifice may indeed have oriented ethical thinking in the past, this does not mean that we can continue to rely upon them in the future.[33] As new phenomena emerge, we are forced to relinquish "categories and formulas that are deeply ingrained in our mind but whose basis of experience has long been forgotten and whose plausibility resides in their intellectual consistency rather than in their adequacy to actual events."[34] Instead of relying on these "safe guiding lines," Arendt insists that we are capable of thinking without these inherited constructs—"without a banister."[35] In this chapter, I suggest that nature and artifice—conceived as discrete concepts between which a barrier must be erected—are precisely the sort of "deeply ingrained" categories of which we should be wary. The problem with such preconceived notions, Arendt reminds us, is that they actually interfere with our capacity to "understand," "comprehend," and "think" events in their "originality."[36]

It is important to note that Arendt's is a call to think *without* a banister—not to construct a new one. Hers is no simple appeal to her readers to find new concepts and categories more suited to contemporary reality. As we relinquish time-worn "categories and formulas," we take on the far more difficult tasks of "thinking and judging."[37] In this way, the turn to Arendt compels us to move away from philosophical-conceptual questions and toward more political ones.[38] As such, hers is a challenge to displace an entire analytical framework that seems more interested in conceptual fidelity than political potency. My concern is not to articulate the "correct" relationship between nature and artifice given new reprogenetic technologies but to *reorient* our thinking. I leave aside the question of whether a conception of human nature (let alone second nature) is ever useful for political theorizing and assert only that this framework need not be the only one through which we approach reprogenetics. What I suggest is that the nature/artifice dualism acts like the spotlight on a stage set, directing the audience's attention toward certain tableaus (or interpretations) and away from others. In the case of reprogenetics, I suspect that what is going on in the shadows—still on stage, but not necessarily the center of attention—is still in need of illumination.

Arendt is an admittedly strange ally to enlist in this project. Given the many distinctions she draws in *The Human Condition*—between labor, work, action, public, private, social, etc.—it is tempting to read her work as if she, too, desires a clear-cut demarcation between nature and artifice. She often seems to call for a shoring up of boundaries—a reinscription of distinctions that modernity has obscured. Indeed, in an insightful essay, Kimberly Curtis turns to Arendt's work to offer a compelling critique of assisted reproductive technologies precisely because they confound our ability to distinguish between freedom and necessity.[39] However, I argue that, despite the value of works like Curtis's, such a reading of Arendt remains mired in the same philosophical-conceptual framework I wish to displace. In the pages that come, I offer an alternative reading.

Instead of understanding Arendt's conceptual work as a chronicle of loss, we might read her concepts as provisional attempts to grasp multidimensional phenomena that defy simplistic description.[40] In this sense, concepts intrude upon phenomena—organizing and articulating but never fully representing them. Because concepts are "thought words" that try to fix in language invisible and ever-changing ideas (*LM*, 52), they exist in an uneasy tension with the phenomena they try to depict. Instead of attending to the definitions of the different concepts Arendt lays out in *The Human Condition*, I draw attention to those moments in which these concepts appear and disappear—intertwine and intersect. In this context, nature and artifice emerge not as clear-cut historical categories she attempts to impose on modernity but as provisional attempts to articulate this phenomenon.[41] While I doubt Arendt herself could ever take this kind of "pleasure in the confusion of boundaries,"[42] I use her work to approach reprogenetics not out of an attitude of fear and revulsion—afraid of what we might lose—but with a posture of resolved inquisitiveness—curious about what we might learn about ourselves and the world in which we dwell.[43]

In the introduction to *The Origins of Totalitarianism*, Arendt suggests that "comprehension . . . means the unpremeditated, attentive facing up to, and resisting of, reality—whatever it may be" (*OT*, viii). An attitude of resolved inquisitiveness requires just this sort of "facing up to" the realities of reprogenetics. Instead of starting with preconceived concepts and categories and trying to understand how phenomena complicate and contest them (as do Kass, Fukuyama, and Habermas), I argue that the phenomena themselves should be our primary concern. In other words, Arendt's categories and concepts are important tools of articulation, but they emerge from phenomena, not the other way around. Rather than seeking refuge in the familiar, I argue that we must be prepared to recognize the complexities and ambiguities inherent in the reprogenetics phenomenon and resist the temptation to understand it through "analogies and generalities" (*OT*, viii). At the same time, we cannot look away from potentially uncomfortable truths this phenomenon might reveal.

In the pages to come, I suggest that whereas interpreters like Curtis are right to see in Arendt's thinking a deep appreciation for the protection the human artifice offers us from the unpredictability of nature, Arendt's conceptions of both nature and artifice are far more complicated than often allowed. Thus, I suggest that blurring the distinction between nature and artifice need not render us incapable of making ethical and political judgments about reprogenetic technologies. Instead, reprogenetics represents a unique phenomenon that must be understood in all its singularity and originality. Like totalitarianism—the particular historical constellation of events that inspired Arendt's thinking—reprogenetics confronts political theorists with a peculiar dilemma in that "the very event, the phenomenon, which we try—and must try—to understand has deprived us of our traditional tools of understanding."[44]

From Nature to Natural Processes

Turning now to Arendt's discussion of nature and artifice, the first thing we notice is that this dualism maps awkwardly onto the tripartite structure of *The Human Condition*. In her discussion of labor, work, and action, it is difficult to locate nature and artifice with regard to these activities. If we make the usual move to connect nature to labor and align artifice with work, something appears to be missing. Not only do we notice the conspicuous absence of a third term corresponding to action, but we would have to collapse Arendt's complex understanding of both nature and artifice into one-dimensional concepts to make them fit. Rather than spend our time searching for a nonexistent third term—a futile attempt that remains at the level of philosophical-conceptual analysis—I argue in the coming sections that we need a more complex understanding of Arendt's discussions of both nature and artifice. Rather than representing distinct spheres, nature and artifice should be understood, I suggest, as always already intersecting, thereby traversing all three of Arendt's modes of human activity—labor, work, *and* action.

How, then, does Arendt use the terms nature and artifice? Unsurprisingly, Arendt attributes the distinction between nature and artifice to Aristotle and briefly appropriates the concepts of *physis* and *nomos* in her discussion of work (*HC*, 150).[45] Unlike the triad of thinkers mentioned previously, however, she highlights the activities of nature—not the entity itself:

> It is characteristic of all natural processes that they come into being without the help of man, and those things are natural which are not "made" but grow by themselves into whatever they become (This is also the authentic meaning of our word "nature," whether we derive it from its Latin root *nasci*, to be born, or trace it back to its Greek origin, *physis*, which comes from *phyein*, to grow out of, to appear by itself). (*HC*, 150)

Where Habermas's, Fukuyama's, and Kass's works refer to nature as a noun, a static entity, Arendt emphasizes the verb from which it originates. Instead of "*the* natural," "*the* grown," or "*what* has come to be," Arendt refers to the activities of nature—its growing and becoming. In her description of biological life, she says that nature is characterized by continuous activity—a constant cycle of creation and destruction, birth and decay (*HC*, 96). Where natural processes reign, there exists "no beginning and no end" (*HC*, 96). This insistence on the motion inherent in nature's activities immediately calls into question both the stability for which theorists like Kass and Fukuyama yearn and the separation of nature and artifice upon which they rely. In the context of the activities of nature, calls to return to the "natural order" of things make little sense.[46]

Looking beyond Arendt's discussion in *The Human Condition*, we recognize what appear as deep inconsistencies in her many references to "nature."[47] At times it is "hostile," a "silent wilderness" that makes eking out even the paltriest existence almost impossible (*OT*, 191). Elsewhere, nature is described as a source of respite from the superficiality of society. It is "majestic" (*OT*, 192) and can occasion "boundless delight" (*RV*, 151). Nature consists of "good" (*HC*, 120) and "green things"—it is one of the "true realities" of existence (*RV*, 151).[48] It can be reveled in (*RV*, 152; *HC*, 120) or sunk back toward (*OT*, 207). The forces of nature are "elemental" and "powerful" (*HC*, 148) yet also monotonous—"swing[ing] in changeless, deathless repetition" (*HC*, 96). Natural processes are "cyclical" (*HC*, 98) and "destructive"—"devouring" matter (*HC*, 100)—but nature's household is characterized by "superabundance" (*HC*, 106). Needless to say, nature is not, for Arendt, simple.[49]

More importantly, even within *The Human Condition*, specific references to "Nature" are rare. Instead, Arendt refers to the earth (*HC*, 2), "natural things" (*HC*, 96), "nature's forces" (*HC*, 148), nature's "household" (*HC*, 97),[50] and, most often, "natural processes" (*HC*, 148, 231, *pas-*

sim). She explicitly disavows a conception of human nature (*HC*, 10; *OT*, 347) and at times seems almost to mock the attribution of "naturalness"—particularly with regard to imperial encounters with indigenous peoples (e.g., *OT*, 192).

This move to think of nature in terms of forces and processes again highlights the sense of motion inherent in Arendt's understanding and suggests that hypostatizing the concepts into "spheres" would be a mistake. Instead of questioning whether any particular entity should be classified as natural or artificial, I draw our attention to the different modes of activity natural and artificial processes entail. Her eclectic discussion of "natural processes," "green things," and human nature suggests that we can read her not as trying to uphold a categorical distinction between nature and artifice but rather as trying to emphasize the power and sense of inevitability associated with those things we call "natural."

Arendt's emphasis on processes and activities also helps explain the antipathy toward nature often attributed to her. Although many feminists read Arendt as hostile toward the bodily dimensions of human existence and thereby construct a hierarchical relationship between labor, work, and action,[51] her hostility now appears directed toward processes—particularly historical processes that take on the appearance of natural ones—not nature itself.[52] As facts of human existence, processes stand in stark opposition to action.[53] Where she can wonder at the majesty of nature and the *cosmos*, Arendt's attitude toward processes is more uniformly negative.

The problem with processes, for Arendt, is twofold. First, they are inherently destructive—"ruinous," she calls them (*WF*, 168). The "natural life process that drives our organism . . . leads from being to non-being, from birth to death" (*WF*, 168). This destructive trajectory is all the more worrisome to her given its automatism. If we take freedom as a guiding principle of Arendt's work, the inevitability associated with processes is understandably troublesome (*WF*, 168). Although they *can* be interrupted, processes, particularly when viewed from within, make the unexpected appear "infinitely improbable" (*WF*, 168).[54]

However, Arendt levels this charge against all processes—regardless of whether they occur in nature or in human affairs. In this way, her work helps call into question attempts like Kass's and Fukuyama's to put nature and artifice into a hierarchical relationship that accords one greater moral or epistemic value. Arendt also explicitly refuses to locate human beings on one side of a nature/artifice dualism. For her, the relationship between these natural processes and humans is a complicated one. Whereas the nature/artifice dualism allows thinkers like Kass and Fukuyama to code human beings as entirely natural—and thereby in need of protection from the unnatural—Arendt helps us to recognize that humanity exists at the intersection of nature and artifice. As *animal laborans*, humans are creatures of nature—subject to the same processes of birth and decay as any other living being. "Nature seen through the eyes of the *animal laborans*" is coterminous with life; it is simply that with which human beings "mix" in order to exist (*HC*, 134). But acting as *homo faber*, human beings separate themselves from nature; it appears as the raw material out of which the world is built (*HC*, 135). Arendt suggests that modern technoscience has made it "more difficult to remain aware of the urges of necessity" (*HC*, 135), but humans are nonetheless both growing and making beings.[55]

It is precisely because human beings cannot be assigned to either side of a nature/artifice dualism that Arendt refuses the language of "human nature" and speaks instead of the "human condition" (*HC*, 10). Only the fact that we live on this earth (and not even that) allows us to say that we are human as opposed to something else. The only thing human beings have in common, according to Arendt, is that they are conditioned beings—conditioned by what they themselves create (*HC*, 9).[56]

I note Arendt's emphasis on the perspective from which nature is viewed (the eyes through which it is seen) because it underscores the fact that natural processes appear differently depending on the comportment of the viewer and further complicates attempts to understand nature and artifice as separate spheres. Although Arendt is inconsistent on this point, she at times seems to suggest that nature only "become[s] a process" because modern science needed it to appear in this way (*HC*, 296). Elsewhere, she argues that nature "appears" as automatic only "if we see these processes against the background of human purposes," which have an altogether linear trajectory (*HC*, 151). Just as events are subsumed by processes when history becomes obsessed with the concept of development, so too does it seem that natural things begin to "derive their significance and meaning solely from their functions in the overall-process" only with the advent of modern science (*HC*, 296).

Even the destructive aspect of natural processes only makes sense from the viewpoint of *homo faber*. Because they are inherently cyclical, endless "small" and "single" natural processes work together to form the "over-all gigantic circle of nature" (*HC*, 96). From the perspective of nature's "metabolism" (*HC*, 100), dead matter is simply food for consumption—to be incorporated into another process. The time structure of natural processes is thus circular—without beginning or end. The ideas of birth and death, however, impose linearity on this circular motion. Only from the perspective of the world do the ideas of birth and death even make sense:

> It is only within the human world that nature's cyclical movement manifests itself as growth and decay. Like birth and death, they, too, are not natural occurrences, properly speaking; they have no place in the unceasing, indefatigable cycle in which the whole household of nature swings perpetually. Only when they enter the man-made world can nature's processes be characterized by growth and decay. (*HC*, 97–98)

Because birth and death represent absolute beginnings and endings, they punctuate nature's cyclical movement and can only be conceived in the linear terms of the world.

Modern Technoscience: Unleashing Natural Forces

Arendt's shift away from nature writ large and toward the idea of natural processes is crucial for understanding the distinctiveness of modern technoscience. In *The Human Condition*, Arendt distinguishes three stages of modern technological development: the invention of the steam engine, the use of electricity, and automation (*HC*, 147–150). I argue that each of these stages can be understood not in terms of a hard and fast distinction between nature and artifice but by a different relationship between human fabrication and natural processes. From this perspective, nature and artifice are always already intersecting. What changes is their interaction.

Take, for example, the steam engine. Via Arendt's interpretation, the steam engine "imitates" natural processes. Electricity, which characterizes the second stage of mechanical development, more directly interferes with natural processes, "killing" and "interrupting" them; electricity is thereby an attempt at "denaturalization" (*HC*, 148).[57] In contrast to these earlier forms of technology, Arendt suggests that technologies like the atom bomb and genetics constitute a different relationship to natural processes. In Arendt's thinking, humans do not simply appropriate naturally occurring activities; "acting into nature," they "provoke" them. They initiate "'natural' processes which without men would never exist" (*HC*, 231).

Whereas Habermas, Fukuyama, and Kass worry that reprogenetic technologies "denaturalize" human beings by making them into something less "natural,"[58] Arendt's concern is the "unnatural growth of the natural" (*HC*, 47).[59] Inherent in this formulation is *both* the "denaturalization" of what we take as natural (the "unnatural growth") *and* the naturalization of the artificial (the "growth of the natural"). Given her experience with totalitarianism, Arendt is particularly attuned to the ways in which matters of choice become transformed into "biological fatality."[60] The concern is not that we are "overcoming nature"[61] but that we are "unleashing" natural processes and "channeling" them into the human artifice (*HC*, 150). Despite her earlier characterization of processes as repetitive and predictable (*HC*, 96), they acquire an element of unpredictability as soon as they are "unleashed." This element of unpredictability is what allows Arendt's interpreters to characterize technoscientific inventions as "technological actions."[62]

An understanding of uncontained natural processes as powerful forces beyond human control further underscores the difference between an Arendtian-inspired critique of reprogenetic technologies and the concerns registered by Habermas, Fukuyama, and Kass. Habermas, in particular, worries that reprogenetic technologies allow for too much predictability—essentially enabling "genetic designers" to determine the life changes of future generations.[63] Whereas he, Fukuyama, and Kass worry that reprogenetics represent an attempt to "overcome" nature and bring it under human control, Arendt's additional concern is that we have let loose processes we can never hope to master. Although new reproductive technologies confound the ability to *recognize* ourselves as subject to nature, Arendt does not commit the concomitant fallacy of suggesting that we are no longer—at least in some part—at nature's mercy. As Kimberly Curtis notes, "the bald assertion that nature now lies, prostrate, in human hands awaiting its fate appears to be foolish hubris."[64]

Although Arendt, too, sees reprogenetic technologies as borne of a *desire* for control (*HC*, 2), a critique inspired by her works must also recognize that we can "channel" natural processes that we cannot even comprehend, let alone master. Reprogenetic technologies represent a supreme example of this ability to use natural processes without understanding how they work. The very activities of DNA sequencing and replication used to conduct genetic tests make use of the natural properties of DNA to cut and paste sequences of nucleotides. Yet scientists still have only limited comprehension of why and how we can do so. From this perspective, the unleashing of natural processes into the human artifice is thereby troublesome not because it represents a transgression of boundaries but because it signifies a disjuncture between what we can do and what we can understand and talk about. This disjuncture raises a relational concern: it inspires questions about our ability to understand and articulate technoscientific action rather than questions about the extent of our technoscientific capabilities.

Arendt's work suggests that the desire for control acts as an impetus for technoscientific development. Via this interpretation, reprogenetics represents an attempt at mastery that can never be realized. Although they fail to recognize this point, Kass's, Fukuyama's, and Habermas's insistence on the need for the "stability" provided by the nature/artifice dualism is emblematic of a similar urge to mastery.[65] For them, stability is a necessary prerequisite to ethical thinking, and they seek to control reprogenetics so as to provide a stable background for thinking.[66] It is this assumption that thinking requires a stable background that Arendt's works help me explicitly complicate. Given the motion inherent in her conception of natural processes, Arendt shows that human beings exist in a perpetual state of instability. The challenge is to think and judge in the context of this unpredictability—not to control it.

Kimberly Curtis suggests that this emphasis on the need to "hold . . . in tension" the desire for self-determination and the "continued relevance of the unintended and unknown" is one of Arendt's greatest contributions to debates surrounding reprogenetics.[67] In her essay, Curtis uses Arendt to assert a qualitative difference between those reproductive technologies that attempt to prevent life (birth control, sterilization, and abortion) and those that actually produce it (in vitro fertilization, artificial insemination, surrogate motherhood, and genetic engineering).[68] This distinction enables us to differentiate between those technologies that enable the self-determination of women (the former) and those that actually interfere with the conditions for freedom (the latter).[69]

Despite the complexity we have seen in Arendt's account of nature, Curtis's account is driven by what she sees as Arendt's "division between things created by nature and things created by humans." Like Habermas, Fukuyama, and Kass, Curtis, too, suggests that attempts to produce nature undermine the function of the nature/artifice distinction. In Curtis's words, "we subvert the age-old purpose of the human artifice which was . . . to stabilize . . . our otherwise evanescent human life."[70]

Curtis is right to see that Arendt rarely suggests that nature needs to be protected from human manipulation (as Kass, Fukuyama, and Habermas argue).[71] Instead, Arendt argues that *the human artifice* needs to be insulated from the relentless processes of birth and death that characterize nature. For Arendt, the human artifice needs this sort of protection because it in turn shields human beings from the unpredictability and uncertainty of action. By providing "permanence" and "stability" to ephemeral human existence (*HC*, 173), the world "offer[s] mortals a dwelling place more permanent and more stable than themselves" (*HC*, 152). The problem with modern technoscience is that "instead of carefully surrounding the human artifice with defenses against nature's elementary forces, keeping them as far as possible outside the man-made world, we have channeled these forces, along with their elementary power, into the world itself" (*HC*, 148–149).[72]

However, Curtis suggests that we need the nature/artifice dualism to appreciate the difference between the necessity of the natural world and the freedom inherent in political action.[73] In this way, Curtis effectively connects the distinction between freedom and necessity to the nature/artifice dualism.[74] She then moves to connect this dualism to our ability to "take our bearings"—a metaphor Arendt uses frequently to signify how we come to terms with and think the world that surrounds us.[75] In tethering the ability to distinguish between nature and artifice to taking our bearings, Curtis makes a move that should be familiar by now, given that it mirrors (albeit in a far more nuanced manner) Kass's, Fukuyama's, and Habermas's similar attempts to connect the nature/artifice dualism to ethical thinking.

Like Kass, Fukuyama, and Habermas, Curtis responds to the dedifferentiation of nature and artifice by insisting on the need to shore up this conceptual distinction. She concludes by suggesting that we need to "articulate principled limits to our efforts to control nature lest we lost [*sic*] important dimensions of what makes us human."[76] Via her interpretation, Arendt "insists" on the "importance of designing social practices and making political judgments which ensure that a protective wall—porous but real enough—can be sustained between nature and the human artifice."[77]

Curtis's call for a barrier (however porous) between nature and artifice puts her, too, in an uncomfortable position with regard to the technologies that most concern her. In a contemporary context, worries about in vitro fertilization, artificial insemination, and surrogacy seem to many alarmist and outdated. As commonplace techniques, they are considered relatively ordinary tools of the fertility specialist and have been used by many to create precisely the kinds of "new family forms" that so worry Kass and interest many feminists. Along with amniocentesis and the ultrasound, these techniques require little by way of technical explanation and justification.[78] If these technologies are examples of fissures in a nature/artifice barrier, this is a barrier that was breached long ago. Despite having started her piece with the explicit intention of overcoming the "particular problem for feminist theory" presented by new reproductive technologies, Curtis's interpretation can be read as yet another lament that requires a defensive posture on the part of the theorist.[79]

Reorienting Ourselves without Nature and Artifice

As I hope the preceding sections have shown, my reading of Arendt's texts complicates this insistence on a nature/artifice dualism. In my emphasis on the interconnectedness of these two concepts and the need to move away from a philosophical-conceptual level of analysis, I suggest that there might be other ways to orient ourselves in the absence of this conceptual construct. My insistence that we need to think reprogenetics without this banister requires that we refocus the spotlight on aspects of reprogenetics that might be missed in the emphasis on nature and artifice. Take, for example, Curtis's discussion of assisted reproductive technologies. In pointing to the stability the human artifice provides, Curtis draws our attention to the world-building and stabilizing activities to which Arendt ascribes importance. The concepts of nature and artifice enable Arendt to articulate the significance of these activities. It is the significance of these stabilizing activities that Arendt wants to maintain even as the particular relationship between nature and artifice that heretofore enabled them is always already in flux.

On this interpretation, the problem with reprogenetic technologies is not that they call into question some abstract and amorphous conception of what it means to be human but that they make more difficult specific activities to which we have formerly ascribed importance. Whereas the former inspires a sort of paralytic fear, the latter interpretation demands another response: it encourages us to question whether these are still activities we value. But instead of attending to these *activities*—asking whether they are still important and how we might enable them given the new relationships reprogenetics crafts, Curtis moves in another direction: to protect the *concepts* of nature and artifice. Despite her many insights into reprogenetics, she, too, remains mired in a philosophical-conceptual framework. I want to ask what we might learn if we detour from Curtis's argument at this crucial point. What happens if we attend to the *activities* the nature/artifice dualism enables? Instead of focusing on the concepts themselves and asking whether nature and artifice can be differentiated, we can question what this conceptual construct has previously authorized.[80] Are there other ways to engage in these activities without relying on a strict demarcation of nature from artifice? This detour leads us to ask a different question of Arendt's works: how are these activities affected by reprogenetics?

There are many ways to approach this question. In the coming pages, I focus on but one of the many activities Arendt describes. For Arendt, one of the primary purposes of the human artifice is stabilizing—it enables human beings to "orient" themselves in a world that is, in some sense, always moving. This is not a matter of controlling one's surroundings but of finding a way to locate ourselves within a world that is always already in motion. Think of the ability to right an airplane in conditions of turbulence or a hold a boat steady in stormy seas. The challenge is to ride the wind and water—not to fix their movements. Whereas Kass, Fukuyama, and (to some extent) Habermas seek stable ground upon which to base ethical decisions, I ask how we keep ourselves oriented in conditions that are never fixed or motionless.

This ability to orient ourselves, or "take our bearings," as Arendt puts it, is crucial; without it, we allow ourselves to be "swept away" by "what everybody does and believes in" (*LM*, 192).[81] But this ability is not simply connected to the nature/artifice dualism. In Arendt's discussions of both thinking and acting, there are continual references to the "stabilizing forces" that allow us to "orient" ourselves in the realm of human affairs (*HC*, 198).[82] Not just the human artifice but reality, promises, and even language and metaphors all act as "guideposts of reliability" (*LM*, 50, 100; *HC*, 204).[83]

What is important to recognize, however, is that it is the *world*—not simply the objective human artifice—that Arendt implicates in her discussion of "stabilizing forces."[84] For Arendt, the world is only partially created by objects. Offering a way for people to "relate" and "bind[ing] them together, they constitute a physical, worldly in-between" (*HC*, 182) that exists among human beings when they are dealing with tangible things. In addition to this "in-between," "overgrown" on top of it Arendt posits another "subjective" and (at least partially) "intangible" web that "consists of deeds and words" (*HC*, 183); this is what she calls the "the 'web' of human relationships" (ibid.). It is into this web that Arendt's actors insert themselves when they act; thus the web itself enables the activity of self-disclosure. Yet it is also here that our actions become subject to "innumerable, conflicting wills and intentions" (*HC*, 184) and are transformed—hence the unpredictability of action. By collapsing Arendt's multifaceted understanding of the world into a purely material artifice, we fail to recognize that this web of other human beings in which we are, existentially, situated enables many of the same stabilizing activities as the nature/artifice dualism.[85] If we accept that this dualism is problematic, we might now turn our attention to questioning how reprogenetics affects this web and our interactions with others.[86] Given the important role this web plays in enabling political action, this becomes a political question of the highest order.

Conclusion: An "Assault on Plurality"?

Once we shift the discussion away from nature and artifice—and toward questions of interaction—different concerns regarding reprogenetics emerge. Where Kass, Fukuyama, and Habermas seek to shore up conceptual barriers in an attempt to defend ethical thinking from the realities of reprogenetics, I have argued that this effort is not only unfeasible but rests on an impoverished understanding of ethical thinking. By contrast, the approach I have developed here calls us to attend to the uniqueness of the phenomenon of reprogenetics—asking questions about how these technologies affect our capacity for political (inter)action. For Arendt, the web of human relationships is characterized above all by the condition of plurality—a fact of our togetherness. In her terms, plurality has a "twofold character of equality and distinction" (*HC*, 175); that is, "we are all the same, that is, human, in such a way that nobody is ever the same as anyone else who ever lived, lives or will live" (*HC*, 8). Because plurality is "specifically *the* condition . . . of all political life" (*HC*, 7), it is crucial to understanding the singularly political implications of reprogenetics.[87] In this last section, I question briefly how reprogenetic technologies might affect the qualities of equality and distinction that undergird Arendt's conception of plurality.

Take, for instance, Habermas's concerns about asymmetry. In his focus on the relationships forged by reprogenetics, he registers the concern that these technologies might institute inequalities heretofore unknown. In his text, he deals primarily with the relationship between child and parent. While we can assume that children would consent to therapeutic interventions that would prevent painful and debilitating conditions, Habermas suggests that enhancement is a different matter. In the former case, "the presumption of informed consent transforms egocentric action into communicative action."[88] In the latter, there is a lack of reciprocity, and the communicative relationship between child and parent is thereby stunted. Habermas argues:

> with genetic enhancement, there is no communicative scope for the projected child to be addressed as a second person and to be involved in a communication process. From the adolescent's perspective, an instrumental determination cannot, like a pathogenic socialization process, be revised by "critical reappraisal."[89]

There are numerous problems with this formulation of the dilemma posed by reprogenetics. Aside from the sense of genetic determinism that permeates the above passage, the focus on informed consent fails to do justice to the kind of communicative interaction Arendt (and Habermas, in other contexts) prizes.[90] Nonetheless, concerns about asymmetry remain—particularly with regard to access to these technologies and the potential relationships they might forge not simply between "designer" and "designed" (Habermas's terms) but also between those who make use of such technologies and those who do not. In this way, reprogenetic technologies might call into question the equality upon which plurality's "twofold character" rests.

On the flip side, commentators also worry that reprogenetics could lead to a leveling out of difference—an attempt to constrain the myriad possibilities inherent in every birth.[91] In this way, reprogenetics might call into question the quality of distinction that constitutes the second part of Arendt's definition. Given reprogenetics' current emphasis on eliminating defects in potential offspring, the specter of normalization weighs heavily. It is quite possible that genetic variation could be understood in terms of deviation—with the human genome acting as the norm against which differences are measured.[92] Many disability advocates worry that these technologies could restrict the range of acceptable human difference because children born with conditions like Down syndrome or dwarfism might come to be seen avoidable mistakes. There is thus the potential that these technologies could exacerbate the already existing prejudices of society in favor of the able bodied.[93]

On a related note, theorists have also noted that scientific discussions of variation tend to reinscribe traditional conceptions of racial and ethnic difference.[94] Although she never suggests, as Fukuyama does, that reprogenetic technologies constitute an attempt to "breed some people with saddles on their backs, and others with boots and spurs," Curtis worries that "radical assaults on human plurality in the interest of the life process become, if not logical, at least difficult to distinguish from more limited interventions."[95]

Aside from the potential to forge asymmetrical relationships and encourage normalization, there is yet another way that reprogenetic technologies might affect our conceptions of plurality. Because it promotes a molecular understanding of disease—where diagnosis is based primarily on genetic tests rather than on physical symptoms—reprogenetics shift attention away from the outward manifestation of human difference.[96] Instead of focusing on how human beings are able to comport themselves in the world, this understanding of disease is concerned with an individual's intrinsic characteristics. In Arendt's terms, reprogenetics might thereby encourage attention to "what" a person is—"his qualities, gifts, talents, and shortcomings"—at the expense of the "who" that is disclosed through speech and action (*HC*, 179).[97]

These worries are exacerbated if we take into account Arendt's concerns regarding the relationship between technoscientific action and language. Whereas speech and language are the media of *political* action, technoscientific actions are, in some sense, wordless. In "The Conquest of Space and the Stature of Man," Arendt suggests that the problem with technoscientific action might be "that man can *do*, and successfully do, what he cannot comprehend and cannot express in everyday human language."[98] Because they "enter not into the web of human relationships and specifically political actions, but into the mute natural world," it is possible that technoscientific actions lack the "revelatory" character of political actions.[99]

The potential wordlessness of the actions initiated by reprogenetic technologies is troublesome not simply because language is a tool of communication. More importantly, language, for Arendt, allows the disclosure of the "who" to other human beings. It is only through speaking that individuals can make their distinctness known. Absent speech, Arendt suggests that action would lose its ability to disclose individuals "as subjects, as distinct and unique persons" (*HC*, 183).[100] For Arendt, action without speech "would not only lose its revelatory character, but, and by the same token, it would lose its subject . . . not acting men but performing robots would achieve what, humanly speaking, would remain incomprehensible" (*HC*, 178).

These concerns over the creation of meaning and our appreciation of human plurality are again political questions that call out for further thinking and judging. In shifting attention to the ways in which reprogenetics might affect our interactions with other human beings and our appreciation for human distinction, I have attempted to reorient our thinking away from philosophical-conceptual concerns and toward political ones. Rather than merely questioning what is natural and what is not, I have argued that we need to interrogate how reprogenetic technologies might affect the web of human relationships that both enables and is created by political action. It seems to me that if we're going to think reprogenetics, let us think and question on this basis—not because these technologies are "unnatural" but because they might interfere with our appreciation for "the fact that men, not Man, live on the earth and inhabit the world" (*HC*, 7).

CHAPTER 5

Potentialities of Second Nature: Agamben on Human Rights

Ayten Gündoğdu

Human rights have become a predominant discourse in global politics, particularly in the post–Cold War era, in addressing various questions of injustice. If this transformation has been welcomed by various scholars who identify it with the promise of a postnational, transnational, or cosmopolitan future,[1] it has also become the target of several critics who underline its insidious effects as a new form of power. The cosmopolitan aura of human rights has been increasingly demystified as various scholars pointed out their deployment in the justification of neoimperial interventions,[2] their masking of a political power constituting subjects in need of political protection and undermining political projects of collective empowerment,[3] and their hegemonic appropriation of "the field of emancipatory possibility."[4]

Giorgio Agamben makes a distinctive contribution to these contemporary debates with his analysis aiming to demonstrate how human rights, perceived as normative guarantees against the state, actually participate in rendering human lives vulnerable to sovereign violence. Agamben locates the starting point of this troublesome development in modern rights declarations, which make natural life the foundation of the modern nation-state. As a result, every aspect of life becomes politicized and subjected to sovereign power to an unprecedented degree. Sovereign decisions with regards to who is to be included in and excluded from citizenship and humanity produce various categories of human beings as "bare life," or life that is left at the threshold of political and natural, law and life, right and fact, and, as such, vulnerable to an unpunishable violence. Agamben concludes his critique with a call for a politics beyond human rights to sever the link that holds human life in the grip of sovereign power.

In many ways, Agamben's critique of sovereignty and human rights shares the concerns and orientations of this volume. Taking his starting point from the de-essentializing turn in political thought, Agamben's analysis reveals that what we take to be "nature" is always already "second nature," acquired through a set of practices, conventions, customs, and habits. He shows, for example, how biological life has always been the site of political decisions. In line with the goals outlined by the editors of this volume, Agamben moves beyond this de-essentializing move and engages in a critique underscoring the mutual imbrication of politics and nature. As modern politics has turned "nature," especially biological life, into the foundation of politics, the line between "political" and "natural" has increasingly blurred. Agamben's assessment of the effects of this blurring, however, diverges from the conclusions that the editors of this volume draw about the political possibilities engendered by the hybrid terrain of "second nature." Since Agamben sees in the "second nature" created by modern politics an irredeemably violent site threatening human life, what he offers is not "a *positive* picture of the important political capacities generated through the hybridity of nature and politics."[5] This hybridity, at least in the form it takes in modern politics, Agamben's work suggests, becomes a resource for revitalizing sovereignty: the more blurred the line between "politics" and "nature" becomes, the more incentive sovereign power has to redraw and entrench that line. The zone of indistinction, or the hybrid and impure realm of "politics" and "nature," according to Agamben, becomes a site of sovereign decisions determining which lives are worth living and which lives can be rendered vulnerable to arbitrary violence. To the extent that human rights discourse participates in, covers up, and legitimizes the sovereign decisions about life in this zone, it is complicit in the perpetuation of sovereign violence. We can begin to imagine an alternative politics, Agamben concludes, only if we reject the "second nature" we come to acquire with sovereignty and human rights.

This chapter aims to provide a critical evaluation of Agamben's inquiry into the underlying assumptions, constitutive terms, and political effects of human rights. My goal is not only to understand Agamben's distinctive intervention in the contemporary debates on human rights but also to inquire into the problematical aspects of his concluding call for a "politics *beyond* human rights." I argue that this call is necessitated by a counternarrative of Western politics that ties human rights inextricably to the "logic" Agamben ascribes to biopolitical sovereignty. Within this stringent logic, any politics organized around human rights cannot help but reproduce sovereign violence. It is this logic of necessity that erases the political possibilities and capacities engendered by human rights (and sovereignty) as "second nature." I question this counternarrative in two ways. First, I show how this counternarrative, which aims to demystify or unveil all the myths that sustain sovereignty, ends up repeating what it identifies as the distinctive mythologizing gesture: rendering the contingent necessary. Second, I highlight how this gesture is at odds with Agamben's own efforts to rethink the past in terms of contingencies and inexhaustible potentialities. Agamben's rethinking of "potentiality" as a capacity that is not consumed in any of its determinate actualizations can provide us with a better framework for capturing the contingent, complex, and unfinished histories of sovereignty and rights.

The critical evaluation of Agamben in this essay aims to proceed in the mode of an "immanent critique," understood in its broad sense: Instead of contesting Agamben's counternarrative by constructing an alternative historical account or by resorting to the conceptual resources of other theoretical traditions—two major routes taken by his critics—I intend to read Agamben *against* Agamben. By taking into account the tensions or paradoxes in Agamben's critique, I deploy his own terms (for example, "potentiality") to question some of his arguments and conclusions about human rights and sovereignty. This critical reading of Agamben strives to open a political space for thinking the "second nature" that we acquire with human rights and sovereignty in terms other than fated necessity. What if, I propose, we were to take Agamben's account of a "potentiality" that is not consumed in any of its determinate actualizations as our starting point and think of the "second nature" of human rights and sovereignty in terms of such inexhaustible potentialities? What kinds of political possibilities, rendered invisible or unfeasible within Agamben's narrative of fated necessity, come to view with this more indeterminate and contingent "second nature"?

Bare Life at the Intersection of Biopower and Sovereignty

In 1998, France introduced an amendment to its law on the "Conditions of Entry and Residence of Foreigners." This legal amendment granted residency permits to different groups of noncitizens who live in France and who have "life-threatening" pathologies that would not be properly treated if they were to be deported to their home countries. The amendment was motivated by humanitarian concerns; indeed, it was groups such as Médecins sans Frontières and Médecins du Monde that pushed for such a legal change. This humanitarian provision, aiming to care for the suffering body, however, had some unanticipated and paradoxical effects, as Miriam Ticktin points out in her insightful analysis of the violence of humanitarianism. Introduced at a time when strict asylum and immigration policies made it increasingly difficult for noncitizens to reside legally in France, this "illness clause" was indeed one of the few available options for securing basic human rights. One of the most troubling effects of the provision came to the fore with cases of willful self-infection and maiming. Increasing numbers of undocumented immigrants, Ticktin argues, started to infect themselves with HIV, reject treatment for illnesses such as cataracts, or take on the identity of people with AIDS to be able to get residence permits.[6]

This recent case, illustrating how a humanitarian politics aiming to care for life can have the paradoxical effect of producing disabled and infected bodies, provides significant insights into the pertinence of Giorgio Agamben's account of sovereignty in the current political context.[7] Agamben, particularly in his *Homo Sacer*, argues that sovereignty consists in a decision over life and that this decision always produces bare lives that can be irredeemably exposed to violence.[8] One of the most controversial claims he makes is that human rights and humanitarianism, usually conceived as normative setbacks to sovereign power, actually work in ways to reinscribe it. They do this precisely by valorizing life and turning it into a site of political decision. In the case of the humanitarian provision in France, for instance, to be able to grant residence permits on the basis of "life-threatening" pathologies, there needs to be a decision about what "life" is in the first place.[9] These vital decisions and their effects are at the center of Agamben's analysis of the inimical effects of the "second nature" that we acquire with sovereignty and human rights. Below, I will outline the main contours of Agamben's analysis of biopolitical sovereignty to provide the groundwork for a discussion of his arguments regarding the complicity of human rights in the perpetuation and augmentation of sovereign violence.

To understand the insidious effects of a power that makes the care of life its central task, Agamben draws on the work of Michel Foucault (*HS*, 3). Of particular interest is Foucault's contention that in modernity we see the emergence of biopower, which differs from the archaic sovereign power that relies on the threat of death and is instead centered on regulating and managing the biological life of the individual and species.[10] Contra Foucault, Agamben argues that biopower is not a distinctively modern form of power but is always already implicated in sovereignty. It is the type of power at work not only in modern democracies but also in absolute monarchies. To the extent that sovereignty, in its archaic and modern forms, always consists in a decision on *life*, it is indeed inseparable from biopower. Agamben argues that Foucault's failure to analyze the ways in which these two forms of power have always interacted with each other is a "blind spot" or a "vanishing point" in his theory (*HS*, 6).[11] It is this theoretical contestation that provides the starting point for Agamben's inquiry of the intersection between juridico-institutional power and biopower.

Agamben starts his analysis of this intersection with the premise that "*the production of a biopolitical body is the original activity of sovereign power*" (*HS*, 6; emphasis in the original). As he works on this premise, he leaves aside Foucault's genealogy and articulates a "logico-formal" thesis that aims to delineate what is always already biopolitical in the permanent structure of sovereignty throughout Western politics (*HS*, 109). To do this, he draws on Carl Schmitt's definition of sovereignty as the decision on the exception (*HS*, 19, 67, 83).[12] For both Agamben and Schmitt, sovereignty cannot ground itself in legal norms; it is in need of an "exteriority" or "factuality" to ground itself. To understand the relation between sovereign law and this exteriority, Agamben turns to the etymological origins of "exception." Exception literally means "*taken outside* (*ex-capere*)." This etymology indicates that sovereign exception is not merely exclusion; it is more precisely an "inclusive exclusion," which signifies a double movement—maintaining or capturing at the very moment of excluding (*HS*, 21). On the basis of this etymology, Agamben argues that the logic of sovereignty consists in capturing, taking in, what is outside of or exterior to the juridico-political order.

What is this "exteriority" or "factuality" that is captured in sovereign law? This question is indeed key to Agamben's inquiry of the intersection between biopolitics and sovereignty. The simple answer is "life." Agamben analyzes the concrete substance or content of the formal structure of sovereignty by drawing partly on Carl Schmitt and mainly on Walter Benjamin. From Schmitt, Agamben draws the idea that law cannot have a concrete meaning or a determinate application without a relation to life: The "law truly 'has no existence in itself, but rather has its being in the very life of men'" (*HS*, 27). Drawing on Benjamin, he concludes that this relationship between law and life always necessitates the isolation of a "bare life" that can be killed with impunity.[13] Life has always been included in the political sphere only in the form of an exclusion, or the capacity to be killed (*HS*, 8). On the basis of this "logico-formal" analysis, Agamben establishes the intersection between biopower and sovereignty and asserts that the distinctive activity of biopolitical sovereignty has always been the production of a bare life.

To explain how "bare life" is produced and to underline the historical continuity of biopolitical sovereignty, Agamben turns to the ancient opposition between *zoē* and *bios:* Whereas *zoē* refers to the "simple fact of living common to all living beings (animals, men, or gods)," *bios* denotes exclusively "the form or way of living proper to an individual or a group" (*HS*, 1). Drawing on Aristotle's *Politics*, Agamben claims that this opposition underlies the exclusion of natural life from the polis and its relegation to the *oikos* (*HS*, 2).[14] On the basis of this opposition, the polis was founded as the site where the living being could become fully "human" only by participating in the activities of the political association (*HS*, 7). It is this biopolitical division of political and natural life that always produces remainders and turns certain categories of living beings into "bare life."[15] Bare life, then, is neither the simple natural life of *zoē* nor the politically qualified life of *bios* (*HS*, 90, 106, 109); rather, it is a life that is left at the threshold of these two, dwelling in a "zone of indistinction" and marking a "continuous transition between man and beast, nature and culture" (*HS*, 109). The production of bare life constitutes the foundation of Western politics and metaphysics, according to Agamben. In both individual and collective terms, sovereignty consists in separating a "natural" life that will be set in opposition to a "political" way of life.[16] Since it is this originary exclusion that founds, sustains, and defines the political community, Agamben uses the term "inclusive exclusion," reminding us again of the etymological origins of "exception," to describe the relationship between bare life and political life (*HS*, 7).

By arguing that the "inclusive exclusion" of life has been the permanent characteristic of biopolitical sovereignty, Agamben contests Foucault and claims that the novelty of modern biopolitics consists neither in the inclusion of *zoē* in the political sphere nor in the fact that politics is concerned with life (*HS*, 9). What is the distinctive nature of modern power, however, if not, as Foucault suggests, the inclusion of natural life in mechanisms and calculations of state power? Agamben argues that with modernity the meaning of politics goes through a dramatic transformation, as natural life, which was confined to the sphere of the *oikos* in the classical world, becomes the foundation of politics. Healing the biopolitical fracture between political and natural life becomes the distinctive goal of modern democracies, which dedicate themselves to the task of "vindication and liberation of *zoē*" (*HS*, 9). However, in doing this, modern democracies end up subjecting every aspect of life to sovereign power and turn each political subject virtually into bare life (*HS*, 111). Agamben attributes a significant role to some modern juridico-political innovations such as *habeas corpus* and declarations of rights in this major historical transformation, and it is to these I now turn to discuss Agamben's distinctive contribution to contemporary debates on human rights.

Modern Rights Declarations and the Dissemination of Bare Life

Agamben's analysis of modern juridico-political developments, including rights declarations, aims to reveal the inimical effects of the often celebrated transformation of the "subject" into a "citizen" with the birth of modern democracy. He argues that with this transformation modern democracy does not abolish bare life but instead "shatters it and disseminates it into every individual body" (*HS*, 125). With the introduction of *habeas corpus*, for example, modern democracy turns *corpus* or body into the new political subject (*HS*, 124) and repeats the fundamental biopolitical fracture at the heart of Western politics: it isolates a *corpus*, compels its physical presence before a court of law, and renders it subject to the violence of sovereign decision. Challenging contractarian accounts, Agamben asserts that it is not the freely consenting individuals but rather the bare lives that can be killed with impunity that constitute the foundation of modern democracy. Thus, what lies in this passage from "subject" to "citizen" is not "man as a free and conscious political subject but, above all, man's bare life" (*HS*, 128).

If *habeas corpus* introduces *corpus* as the bare life founding the body politic, modern rights declarations identify this body politic with the nation-state (*HS*, 127).[17] With these declarations, natural life, which was distinguished as *zoē* and relegated to the realm of *oikos* in the classical world and considered politically neutral during the *ancien régime*, becomes the "earthly foundation" of sovereignty in the modern nation-state (*HS*, 127; *MWE*, 20). Through a brief and provocative examination of the French Declaration of the Rights of Man and Citizen of 1789, Agamben suggests that "it is precisely bare natural life—which is to say, the pure fact of birth—that appears here as the source and bearer of rights" (*HS*, 127).[18] He concludes that these rights declarations inaugurate modern biopolitics, in which bare life moves from the margins of the political order to its center.

Agamben's critique of modern rights declarations draws primarily on Hannah Arendt. Both authors take the problems of human rights, especially the precarious condition of refugees, as their starting point; instead of seeing these problems either as accidental incidents or implementation failures, they take them as symptoms revealing the deeply embedded paradoxes of human rights in a nation-state system. Of particular importance is the following conceptual dilemma at the heart of modern rights declarations: On the one hand, these declarations assume "man" in his natural condition to be the source and bearer of rights that he is born with. On the other hand, they presuppose this man to be a "citizen" with membership in a sovereign nation-state (*HS*, 128).[19]

Although both Arendt and Agamben have similar starting points, they proceed differently in their critique and reach divergent conclusions. Arendt presents a more historically oriented inquiry, attending to the effects of important events such as the rise of imperialism on the conceptual paradoxes of human rights. She does not take the rightlessness of the stateless as an inevitable condition given the premises of modern rights declarations or conceptual dichotomies of Western metaphysics; instead, she treats it as a historically contingent problem that urges us to inquire into the paradoxes of human rights. Indeed, her critique ends with a call for rethinking, not abandoning, human rights.[20]

Agamben, however, interprets the conceptual dilemma in rights declarations—that is, equivocal invocation of man and citizen—as another instance revealing the biopolitical fracture (*bios/zoē*) defining Western politics and metaphysics for centuries. Hence, he calls for nothing less than a politics that renounces all concepts, including human rights, that hold life in the grip of sovereign power. Indeed, in his account, far from disrupting the logic of biopolitical sovereignty, rights declarations aggravate its violence by politicizing natural life or *zoē*. Agamben argues that as modern democracy attempts to heal the biopolitical fracture between political and natural life by stipulating a fictional unity between man and citizen, birth (*nascere*) and nation, it ends up turning virtually everyone into bare life (*HS*, 128). With these declarations, questions of inclusion and exclusion—which *man* is a *citizen*?—become essentially political (*HS*, 131). These questions need constantly to be settled through sovereign decisions on the "inclusive exclusions" of the national political community. As a result of these sovereign exceptions or inclusive exclusions, there are various categories of people who inhabit the political space of the sovereign nation-state without being entitled to political rights. Agamben insists that these inclusive exclusions should not be understood as "a simple restriction of the democratic and egalitarian principle, in flagrant contradiction to the spirit and letter of declarations" (*HS*, 131). If this was the case, one could still refer to these declarations to criticize their violence. They are instead necessitated by the modern biopolitical order inaugurated by these declarations.

As Agamben analyzes the historical and political effects of these conceptual presuppositions, he puts a particular emphasis on the crisis of the nation-state. Since the end of World War I, he argues, we have witnessed a dissolution of the fictional unity between birth and nation, man and citizen (*HS*, 131–132). His argument again closely resembles Arendt's analysis of the crisis of the nation-state, which specifically focuses on the emergence of statelessness as a mass phenomenon in the aftermath of World War I, with the introduction of various juridical measures allowing mass denationalizations and denaturalizations.[21] These denationalizations and denaturalizations, Agamben claims, showed that one's birth does not guarantee membership in a nation-state; in other words, "man" is not identical with national "citizen." With these historical developments, it became clear that there is indeed an "interval of separation [*scarto*]" (*HS*, 128) between birth and nation, or man and citizen, which cannot be remedied by the fictional unity established between these terms in the rights declarations.

If modern biopolitics was linked intricately to the nation-state in its origins, does the crisis of the birth-nation link bring it to an end? Agamben answers this question in the negative and demonstrates how this crisis has actually intensified the politicization of natural life. One of the problematic effects of this crisis is the increasing deployment of human rights outside the context of citizenship. The dissociation of human rights from citizenship paves the way for modern humanitarianism, in which human rights stand for the rights of those who are isolated as bare life—for example, refugees (*HS*, 131–134). We can think of the French humanitarian provision, cited in the first section, to understand how a seemingly depoliticized humanitarianism can actually end up exacerbating the politicization of natural life and production of bare life. Tying the human rights of undocumented migrants to "life-threatening diseases," the provision illustrates the attempts to turn human rights into the rights of those who are denied a political life. From Agamben's perspective, such attempts risk reducing humanity to a biological minimum that is to be represented and protected by a compassionate humanitarianism that posits itself as apolitical.

Another effect of the dissolution of the fictional unity between birth and nation is the regulation and administration of life in the name of its valorization to an unprecedented degree. Once the fictional unity loses its "mechanical force and power of self-regulation," nation-states need more than ever to be engaged in sovereign decisions discriminating between "a so-to-speak authentic life and a life lacking every political virtue" (*HS*, 132). One of Agamben's most controversial claims is that these decisions, the lethal consequences of which became most explicit with modern eugenics and concentration camps, need to be understood within the context of modern biopolitics inaugurated by rights declarations that invest life with the principle of sovereignty: Life itself can become "the place of a sovereign decision" only because it is politicized, valorized, and sacralized to an unprecedented degree in the first place (*HS*, 142). As it constantly attempts to define the juridical value of life (*HS*, 139), modern biopolitics turns human populations into *homines sacri*, or sacred man, who can be killed with impunity and whose death cannot be memorialized as sacrifice (*HS*, 71, 82). In Agamben's words,

> [it] is as if every valorization and every "politicization" of life . . . necessarily implies a new decision concerning the threshold beyond which life ceases to be politically relevant, becomes only "sacred life," and can as such be eliminated without punishment. Every society sets this limit; every society—even the most modern—decides who its "sacred men" will be. (*HS*, 139)

At the end of his critical analysis of rights declarations, Agamben concludes that modern democracy has not only failed in healing the biopolitical fracture between *bios* and *zoē* but also repeated it in an unprecedented fashion precisely by valorizing life. Modern rights declarations have turned "the care of nation's biological body" (*HS*, 142) into an essentially political task because they attributed the principle of sovereignty to life. Insofar as these declarations have made it possible for the sovereign state to extend its regulative powers into every sphere of life, Agamben suggests, they have become complicit in the production of bare life.

By insisting on the political effects of human rights and humanitarianism that have come to be celebrated as moral shields against the vagaries of politics, Agamben joins several other prominent critics: Wendy Brown, for instance, has argued recently that the discourse of human rights, which presents itself as "an antipolitical and expressly moral antidote to abusive political power," works instead as a form of political power when it constitutes us as subjects in need of protection and undermines political projects of collective empowerment.[22] Along similar lines, Jacques Rancière, leaving aside his disagreements with Agamben's account, has also criticized the ascendancy of a depoliticizing humanitarianism that turns the "rights of man" into humanitarian rights and represents the subjects of these rights as lacking the power to enact or actualize them.[23]

Agamben's distinctive contribution to this critical scholarship has been his analysis of the exceptions or remainders of progressivist histories of human rights—for example, the comatose, refugees, concentration camp inmates—so as to point to a more sinister aspect of the ascendancy of human rights and humanitarianism: what is at stake in the "second nature" that we come to acquire with human rights is not merely depoliticization or disempowerment, as various critics have already suggested, but also "life" itself. Agamben aims to show how human rights, by making life itself the place of sovereign decision, increasingly pave the way for the blurring of the line between biopolitics and thanatopolitics, or between politics of life and politics of death (*HS*, 122). In contemporary politics that valorizes life, Agamben's analysis suggests, the putatively archaic sovereign "right to take life" merges perniciously into the modern "right to intervene to make life."[24] Situating human rights and humanitarianism within the project of biopolitical sovereignty, Agamben's account achieves an eerie pragmatic soundness with cases such as the French humanitarian provision, which paradoxically end up abandoning life at the "no-man's land" between life and death (*HS*, 90). Valorization of life entails a sovereign decision on its value and nonvalue. This question of value can be decided by the sovereign only with "an incomprehensible intrusion of biologico-scientific principles into the political order" and in cooperation with juridical, medical, scientific, and religious experts (*HS*, 122). Indeed, in the French case, what a "life-threatening" disease meant could not be decided without recourse to such biologico-scientific principles and medical experts. Agamben's distinctive contribution to the contemporary debates on human rights lies in his attentiveness to the vulnerability of lives that are left at that borderline between biopolitics and thanatopolitics.

The current global political context in which we can no longer be dismissive of such cases as mere exceptions to be remedied on the way to a more universal conception of human rights requires us now more than ever to question the constitutive terms and conceptual presuppositions of these rights, if we are to be able to understand their political effects. Agamben's critical scrutiny of the constitutive terms ("man" and "citizen") and conceptual presuppositions (for example, the biopolitical fracture of *bios* and *zoē*) of human rights helps us understand the inclusive exclusions of our prevailing conceptions of "human." More than any other contemporary critic of human rights, Agamben effectively demonstrates how the division of human/nonhuman passes through living beings to leave aside some as less than human. As such, he points out how even the well-intentioned attempts to define a human essence or nature by identifying a set of human values, functions, and needs can render certain lives as invaluable and unlivable.

Agamben's critical analysis of human rights indicates that we need to inquire into the underlying assumptions, constitutive terms, and political effects of human rights precisely to be able to recognize that we do not yet understand all the ways of being "human" and that we need to understand our "humanness" instead as always "in the making" and as an "ongoing task."[25] It underscores the need to look into the ways in which human rights can entail divisions between political/natural, human/nonhuman, and man/citizen to the effect of banning certain categories of people from politics and rendering their lives unworthy of living.

At the end of this critical inquiry, Agamben calls for a "politics beyond human rights" (*MWE*, 15–26). He suggests that any struggle organized around human rights cannot help but reproduce the sovereign violence that it aims to counter. His critical remarks about historical rights struggles are indicative of his negative stance toward any politics organized around human rights:

> It is almost as if, starting from a certain point, every decisive political event were double-sided: the spaces, the liberties, and the rights won by individuals in their conflicts with central powers always simultaneously prepared a tacit but increasing inscription of individuals' lives within the state order, thus offering a new and more dreadful foundation for the very sovereign power from which they wanted to liberate themselves. (*HS*, 121)

Thus, Agamben asserts, rights struggles cannot help but reproduce the logic of biopolitical sovereignty: the "second nature" that we take on with the rise of human rights is an iron cage in which we are entrapped and from which we desperately need to seek an exit. Yet, if human rights can become "second nature" only through frequently repeated practices—practices such as declaring, claiming, vindicating, and reappropriating rights—what can guarantee that these practices will always produce a singular effect (that is, the reproduction of biopolitical divisions)? In other words, how does the dependency of human rights on such political practices instill in them an unpredictability and instability? What are some of the political capacities engendered by the intertwinement of "politics" and "nature" in the discourse of human rights? And why does Agamben's analysis overlook such capacities and foreclose the possibility that rights struggles might call into question the biopolitical divisions that relegate certain categories of human beings to bare life? With these questions in mind, I now turn to Agamben's account of Western politics, which establishes inextricable links between sovereignty, human rights, and bare life and renders any politics organized around human rights either unfeasible or complicit in biopolitical violence.

Agamben's Counternarrative of Western Politics and the Problem of Mythologization

In his analysis of biopolitical sovereignty, Agamben provides us with a "counternarrative" of Western politics with the explicitly stated goal of "unveiling" or "unmasking" what has become mystified, hidden, secret, or invisible, particularly within prevalent contractarian accounts of political power (*HS*, 8).[26] Agamben describes this critical task in terms of "disenchantment," or the "patient work" of unmasking the fiction or myth that covers up and sustains the violence of sovereignty (*SE*, 88). What underlies this urge to unmask, demystify, and unveil is a particular understanding of myth as a deceptive narrative naturalizing and legitimizing violence in the name of the preservation of life.

I use the term "counternarrative"[27] to call attention to what Agamben's account aims to do: this is a critical analysis, as Agamben himself insists, that does not offer "historiographical theses or reconstructions" but instead treats some historical phenomena as "paradigms" so as to "make intelligible a broader historical-problematic context";[28] to do this, it proceeds at "a historico-philosophical level" (*HS*, 11). In that sense, it is not an account that claims historical accuracy or factual verifiability. This is a crucial point that is overlooked by some of Agamben's critics who call into question his inaccurate treatment of historical phenomena such as the concentration camps.[29] Indeed, most of Agamben's critics either turn to history or to the conceptual resources of another theoretical tradition in contesting his analysis.[30] In analyzing Agamben's account as a counternarrative, I aim to attend to the goals that it sets for itself. It is these goals—particularly the goal of freeing human potentialities from myths that render the contingent necessary and mask other possibilities—that provide the starting point for my critical engagement with Agamben. Instead of resorting to an "outside"—whether this be an alternative historical account or another theoretical tradition—I aim to read Agamben on his own terms, and I suggest that as he tries to free human potentialities from contractarian myths, he might be entrapping them in another myth that ends up casting the contingent as necessary.

As Agamben identifies the production of bare life as the "originary," or constitutive and foundational, activity grounding sovereign power (*HS*, 83), he aims to provide a counternarrative of the origins of political power, targeting in particular the contractarian "myth" of founding: "The time has come . . . to reread from the beginning the myth of the foundation of the modern city from Hobbes to Rousseau" (*HS*, 109). Agamben's characterization of this contractarian tradition, leaving aside its problems of overgeneralization, targets two presuppositions about sovereign power: that it marks a clear transition from the state of nature to a civil state for the protection of individual subjects from arbitrary violence, and that it establishes a legitimate rule relying on the consent of equal and free individuals.

In his rereading of Hobbes, Agamben points out how the state of nature, which is usually presumed to be chronologically prior to the civil state, survives as a principle internal to sovereignty after the founding moment and becomes manifest in the state of exception when the civil state is considered "as if it were dissolved" (*HS*, 36; see also 37, 106, 109). The foundation of sovereignty then does not indicate the transcendence but rather the incorporation of this condition. If life is irreparably exposed to a death threat in the state of nature because of the limitless right of everybody over everything, it is still under this threat once the civil state is founded, because the right of life and death is now exclusively held by the sovereign (*MWE*, 5). By drawing an analogy between the state of nature and state of exception, Agamben aims to unsettle the *physis/nomos* (nature/law) antinomy, which establishes an identity between violence and the state of nature, opposes this to the juridico-political order of the civil state, and, thereby, legitimates the absolute power of sovereign as necessary to overcome this natural violence (*HS*, 35). Sovereignty can assume the character of "second nature" or create the effect of innateness and inevitability only by incorporating a "first" nature that it invents to naturalize and justify its violence. Agamben underlines the inimical effects of this "second nature" especially when he points out that the sovereign power does not protect its subjects from violence but instead "abandons" them. He draws on Jean-Luc Nancy to suggest that "abandonment" does not mean merely to be excluded or set outside; that would indeed indicate the possibility of being outside of or indifferent to law. Instead, with the institution of sovereignty, individual subjects are "abandoned" in the sense that they are at the mercy or free disposal of the absolute power of sovereign law.[31] It is this abandonment that leaves them exposed to sovereign violence.

When Agamben points out that it is the bare life of *homo sacer* that lies at the foundation of the political community, he challenges the contractarian assumption that it is equally free individuals who establish legitimate rule with their consent. In his interpretation of "*vitae necisque potestas*," or the "right over life and death," which indicates the unconditional authority that fathers had over their sons in Roman law, Agamben implicitly targets the contractarian assumption of natural equality (*HS*, 88). He draws an analogy between the status of citizens or political subjects and that of sons as they both find themselves "in a state of virtually being able to be killed" (*HS*, 89). Agamben's reading of Hobbes also underlines that it is bare life, understood in terms of the fragility of the human body and its capacity to be killed, that underlies both the presumed natural equality and the necessity to found the civil state (*HS*, 125). Agamben also puts into question the principle of consent when he challenges the assumption that subjects freely renounce their natural rights to gain civil rights. The founding of the sovereign power does not consist in such a pact but rather in "the sovereign's preservation of his natural right to do anything to anyone"; thus, the sovereign's right to punish was not "given" but rather "left" to him (*HS*, 106).

Agamben turns to key figures of the contractarian tradition to offer a rereading that aims to demystify or uncover what has become hidden, unveiled, or invisible with "our modern habit of representing the political realm in terms of citizens' rights, free will, and social contracts" (*HS*, 106). These powerful myths, he suggests, posit sovereignty as necessary and inevitable for politics. In other words, what is only "second nature" assumes the character of "first nature" with the inextricable ties that these myths weave between sovereignty and politics.

After unveiling the foundational myths of Western politics, Agamben concludes that we cannot effectively respond to "the bloody mystification of a new planetary order" if we let these myths continue to obstruct our political imagination (*HS*, 12). With his counternarrative presenting a catastrophic view of the historical present—a view that emphasizes how exception has become the rule, that the camp has become the paradigmatic structure organizing political space, and that we have all virtually become *homines sacri* (*HS*, 38, 176, 111)—Agamben aims to convince his readers of the need to think of a "nonstatal and nonjuridical politics and human life" freed from sovereignty (*MWE*, 112). This new politics would require the renunciation of concepts associated with sovereignty (for example, citizenship, state, rights). The contemporary predicament cannot be remedied by a return to conventional political categories, concepts, and institutions, Agamben suggests, since these are deeply involved in the creation of this catastrophe in the first place. Almost anticipating those of his critics who would be puzzled by his renunciation of the rule of law and rights, particularly at a time when the problem of legal dispossession increasingly threatens populations around the world, he explicitly states that the response to the current permanent state of exception cannot consist in confining it within constitutionally defined boundaries and reaffirming the primacy of legal norms and rights (*SE*, 87).[32] As legal norms and rights are ultimately grounded in the originary violence of separating a bare life, legal dispossession is already inscribed in them as an inescapable possibility. Neither the liberal remedy of reasserting the rule of law nor the Derridean strategy of "infinite negotiations" with a law that is in force without any significance are viable options. Both are futile, if not lethally dangerous, endeavors.[33] The only politically tenable option is to move out of sovereignty with "a complicated and patient strategy" of getting the "door of the Law closed forever" (*HS*, 54, 55).

Agamben's counternarrative, which aims at the "disenchantment" of social contractarian myths, ties sovereignty, human rights, and citizenship so inextricably to what he deems to be the permanent biopolitical logic that any political strategy short of exodus becomes indefensible (*SE*, 88). As Agamben lifts the veil of the myths legitimizing sovereign power and invites us to invent a new politics, however, does he end up constructing another myth of origins that is as enchanting and mystifying as those he aims to uncover? In posing this question, I am deploying "myth" in Agamben's sense of the word—that is, as a deceptive narrative rendering what is contingent inevitable and necessary. Agamben's counternarrative risks becoming another myth, I suggest, to the extent that it obscures the contingencies and possibilities in the complex histories of sovereignty and human rights.

It is Agamben's attempt to find out *the* "logic" of sovereignty that entraps his counternarrative in mythology and is in tension with his project of demythologization, which aims to bring out the contingency of what has been justified as necessary.[34] As mentioned above, the central task that Agamben's counternarrative sets for itself is the delineation of the "formal structure" or "logic" of sovereignty as it manifests itself across different spatiotemporal contexts in Western politics (*HS*, 19, 67, 83). The identification of this "logic" endows Agamben's counternarrative with continuity so that it can speak to "24 centuries" of Western political history (*HS*, 11). When Agamben deploys this "logico-formal" structure so as to endow history with a continuity, inevitability, and finality that it ultimately lacks, however, his counternarrative entraps itself in mythology. The paralyzing result of this move can be seen in his statements such as "the river of biopolitics that gave *homo sacer* his life runs its course in a *hidden but continuous* fashion" throughout the history of Western politics (*HS*, 121; emphasis mine).

As Agamben's counternarrative imposes on sovereignty a stringent logic on the basis of a problematical reading, glossing over the ambivalences, discontinuities, and unpredictabilities in its history (or, more precisely, histories), it cannot help but repeat, albeit unwittingly, the distinctive gestures that he associates with "myth": what was contingent seems as if it was necessary and inevitable. Agamben's account yields to "the principle of the fated necessity," to use the words of Horkheimer and Adorno, who alert us to how an antimythical posture itself can turn into myth: "This barren wisdom merely reproduces the fantastic doctrine it rejects: the sanction of fate which, through retribution, incessantly reinstates what always was. Whatever may be different is made the same."[35] Any politics organized around sovereignty and human rights cannot, within the confines of Agamben's stringent logic, help but reinscribe the originary violence repeated since the beginning of Western political history.

The imposition of such a "logic," which ends up imputing a preordained trajectory to any politics organized around sovereignty and human rights, however, is at odds with Agamben's attempts to understand time and history in terms of contingency. Indeed, Agamben's notion of "potentiality" might help us in breaking the binding spell of his own myth and in rethinking the "second nature" that we come to acquire with sovereignty and human rights in ways differing from a narrative of "fated necessity," which dooms them to reinstate the biopolitical divisions that produce and reproduce bare life.

Potentialities of Sovereignty and Human Rights: The Indeterminate Politics of "Second Nature"

Agamben develops his distinctive notion of a potentiality that is not consumed in its determinate actualizations by critically engaging with Aristotle. In Book Theta of *Metaphysics*, Aristotle argues against the Megarians who identify potentiality with actuality to the effect of denying any potentiality that is not actualized. The Megarian position, Aristotle suggests, would take us to the unreasonable conclusion that a builder has a potentiality for building only when he engages in the act of building and that he is not a builder when he is not building. One of the major reasons why Aristotle resists the Megarians' denial of potentialities that are not actualized is that this would bring all movement, change, and becoming to a paralyzing stasis: "So our brilliant Megarian friends will now have done away with all process and generation! The standing will remain on their feet, and the seated on those places where the Megarians keep their brains to eternity."[36] To resist this indistinction between potentiality and actuality, Aristotle insists on understanding potentiality in terms of not only *dynamis*, or a power to become, be, or actualize, but also *adynamia*, or a power not to become, be, or actualize (*HS*, 45–46; *P*, 184).

Aristotle's critique of the Megarians and his notion of a "potentiality-not-to" are crucial for understanding Agamben's own attempts to think of a potentiality that is not annulled or destroyed in any of its determinate actualizations. For potentiality to have "its own consistency," Agamben argues, it should not "disappear immediately into actuality" (*HS*, 45). However, from Agamben's perspective, Aristotle falls short of giving potentiality its full due because he still privileges actuality, being, and presence.[37] Indeed, Agamben locates in Aristotle's notion of "potentiality-not-to" the metaphysical origins of the sovereign ban. Aristotle's formulation of a potentiality that maintains itself in the form of withdrawal or suspension comes very close, at least in Agamben's peculiar reading, to the ban structure in the Schmittian sovereign exception, in which the law subjects life to its power precisely by way of suspension or withdrawal.[38] Agamben's goal then becomes to uncouple potentiality from the sovereign ban by refusing to tie it to any notion of being and presence.

Agamben's ontological reflections, especially his efforts to rethink potentiality, have been carefully analyzed by other scholars.[39] What is crucial for the purposes of my argument is that, as Agamben reappropriates Aristotle's "potentiality-not-to," he sets himself a task that is at odds with the narrative of fated necessity that shapes his counternarrative of Western politics. Agamben's goal in rethinking potentiality is precisely to understand history in terms of contingency. In doing this, he counters two traditional principles—"the irrevocability of the past" and "conditioned necessity"—that are invoked to annul the contingencies of the past (*P*, 262). The principle of "irrevocability" suggests that the potentialities of the past cannot be realized retroactively, presenting what happened as complete and overlooking the possibility that things could have happened otherwise; it presents us with "an impossibility of realizing the potentiality of the past" (*P*, 262). The principle of "conditioned necessity" casts future events as necessary occurrences, cancelling again the contingencies in the past (*P*, 262). Agamben argues against both of these principles and rethinks the past in terms of multiple possibilities that can be reactivated. Hence, his notion of potentiality suggests that no past event is a "simple element in a historical archive but a potentially dynamic means of understanding—and changing—the present situation."[40]

I suggest that Agamben's efforts to rethink potentiality so as to redeem the contingencies of the past can actually be a more promising way to interpret the complex, multiple histories of human rights—one that can also question the narrative of fated necessity he attributes to rights struggles. This interpretation, guided by Agamben's insights into the "potentialization" of the past, recasts rights struggles as events with possibilities that are not fully consumed in any of their determinate actualizations (P, 267). To illustrate how understanding potentiality in terms of its different modalities of existence can help us reclaim the indeterminate temporality of sovereignty and rights, I want to point briefly to the contemporary rights struggles of noncitizens, particularly to the *sans-papiers* movement in France.

In 1996, a group of *sans-papiers* (literally, "without papers"; undocumented) occupied various churches to protest the administrative decrees that put them in a legal limbo, or, as Agamben would put it, in a zone of indistinction between law and violence.[41] One of their occupations, the one at the Church of Saint-Bernard de la Chapelle in Paris, ended with their forceful eviction by police forces. In November 1998, Madjiguène Cissé, a leading spokesperson of the *sans-papiers*, lodged an application with the European Court of Human Rights, complaining that her right to freedom of peaceful assembly, guaranteed under Article 11 of the European Convention of Human Rights (ECHR), was infringed by the forceful eviction. The court agreed with Cissé that the evacuation of the church amounted to an interference with the exercise of freedom of assembly. However, the court added, "the interference pursued a legitimate aim: the prevention of disorder." In conclusion, "although it regretted the sudden and indiscriminate manner in which the police intervened . . . the Court found that the interference with the applicant's freedom of assembly was not disproportionate. Therefore there had not been a breach of Article 11."[42]

This case manifests the strengths and limits of Agamben's biopolitical analysis as well as the promise of his reconceptualization of "potentiality." The court decision clearly shows how sovereign exception continues to pervade human rights norms, challenging conventional accounts that see them as normative restraints on sovereign power: Freedom of assembly is recognized in Article 11 of the ECHR, yet the exception clause of the same article explicitly allows armed forces, police, and state administration to impose restrictions on the exercise of this right on very ambiguous grounds, including "national security or public safety," which can easily pave the way for arbitrariness. These exceptions underscore the significance of Agamben's argument that the force of law needs to be understood in terms of not only its application but also its power to suspend itself. The court's justification of the forceful police eviction with references to sanitary conditions and strikers' health also confirms his argument that the valorization of life can indeed participate in the production of bare lives that can be exposed to sovereign violence.

If the forceful eviction and the European Court of Human Rights' decision were to exhaust the potentiality of the *sans-papiers'* struggle, we could have concurred with Agamben's concluding call for a politics beyond human rights. However, both the beginnings and the ongoing effects of the *sans-papiers* movement are caveats against collapsing potentiality into actuality. The *sans-papiers* movement started its demonstrations at the Church of Saint-Ambroise on March 18, 1996, and it is interesting to note that it was on March 18, 1871, that the Paris Commune seized power in the city. March 18 holds a symbolic power in the political imaginary of the *sans-papiers;* a recurring slogan of the movement has been "March 18, 1996, *on c'est levé*" (we have risen).[43] The *sans-papiers* demonstration illustrates that the potentiality of the Commune was not consumed in the summary executions, deportations, and imprisonment of thousands of Communards in May 1871. What survived the violent repression of the Commune was the memory of a quite different understanding of "sovereignty," which consists of the constitution of a self-governing, free political association and has been invoked by several political movements throughout history. Not only the beginnings but also the ongoing effects of the *sans-papiers* mobilization reveal the need to understand political events, names, institutions, and practices as containing potentialities that cannot be consumed in their determinate actualizations. The forceful eviction did not end *sans-papiers'* demonstrations; it turned out to be just the beginning of a European-wide mobilization that continues to question the limits of existing conceptions of rights and citizenship.

Multiple, conflicting, and unpredictable invocations of sovereignty and human rights in this particular case point to the need for an assessment diverging from Agamben's conclusions. In the court's deployment of sovereignty and human rights, we see an attempt to reinscribe biopolitical divisions exposing certain lives to an unpunishable violence (yet this is, by no means, an unrisky attempt as it also involves a critique of the extremity of the violence used). What survives this attempt, however, is a "potentiality-not-to," indicating the possibilities of withholding or suspending the affirmation of such biopolitical divisions as well as the possibilities of contesting and transforming them. Precisely such possibilities come to the fore in *sans-papiers*' invocation of human rights in ways to contest the "clandestinity" imposed on them because of lack of proper documentation. The words of Madjiguène Cissé are telling in this regard:

> In France up until now our fate as immigrants was: either take part in the Republic's process of integration, or be deported like cattle. At the heart of this approach was the notion that we are "underground," which has a very negative charge. . . . We have made ourselves visible to say that we are here, to say that we are not in hiding but we're just human beings.[44]

Clandestinity is precisely the condition that forces migrants without proper documentation to dwell, in Agamben's words, in a "zone of indistinction" between *physis* and *nomos*, *bios* and *zoē*, human and nonhuman. At this threshold they are irreparably exposed to sovereign violence (that is, always ready to be deported as "cattle"). Clandestinity of undocumented migrants, then, is part and parcel of biopolitical sovereignty in its inclusive exclusion of "bare life": these migrants are excluded from political life, yet they are also included since they are subject to laws and since their exclusion founds, sustains, and defines the political community. What escapes Agamben's biopolitical narrative, however, is the *sans-papiers*' contestation of their clandestinity, or their isolation as bare life precisely by resignifying the constitutive terms of rights declarations—"man" and "citizen"—in their claims to human rights and democratic liberties.[45]

Such reappropriations call attention to the problems of understanding rights declarations and struggles in terms of a narrative of "fated necessity." We can remember here Agamben's own characterization of rights declarations and struggles as "double-sided" (*HS*, 121). As such, these declarations and struggles have multiple, equivocal, and unpredictable effects.[46] Most importantly, the novelty of rights declarations lies not only in their politicization of life, but also in their introduction of the idea that rights need to be declared, proclaimed, and publicly granted. As speech acts, these declarations contain a contingency and vulnerability proper to language and politics. They lack finality and closure precisely because of their dependency on our practices of declaring, inventing, claiming, vindicating, and reappropriating them.[47] In addition, conceptual equivocations of modern rights declarations (that is, man/citizen, nature/politics), taken by Agamben as another sign of the biopolitical fracture defining Western politics and metaphysics since antiquity, can enable such contestation: it is precisely this ambivalent language that forecloses the possibility of any final authoritative interpretation and can give rise to new appropriations. Such interpretive practices can potentially affirm and reinscribe biopolitical divisions of *bios/zoē*, as can be seen in the court's invocation of human rights and sovereignty. However, we also need to be alert to how rights can be claimed in unanticipated ways, especially by those who are excluded from their constitutive terms ("man" and "citizen") and rendered less than human. Such future reappropriations can put into question the underlying presuppositions of rights declarations; contest the naturalized divisions, hierarchies, and exclusions justified according to their prevailing conceptions; and change our understanding of their constitutive terms.[48]

Struggles such as the *sans-papiers*' point to the problems of two forms of fatalism that figure in contemporary assessments of human rights and sovereignty. On the one hand, there is the fatalistic position of those who turn to them in terms of a pragmatic minimalism in which they stand as our only hope to limit violence, suffering, and cruelty in the global order.[49] This position would indicate nothing less than an unquestioning acceptance of the "second nature" we come to acquire with human rights and sovereignty as our inevitable fate. Then there is the other kind of fatalism, illustrated by Agamben's counternarrative of Western politics, in which sovereignty and human rights are doomed to leave us at the threshold of a catastrophe, where we have no option but to abandon them. Neither of these fatalistic assessments seems to capture the complex and contingent effects of the "second nature" that we acquire with sovereignty and human rights. If the first position is oblivious to how certain lives become unworthy and unlivable because of prevailing conceptions of sovereignty and human rights, the second forecloses an analysis of their unpredictable appropriations and ongoing transformations. Human rights and sovereignty can seem as if they are "second nature" because of various practices that are repeated so frequently as to produce an effect of innateness. Such iterative practices, however, always carry a risk, as they do not merely reinstate what was already there. It is precisely because of the instability introduced by such practices that the operations of sovereignty and human rights can never be secured in advance, and they open themselves to unpredictable futures. It is this indeterminate temporality that urges us to understand the "second nature" of human rights and sovereignty in terms of "potentialities" and not fated necessity.

I am grateful to Çiğdem Çıdam for carefully reading several versions of this chapter. I would like to thank Mary Dietz, Bud Duvall, Bonnie Honig, Bill Scheuerman, and Bruce Braun for their insightful comments on earlier versions. Crina Archer, Laura Ephraim, and Lida Maxwell deserve special thanks for inviting me to participate in this volume and providing helpful feedback throughout the process.

CHAPTER 6

The Utopian Content of Reification: Adorno's Critical Social Theory of Nature

Christopher Buck

The theory of second nature, to which Hegel already gave a critical tinge, is not lost to a negative dialectics. It assumes, *tel quel*, the abrupt immediacy, the formations which society and its evolution present to our thought; and it does this so that analysis may bare its mediations to the extent of the immanent difference between phenomena and that which they claim to be in themselves.

—THEODOR W. ADORNO, *Negative Dialectics*

Introduction

In the afterword to the second German edition of *The Critique of Power*, Axel Honneth notes how renewed interest in the critical theory of Theodor W. Adorno is motivated in part by the conviction that Adorno's later writings "provide the best means for comprehending the conditions for a noninstrumental relation to inner and outer nature."[1] One of Adorno's more suggestive articulations of this relation appears in his essay "On Subject and Object," where he violates his self-imposed taboo on speculating about the possibility of reconciliation between humans and nonhuman entities: "In its proper place, even epistemologically, the relationship of subject and object would lie in a peace achieved between human beings as well as between them and their Other. Peace is the state of differentiation without domination, with the differentiated participating in each other."[2] Honneth, however, exhibits skepticism over the fruitfulness of this turn to Adorno, arguing that it "immediately gives rise to the difficult question of how the idea of an uncoerced relation to nature can appropriately be fit-ted not within the theory of knowledge or aesthetics but rather within the conceptual framework of a critical social theory."[3]

Here, I begin the task of situating Adorno's account of nature within a broader social theory, with the aim of providing a critical intervention into the current state of environmental politics, which for the most part fails to call into question central features of the capitalist social form, as though they are unchangeable aspects of first nature.[4] The key to translating the ecologically promising formulations in Adorno's writings on epistemology and aesthetics into the categories of a social theory, I argue, involves demonstrating how these writings draw heavily on Marx's mature critique of political economy, which takes the commodity form and the phenomenon of commodity fetishism as its starting point.[5] In particular, I focus on an interesting and overlooked aspect of Adorno's thought, namely, his reluctance to embrace a relentless critique of reification as the central strategy of his critical social theory of nature. While Adorno appreciates the importance of denaturalizing the reified products of human activity, he also worries that an unwavering commitment to revealing the fundamentally social character of nature risks throwing out the baby with the bathwater, to borrow the title of an aphorism in *Minima Moralia.* More specifically, Adorno acknowledges that the separation between nature and society functions as a fetish form of capitalist society but insists nonetheless that this false appearance contains an aspect of truth insofar as it projects an image of a world free from alienated labor as the predominant means of self-preservation, a world in which people will no longer be required to sell their labor power as a commodity in order to survive. This image should be understood not as a nostalgic yearning for an unmediated relationship with nature but rather as the possibility, generated by the current state of science and technology, of both reducing the necessary labor time required to generate social wealth and transforming the labor process itself to minimize the alienation as well as the ecological footprint associated with production.

After presenting Adorno's nuanced treatments of reification and nature in his later writings, I address the criticisms of two theorists who develop very different approaches to environmental ethics and politics by thinking with and against Adorno. On the one hand, Steven Vogel uses Adorno as a foil in his argument for an environmental ethic based on his philosophy of practice, which emphasizes the ways in which nature is socially constituted and endorses idealism's account of the active character of knowledge.[6] According to Vogel, Adorno's writings betray a longing for an immediate encounter with nature that is neither possible nor desirable. On the other hand, Jane Bennett takes Adorno to task for his refusal to indulge in moments of naïve realism that can enhance one's appreciation for the ability of nonhuman things to leave an impression on thinking subjects and thus contribute to the act of cognition.[7] Moreover, Bennett implicates Adorno in perpetuating a narrative of disenchantment that fails to acknowledge the vitality that exists in all forms of matter, human and nonhuman alike, and defends commodity fetishism insofar as it has the potential to induce moments of enchantment by attributing the properties of human agents to mere things.[8] What is striking about these criticisms is that Vogel and Bennett depart from Adorno in completely opposite directions. Whereas Vogel accuses Adorno of attempting to depict nature in-itself unmediated by subjectivity, Bennett rejects Adorno's unwillingness to offer a speculative ontology of nonhuman things in an effort to "counter the tendency . . . to conclude the biography of an object by showing how it, like everything, is socially constituted."[9] For Vogel, Adorno says too much about the nature of nature; for Bennett, he does not say enough.

One might follow Vogel in concluding that these conflicting interpretations confirm the failure of Adorno's supposed attempt to reconcile Hegel's idealism with Marx's materialism. Here, however, I argue that these antithetical characterizations of Adorno are symptomatic of an oversimplification of his critical social theory of nature. Adorno does not seek to inhabit an ideal middle ground between idealism and materialism that satisfies neither Vogel nor Bennett. To appreciate the critical potential of Adorno's project, one must shift registers and focus on what these two diverging critics of Adorno nonetheless share in common. Both Vogel and Bennett ground their critiques of ecologically harmful practices with reference to transhistorical aspects of the world as a means to secure an immanent standpoint of critique. Vogel's philosophy of practice emphasizes the ways in which humans are causally and morally responsible for their environment insofar as they constantly transform the world through their thoughts and actions. Bennett invites people to embrace the ecological implications of commodity fetishism's tendency to blur the boundaries between humans and nonhumans through its animation of artifacts. The problem with these approaches is that they lead both Vogel and Bennett to reify historically specific forms of the categories on which they rely for social criticism, despite their claims to the contrary. In other words, both theorists rely on a kind of immanence that makes it difficult for them to imagine a world beyond the existing capitalist social form, thus placing undue limitations on the realm of the possible. This becomes evident in Vogel's tendency to conflate Adorno's critique of the specific form of labor under capitalism with a critique of human transformations of nature in general; it is also evident in Bennett's celebration of the enchanting aspects of commodity fetishism, based on the assumption that the commodity form is a necessary feature of the human condition.

While I share Vogel's and Bennett's aim of articulating an immanent critique of ecological degradation, they do so at the expense of a very particular kind of transcendence that I contend is invaluable for environmental politics. This moment of transcendence refers neither to a pristine nature outside of human society nor a messianic promise but rather to an image of utopian possibilities generated by tendencies immanent to society itself. Adorno's notion of a transcendence mediated by immanence enables him to disclose possibilities that are foreclosed by the one-sided emphasis that Bennett and Vogel place on immanence.[10]

Bringing Marx Back into Adorno's Negative Dialectic

In *Negative Dialectics*, Adorno seeks to rescue dialectic's emphasis on contradiction from its tendency to affirm the culmination of its movement into a positive totality.[11] The contradiction of primary concern for Adorno is the contradiction of nonidentity: the concepts that the thinking subject depends upon necessarily fail to encompass the entirety of the objects of thought; an excess always remains. Adorno explains the necessity of this contradiction in the following manner: "Because of the immanent nature of consciousness, contradictoriness itself has an inescapably and fatefully legal character. . . . This law is not a cogitative law, however. It is real."[12] This turn to reality marks the materialist element of Adorno's negative dialectic as well as its indebtedness to Marx.

The law to which Adorno refers is the principle of exchange elaborated by Marx in his analysis of the commodity form: "The principle of exchange, the reduction of human labor to the abstract universal concept of average labor time, is fundamentally akin to the principle of identification."[13] In the first instance, the commodity is a useful thing; its physical characteristics give it a use value. But not all objects with use value are commodities. While use values "constitute the material content of wealth, whatever its social form may be," in capitalist society "they are also the material bearers of . . . exchange value."[14] This suggests that it is the exchange-value aspect of the commodity that makes it more than a useful product and ties it to the historically specific capitalist social form. Unlike use value, which stems from the intrinsic and qualitative properties of an object, the exchange value of a commodity is relational and quantitative:

one pair of GAP khakis can be exchanged for *x* bottles of Seven-Up (now 100 percent natural!) or *y* pairs of Nike shoes.[15] For Marx, "it follows from this that, firstly, the valid exchange-values of a particular commodity express something equal, and secondly, exchange-value cannot be anything other than the mode of expression, the 'form of appearance,' of a content distinguishable from it."[16] The content for which exchange value serves as a form of appearance is abstract human labor power. If one sets aside the use-value aspect of commodities, all that remains is the labor expended to produce them:

> There is nothing left of them in each case but the same phantom-like objectivity; they are merely congealed quantities of homogenous human labour; i.e. of human labour-power expended without regard to the form of its expenditure. All these things now tell us is that human labour-power has been expended to produce them, human labour is accumulated in them. As crystals of this social substance, which is common to them all, they are values—commodity values.[17]

Value, which exists in all commodities and is the precondition for their very exchange, is the material manifestation of labor, measured as socially necessary labor time, which fluctuates according to a variety of factors, including the degree to which scientific and technological advancements have been incorporated into the production process.

Just as identity thinking fails to do justice to the irreducible gap between concept and thing, the principle of exchange promotes an indifference to the qualitative aspects of labor, leading to the alienation of the worker from the labor process. But this similarity is by no means coincidental: the ideology of identity thinking and the commodity form are deeply intertwined. Adorno clarifies this point in his discussion of "natural history" in *Negative Dialectics*.[18] That Marx sometimes refers to the principle of exchange as a law of nature does not escape Adorno, yet he insists that in this context the category of nature has a critical edge to it:

> That law is natural because of its inevitable character under the prevailing conditions of production. Ideology is not superimposed as a detachable layer on the being of society; it is inherent in that being. It rests on abstraction, which is the essence of the exchange process. . . . What this implies in the real process of life to this day is the necessity of social appearance. Its core is value as thing-in-itself, value as "nature."[19]

This passage provides an excellent example of how Adorno's negative dialectic unfolds contradictions to reveal moments of nonidentity. Here, the claim that the principle of exchange falls under the category of a natural law is simultaneously both true and false. It is true insofar as this principle operates as an external force beyond human control. At the same time, however, Marx's defetishizing critique reveals human labor power as the essence of the exchange principle, which suggests that its natural appearance is false. After all, "that the assumption of natural laws is not to be taken *à la letter* . . . this is confirmed by the strongest motive behind all Marxist theory: that those laws can be abolished. The realm of freedom would no sooner begin than they would cease to apply."[20] But this raises the following questions: If the principle of exchange necessarily takes the form of a law of nature, what motivates the desire to abolish this law? How is it possible to imagine a society other than one in which alienated labor is the measure of wealth?

The Critical Potential of Fetish Forms

A recurring theme in Adorno's thought is that an unwavering critique of reification risks neglecting the critical potential of the fetish forms generated by capitalist society. In *Minima Moralia,* for example, Adorno warns that ideology critique, with its emphasis on demystifying false appearances, can get carried away and negate the critical potential of the deceptions that conceal the gap between the ideals of a society and its actual state, as well as hide the material conditions that prevent society from achieving these ideals. "With the logic of coherence and the pathos of truth, cultural criticism could therefore demand that relationships be entirely reduced to their material origin, ruthlessly and openly formed according to the interests of the participants," but Adorno worries that "to act radically in accordance with this principle would be to extirpate, with the false, all that was true also, all that, however impotently, strives to escape the confines of universal practice, every chimerical anticipation of a nobler condition, and so bring about directly the barbarism that culture is reproached with furthering indirectly."[21] Ideology critique, when pushed to its logical extreme, would call for completely transparent human relationships in which the material interests of the participants are no longer veiled by bourgeois manners. The problem, however, is that these customs do not merely give the false appearance of formal equality in a society that perpetuates substantive inequality; they also prefigure the possibility of reorganizing society so that human relations cease to be primarily relations of production.

Even the fetish forms associated with the principle of exchange itself contain an emancipatory potential. Given its role in the perpetuation of alienated labor and its privileging of ongoing accumulation over the satisfaction of human needs, one might be tempted to reject the principle of exchange altogether. Adorno suggests that this romantic rejection of the logic of equivalence has dangerous implications:

> But if we denied the principle abstractly—if we proclaimed to the greater glory of the irreducibly qualitative, that parity should no longer be the ideal rule—we would be creating excuses for recidivism into ancient injustice. . . . If comparability as a category of measure were simply annulled, the rationality which is inherent in the exchange principle—as ideology, of course, *but also as a promise*—would give way to direct appropriation, to force, and nowadays to the naked privilege of monopolies and cliques.[22]

The promise of the exchange principle is the promise of a qualitatively different kind of equality than the equality that exists in bourgeois society. The principle of exchange is false insofar as it conceals how the accumulated wealth of the few rests upon the alienated labor of the many, but it also contains a moment of truth by prefiguring the possibility of abolishing alienated labor:

> When we criticize the principle of exchange as the identifying principle of thought, we want to realize the ideal of free and just exchange. To date, this ideal is a pretext. Its realization alone would transcend exchange. . . . If no man had part of his labor withheld from him any more, rational identity would be a fact, and society would have transcended the identifying mode of thinking.[23]

Once again, Adorno draws an intimate connection between the principle of exchange and identity thinking and illustrates his particular understanding of the contradiction of nonidentity. In the first instance, nonidentity refers to the contradiction between how things appear and their essence: the essence of value, namely, abstract labor time, appears to be a property of things, and their movement thus resembles a law of nature. The critique of reification seeks to denaturalize this appearance by revealing its social essence in order to demonstrate that things could be otherwise. Adorno, however, goes further: he argues that false appearances themselves can provide insight into *how* things could be otherwise. In other words, nonidentity also refers to the difference between the present manifestation of a concept such as freedom or equality and the form that it could take. If a critique simply discards false appearances in the process of revealing the essence of things, it risks overlooking the potential for false appearances to project a utopian image of a better state of things.

The Promise of Natural Beauty

In *Aesthetic Theory* Adorno provides an analysis of the paradoxes of art and nature, which resembles his treatment of the exchange principle insofar as the paradoxical forms of all three concepts portray the utopian possibility of life beyond alienated labor. Even though works of art are the products of artistic labor and depend upon a social division of labor that influences its content, art appears to be antithetical to labor in its purposelessness. Through his discussion of the relationship between art and society, Adorno offers the following account of the former:

> Art is not only the plenipotentiary of a better praxis than that which has to date predominated, but is equally the critique of praxis as the rule of brutal self-preservation at the heart of the status quo and in its service. It gives lie to production for production's sake and opts for a form of praxis beyond the spell of labor. Art's *promesse du bonheur* means not only that hitherto praxis has blocked happiness but that happiness is beyond praxis.[24]

Art provides a glimpse into a world where human activity no longer primarily serves as a mere means to survival but rather becomes an end itself. Moreover, art also suggests that activities that occur outside of the confines of alienated labor are more capable of enriching the lives of acting subjects. Note that Adorno embraces a form of praxis *beyond* the spell of labor. On the one hand, this passage implies that Adorno is privileging one form of practice over another, *not* immediacy over practice. On the other hand, this form of practice exists beyond, *not* before labor as it exists in the status quo, which guards against a romantic interpretation of his critique. Such an interpretation is further dispelled when he states that "the real possibility of utopia—that given the level of productive forces the earth could here and now be paradise—converges with the possibility of total catastrophe."[25] Adorno thus grounds his utopian vision as a real possibility existing in the present by appealing to the current state of science and technology and also stresses that there is no guarantee that these productive forces will bring about a better world.

While Adorno carefully distinguishes art beauty from natural beauty in *Aesthetic Theory*, he also points out an important similarity between the two:

> Just how bound up natural beauty is with art beauty is confirmed by the experience of the former. For it, nature is exclusively appearance, never the stuff of labor and the reproduction of life, let alone the substratum of science. Like the experience of art, the aesthetic experience of nature is that of images. Nature, as appearing beauty, is not perceived as an object of action. The sloughing off of the aims of self-preservation—which is emphatic in art—is carried out to the same degree in aesthetic experience of nature. To this extent the difference between the two forms of beauty is hardly evident.[26]

When one encounters nature aesthetically, it *appears* to be absent of any trace of labor, even though it has been worked upon thoroughly by humans. Thus, Adorno argues that the separation between nature and society is both true, insofar as it is a real appearance that prefigures a real utopian possibility of a postcapitalist future, and false, insofar as there is no such thing as nature that exists outside of society: "The image of nature survives because its complete negation in the artifact—negation that rescues this image—is necessarily blind to what exists beyond bourgeois society, its labor, its commodities. Natural beauty remains the allegory of this beyond in spite of its mediation through social immanence."[27] This notion of a transcendence meditated by immanence enables Adorno to ground his critique within society while simultaneously pointing beyond it.

In the passages that I have highlighted so far, Adorno raises the possibility of a world beyond alienated labor that focuses on the significance of this possibility for human freedom. That is, he critiques the present manifestation of practice in the name of the emancipation of the acting subject and *not* in the name of a nature that is acted upon. At the same time, however, there is no denying that Adorno also exhibits a concern for nature as an object of labor that can be dominated at the hands of humans. After all, it is his commitment to a relationship of "differentiation without domination" between humans and nature that, according to Honneth, motivates the recent turn back to Adorno. What sort of connection, if any, can be drawn between human freedom from labor under capitalism and the reconciliation of humans and nonhuman nature? Adorno gestures toward a connection in the following passage:

> [Violence toward nature] could be transformed only by a reorientation of technical forces of production that would direct these forçes not only according to desired aims but equally according to the nature that is to

> be technically formed. After the abolition of scarcity [*Mangel*], the liberation of the forces of production could extend into other dimensions than exclusively that of the quantitative growth of production.[28]

Changing the way in which humans interact with the environment involves harnessing the technical forces of production toward ends other than ongoing accumulation, *not* abandoning technological advancements in favor of a more immediate encounter with nature. Once human needs have been met, the aims of production could shift from maximizing surplus value to developing greater attentiveness to the impact of industry on the natural resources that enter the production process as raw materials. Here is a moment where Adorno comes dangerously close to providing an account of what nature *is* as opposed to how nature *appears*. By calling for a reorientation of production in accordance with nature, he seems to put forward a teleological account of nature—without explaining how people can gain knowledge of the purported ends of nature—and then proceeds to suggest that these ends can and should provide normative guidance when it comes to organizing the productive forces of society. The more promising formulation occurs at the end of the quotation: instead of engaging in production for the sake of production, a postcapitalist society could pursue other ends, such as ecological restoration projects, by repurposing the existing forces of production instead of completely abandoning them.

This reconstruction of Adorno's critical social theory of nature differs from other interpretations of Adorno by theorists who engage with his thought in their own contributions to environmental ethics and politics. Despite their advocacy of diametrically opposed approaches to environmentalism, both Steven Vogel and Jane Bennett reject the moment of transcendence preserved in Adorno's negative dialectic and aesthetic theory. This rejection, however, stems from a misunderstanding of his account of nonidentity and its contradictory nature. This misunderstanding does not appreciate the productive tension of the nonidentity between the actual and the possible, leading to an affirmation of the former at the expense of foreclosing the latter. Adorno's critical social theory of nature can contribute to environmental politics by revealing how another world, a world overlooked by both Vogel and Bennett, is possible.

Vogel's Philosophy of Practice

In his highly rewarding book *Against Nature*, Vogel portrays the development of Western Marxism from Lukács to Habermas as a struggle between two opposing attempts to incorporate nature within a critical social theory. On the one hand, there exists a tendency toward romanticism in critical theory insofar as it occasionally appeals to nature as an extrasocial realm, to provide a normative standpoint from which a critique of society can be leveled. On the other hand, the Hegelian influence in critical theory leads to a different approach that

> insists on the active role of a socially situated subject in constituting the field that subject inhabits, it emphasizes the dynamic, the social, and the historically changing in its account of what the world is like and sees the static and putatively "natural" as standing for those aspects of the world whose social character has been hidden or forgotten and that have thus become "reified."[29]

According to this view, nature is the object, rather than the standpoint of critique, and consists of what must be demystified to reveal its fundamentally social character. Vogel insists that these two accounts of nature form an antinomy that even the most sophisticated dialectical maneuvering fails to resolve into a higher synthesis and argues that one must choose between these incompatible approaches. The romantic moments in critical theory presuppose a privileged knowledge of nature that somehow escapes the instrumentalizing impulse of the natural sciences, but critical theorists have difficulties articulating and grounding the possibility of this alternative, nondominating relationship with nature. Given this shortcoming, which threatens the very coherence of the romantic position, Vogel favors the Hegelian understanding of nature as being constituted by social subjects and proceeds to develop a critical social theory of nature on the basis of a philosophy of practice that he reconstructs immanently from the missed opportunities of the Frankfurt School tradition in critical theory.

Like Honneth, Vogel remains skeptical of attempts to develop a critical theory of nature that take Adorno's later writings on epistemology and aesthetics as their starting points. Adorno characterizes Enlightenment and identity thinking as necessarily enmeshed in the domination of nature, but this begs the question of the normative standpoint from which Adorno decries the domination of nature, since the values of the Enlightenment do not escape the wrath of his critique. According to Vogel, Adorno (and Max Horkheimer) can avoid grounding their critique of Enlightenment thinking on the basis of Enlightenment values

> only by appealing to the "nature" that enlightened natural science is supposed to be harming; the trouble is that such an appeal itself

> requires a kind of knowledge of the nature being harmed that would substitute for the natural science they want to reject, and they have nothing to say about what this knowledge might be . . . or how it might be justified.[30]

In other words, this critique in nature's name collapses into incoherence insofar as it provides an account of what nature is while simultaneously insisting upon the irreducible otherness of nature that suffers at the hands of humans. Moreover, the turn to nature is symptomatic of a longing for the impossible experience of an immediate encounter with nature outside the confines of the social world: "What lies behind the surface here is the hope for some access to immediacy other than the cognitive one, a hope that marks this kind of theory finally as romantic."[31] Even though Adorno's later writings shift toward a concern with the violence that human practices (including thinking) inflict upon the nonidentical, Vogel claims that this move reproduces rather than resolves Adorno's trouble with nature. What ultimately distinguishes Vogel's philosophy of practice from Adorno's negative dialectics is the former's commitment to a reflexive mode of thought:

> A reflexive thought in the Hegelian sense recognizes its own involvement in that which it thinks, and in so doing comes to recognize that "otherness" is always a *thought* otherness and hence not really a realm of the "nonidentical" after all, at least not if the latter term is given Adorno's strongly materialist meaning.[32]

By grounding itself in an otherness beyond the realm of thought, Adorno's critique of identity thinking loses its immanent character.

Against Natural Beauty and Its Emancipatory Potential

As I have argued above, however, the nonidentical *is* a thought otherness for Adorno: it is the utopian vision of an emancipated future that arises from a fetish form immanent to society. Even though Vogel claims that Adorno "is at his best" when he argues that "what we see in nature . . . says something more about the social than about any (unknowable) nature in itself,"[33] he rejects Adorno's insistence on the critical potential of natural beauty:

> But natural beauty as proxy of immediacy, as trace of nonidentity, as anamnesis of an in-itself prior to human mediation, as promise of a utopian "*noch nicht*," as allegory for something beyond labor and com-

> modities, even as "glimpse of freedom"—finally these are just rhetorical moves, marvelous ones no doubt, but still ultimately bald assertions about what nature "is" not backed up (nor capable of being backed up) by argument or evidence.[34]

Vogel's conclusion that Adorno's critical theory of nature amounts to nothing more than (marvelous) rhetorical moves is unwarranted for several reasons. First, Vogel conflates natural beauty, the *appearance* that stems from an aesthetic experience of nature, with nature itself. Adorno carefully distinguishes this particular form of mediation from economic and scientific approaches to nature, insofar as nature does not *appear* to be an object of action when experienced aesthetically, while ultimately acknowledging that nature is in fact socially constituted. I agree that Adorno cannot back up claims about what nature *is*, but he is capable of backing up claims about how nature *appears*, which is his concern in his discussion of natural beauty. Similarly, one can draw a distinction between the first three (as a proxy of the immediate, the nonidentical, and the thing-in-itself) and the last three (as a proxy for a utopian vision, a social form beyond capitalism, and human freedom) ways in which natural beauty appears to the human subject engaged in an aesthetic experience. Whereas the first three appearances tell us something about nature, the last three appearances tell us something about society and the possibility of transforming it. Adorno might not provide an adequate argument or sufficient evidence to ground this possibility in the present state of society (he merely asserts that the current state of productive forces are sufficient to abolish want and alienated labor), but that's not to say that doing so would be an impossible task.[35] In other words, Vogel prematurely dismisses Adorno "at his best" by mistaking his discussion of nature's appearance for an account of nature's essence and by neglecting to distinguish the appearances that tell us about nature from the appearances that tell us about society.

Vogel also acknowledges that Adorno turns to aesthetic experience as a different kind of mediation, rather than basing his critique on an appeal to immediacy. At the same time, however, Vogel associates this approach with the shortcomings of deconstruction:

> It wants to reveal the arbitrariness and historical contingency of our mediating acts, and does so by showing the possibility of engaging in very different ones. This is fine as far as it goes, but it still threatens to end up in relativism: all mediations turn out to be arbitrary, so why should we choose "aesthetic" ones over those that dominate nature? . . . Adorno's *es könnte auch anders sein* is moving and powerful as a slogan,

> yet more closely considered it becomes clear that he is absolutely unable to give it any content: what *is* this other way things could be? How *ought* they to be?[36]

In a footnote appended to the end of this passage, Vogel provides an answer to his rhetorical questions: "As we have seen, the only real content Adorno offers involves an appeal to the somatic, which is to say to immediacy."[37] While Adorno undoubtedly turns to bodily experience as an alternative mediation that, as Vogel convincingly argues, amounts to nothing more than a dressed-up form of immediacy, this is by no means the *only* content that Adorno is otherwise *absolutely unable* to provide for his alternative. In my treatment of Adorno, I have shown that he articulates a different mediation in a way that avoids relativism. For Adorno, an aesthetic encounter with nature makes nature appear as though it is separate from society insofar as nature does not appear to be an object of labor. This image of a world beyond labor prefigures the utopian vision of a postcapitalist future that, according to Adorno, can be realized given the current level of scientific and technological advancement. In other words, Adorno does not posit an alternative mediation arbitrarily simply to reveal the contingency of the current state of affairs. Rather, he latches on to tendencies generated by the dynamic of capitalism (the reduction of necessary labor time through developments in science and technology) and highlights the gap between the possibilities that this dynamic unleashes and the present failure to realize them. According to Vogel, the theory of reification has advantages over the method of deconstruction insofar as the former avoids relativism by calling us forward "to *better* mediations that we know and plan and no longer mistake for the immediate."[38] I have argued that Adorno also calls us forward, although along a different road than the one taken by Vogel. The fact that Vogel's philosophy of practice does not even recognize Adorno's better mediation as a mediation leads to my third objection to Vogel's characterization of Adorno.

Vogel claims that Adorno's concern with the domination of nature and the violence to the object perpetuated by identity thinking leads him to retreat from any mediation between humans and nature and oppose any human transformation of the world. He concludes that "Adorno finally hates practice, which is to say he hates labor, associated as it is for him with domination. Art's practice is itself a critique of practice, he says; and he is explicit that it is not merely a critique of contemporary (capitalist, exploitative, dehumanizing) practice that is involved here but rather a critique of practice *as such*."[39] Vogel bases his claim on the passage from *Aesthetic The-*

ory quoted above, in which Adorno characterizes art not only as a proxy for a better form of practice than the current one but also "a critique of praxis as the rule of brutal self-preservation at the heart of the status quo and in its service."[40] But one need not conclude from this quotation, as Vogel does, that Adorno's "position ends by rejecting any *real* human attempt to interact with [the] world, worrying that all interaction is a transformation and so inevitably betrays the egoism of domination, the violence of 'brutal self-preservation.'"[41] What enables Vogel to jump to this unwarranted conclusion is his lack of attention to the nonidentity between the historically specific form of practice that predominates in capitalist society, namely, alienated labor that one sells in exchange for wage in order to survive, and the form that practice could take in a postcapitalist future.[42]

This conflation stems from Vogel's reliance on a relatively transhistorical conception of practice to secure an immanent standpoint of critique. On the one hand, it ought to be noted that Vogel's rich account of practice cannot be reduced to labor in general (let alone its alienated form under capitalism), although in the context of Vogel's critique of Adorno practice and labor become more or less synonymous. On the other hand, there's a way in which Vogel highlights what unites all forms of human practice at the expense of their qualitative differences. In response to his critics, he advocates a reconstruction of Horkheimer and Adorno's critique of the domination of nature that

> would criticize capitalism not for the way it transforms the world humans inhabit—a transformation that all social systems produce (although perhaps not all to the same extent), because it is founded in the very nature of human practice—but rather for the way it systematically occludes humans' recognition that such a transformation is taking place and *is their own doing.*[43]

Even though Vogel acknowledges that there may be differences in the extent to which various social systems transform the world, the emphasis is on the transhistorical nature of human practice. Moreover, it remains unclear whether Vogel would describe the differences between the transformations produced by various social systems as qualitative or quantitative. The main criterion that Vogel provides to distinguish good practices from bad ones is whether or not the practice is recognized as such, which implies that Vogel levels his critique from the standpoint of practice in general. Adorno, by contrast, insists upon the historical specificity of labor under capitalism and preserves the productive contradiction between actually existing practice and the form that it could take. There is no denying that humans must transform the world, but there exists a qualitative difference between the predominant mediation in capitalism and the mediation that could exist in a postcapitalist future. So long as labor time remains the measure of value, there will be a tendency to rely on direct human labor in the production process, even when technological developments render much direct human labor obsolete. A mediation that substitutes the forces of production for direct human labor is qualitatively different than a situation in which people must sell their labor to survive, on the basis that the former ensures that labor-saving technology actually translates into more free time for people to engage in practices other than labor. At the end of *Against Nature*, Vogel calls for new practices and a new form of social organization, but he does not provide these new forms of practice and society with any content beyond an appeal for more opportunities for democratic decision making, despite his claim that the theory of reification equips his critique with a directionality absent in Adorno's critical theory of nature.

A greater appreciation of the potential for the false appearances systematically generated by capitalism to disclose emancipatory possibilities might lead Vogel to rethink his claim that Adorno romantically longs for an immediate encounter with nature. While Jane Bennett shares Adorno's concern that an unwavering critique of reification risks overlooking the ethically and politically laudable aspects of commodity fetishism, she falls into a similar trap as Vogel by characterizing the commodity form as a transhistorical feature of the human condition.

Bennett's Defense of Naïve Realism

Bennett also develops an approach to ecological ethics in conversation with Adorno, but her criticisms of his negative dialectic are nearly antithetical to the concerns that Vogel raises. In particular, she faults Adorno for adhering to Marx's call for the "ruthless criticism of everything existing"[44] when a willingness to suspend one's critical faculties and embrace moments of naïve realism has the potential, according to Bennett, to inspire and motivate ethical and political action. If "all reification is forgetting,"[45] and if, as Bennett contends, "in small, controlled doses, a certain forgetfulness is ethically indispensable,"[46] then Bennett's argument is at odds with Vogel's commitment to a relentless critique of reification.

Dissatisfied with hitherto existing materialisms that insist that the capacity to act solely belongs to humans, Bennett introduces "thing-power materialism," which is a "speculative onto-story, a rather presumptuous attempt to depict the nonhumanity that flows around but also through humans."[47] While she admits that one cannot escape the mediations inherent in subjectivity, "there nonetheless remains something to be said for the naïveté of naïve realism. A moment of naïveté is . . . indispensable for any discernment of thing-power, if there is to be any chance acknowledging the force of matter. A naïve realism . . . allows nonhumanity to appear on the ethical radar screen."[48] By highlighting the way in which matter acts through networks and assemblages composed of both humans and nonhumans, the naïve moment of thing-power materialism blurs the boundary between the two, thus allowing nonhuman entities to be objects of moral consideration. Bennett suggests that thing-power materialism can motivate and inspire people to adopt ecologically sustainable lifestyles. With regards to consumption, Bennett wagers that thing-power materialism

> would increase the deliberateness or intentionality involved—less thoughtless waste, and so perhaps less waste overall. . . . A renewed emphasis on our entanglement with things, an entanglement that renders us to an array of dangers and diseases as well as joys and inspirations, is compatible with a "wise use" orientation to consumption.[49]

In other words, a respect for the vitality of all things will motivate people to minimize their ecological footprints out of respect for the larger web of life in which they are entwined.

While both Bennett and Adorno emphasize the gap between a thing and its concept, they disagree over the location and meaning of that which exceeds thought. According to Bennett,

> Adorno refuses to confine nonidentity to an immanent, material world. . . . [He] seems, then, to maintain the possibility of transcendence by honoring nonidentity as an *absent* absolute, as a messianic promise. A thing-power materialist might respond by invoking the wondrous energy of actants as itself sufficient to warrant an honorable relation to things, or to justify the wisdom of proceeding cautiously in our engagements with the world. To us, resistances and swerves are less gestures of transcendence than manifestations of the vitality of immanent forces that flow through us as well as course over and under us.[50]

I share Bennett's unease regarding the messianic moments in Adorno's thought, but these moments coexist with less theological accounts of transcendence. In particular, transcendence also signifies the possibility of overcoming the capitalist social form. Bennett acknowledges this herself when she notes that one of Adorno's strategies "for training oneself to honor nonidentity" involves "engag[ing] in utopian thinking: [the negative dialectician] imagines emergent possibilities and does not restrict herself to the examination of existing objects. Nonidentity consists in those denied possibilities, in the invisible field that surrounds and infuses the world of objects."[51] By grounding the promise of a postcapitalist future in tendencies generated by capitalism itself, Adorno upsets the dichotomy that Bennett sets up between immanence and transcendence. This is an advantage of his negative dialectics, which "is bound—like Marx's, largely—to be immanent even if in the end it negates the whole sphere it moves in."[52] In other words, Adorno seeks to provide an immanent critique without falling prey to the risk of affirming the present state of the world.

Moreover, Bennett's privileging of immanence over transcendence is somewhat surprising, given how she embraces moments of transcendence in her earlier work, especially in *The Enchantment of Modern Life*. The flight of Andoar, the goat-kite hybrid of Michel Tournier's novel *Friday*, for example, "activates a longing for what Tournier calls '*something else*,' a longing that has been at the heart of a variety of social and liberation movements. One can see how the fantasy of transcendence might have ethically laudable effects."[53] Similarly, Bennett expresses ambivalence over the *meta*physical moment of her speculative ontology, insofar as it implies a departure from her commitment to immanence. At the same time, however, she refuses to abandon completely the "meta" of metaphysics: "I like its utopian gesture, aura, or scent, that is, its willingness to venture above and beyond, onto the plain of virtual things and not-yet realized possibilities."[54] Judging from these passages, interesting similarities exist between Adorno's negative dialectics and Bennett's thing-power materialism. Yet a fundamental difference remains: not only does Bennett affirm the enchanting potential of commodity fetishism; she also seems unwilling to entertain the possibility of a society beyond the commodity form.

The Affirmative Character of Commodity Enchantment

Playing the role of garbage collector by picking up the debris left behind by the disenchantment narrative perpetuated by Adorno and others, Bennett seeks to highlight potential sources of enchantment in the modern world. Perhaps the most controversial site of enchantment she identifies is the commodity and the commercial art that surrounds it. Noting how recent work in cultural studies acknowledges the liberatory potential of consumption, Bennett argues that "the theme of commodity fetishism is not capacious enough to account for our fascination with commercial goods."[55] Marx describes commodity fetishism in the following manner: "The mysterious character of the commodity-form consists therefore simply in the fact that the commodity reflects the social characteristics of men's own labour as objective characteristics of the products of labour themselves, as the socio-natural properties of these things."[56] Capitalist relations of production appear to belong to a second nature, which makes it difficult to appreciate the historical specificity of this social form and the domination it entails, as well as the possibility of overcoming it. Bennett admires how a defetishizing critique primarily seeks to reveal "the pain and suffering embedded in the commodity by virtue of an unjust and exploitative system of production,"[57] but she takes issue with the way in which "it supports an onto-story in which agency is concentrated in humans."[58] By appearing to have properties that actually belong to their producers, "commodified objects are implicated in an unnatural transference of energy from persons to things; commodification operates as a zero-sum game. To respond to things as if they were alive is to steal animus from the humans who own the monopoly rights to it."[59]

Bennett affirms this animation of artifacts associated with commodity fetishism insofar as it has the potential to bring about moments of enchantment by imbuing consumers with a sense of liveliness and drawing attention to the vitality of the nonhuman world. Artistic portrayals of commodities in advertising can capture "an aesthetic of vibrant mobility, of the ever-present possibility of bursts of vitality that violate an order ranking humans incomparably higher than animals, vegetables, and minerals."[60] By bringing artifacts to life, commercials have the capacity to cultivate an ecological ethic despite their role in perpetuating a consumer culture with devastating environmental consequences. Given the multiple and multivalent effects of commodity fetishism, Bennett suggests that debating the relative merits of the commodity-based economy only serves as a distraction from the more important question of *how* to incorporate the commodity properly within our lives:

> the issue is not whether to live with commodities but how to participate in commodity culture, *for there is no vision of capitalist or noncapitalist economy that does not include some role for the commodity form.* The pertinent questions become how to reform commodity culture to render it more just and more ecologically sustainable and how to extract the ethical potential within commodity culture.[61]

Reforming commodity culture might include "efforts to reconstruct an economic infrastructure that demands increasing levels of consumption and waste and regularly overpowers individual efforts toward ecological living."[62] More specifically, Bennett advocates a shift toward a political economy that privileges inclusive goods such as public transportation over exclusive goods such as automobiles without abandoning commercial advertising and its ability to enchant.

While Marx's analysis of fetishism in his early writings does seem to presuppose a troubling ontology according to which the animation of artifacts violates the natural order of things, this concern does not motivate his later critique of commodity fetishism in *Capital.* Nonetheless, a zero-sum game between humans and commodities remains. Lived experience under capitalism is one of domination insofar as people's "own movement within society has for them the form of a movement made by things, and these things, far from being under their control, in fact control them."[63] If capitalists wish to remain capitalists, they must continually sell commodities for the sake of capital accumulation. If workers wish to remain alive, they have little choice but to sell their labor power as a commodity. Moreover, the commodity form generates the impression that this alienated human activity is natural and thus unchangeable. Despite her best intentions to the contrary, Bennett falls into the trap of naturalizing capitalism and its accompanying domination when she insists that the commodity form is a necessary feature of the human condition. Just as Vogel conflates human labor in general with the particular form it predominantly takes under capitalism, Bennett confuses goods produced in *any* society with a complex division of labor (such that these goods are not produced for direct consumption by the producer) with commodities, which only appear under capitalist relations of production. According to Marx, "The product of labour is an object of utility in all states of society; but it is only a historically specific epoch of development which presents the labour expended in the production of a useful article as an 'objective' property of that article, i.e. as its value. It is only then the product of labour becomes transformed into a commodity."[64] Bennett's insistence that even a postcapitalist future will be stamped by the commodity form has the effect of dulling the edge of both Marx's and Adorno's incisive critiques of a society that measures its wealth by the amount of labor time expended in production while simultaneously reducing the amount of labor time needed to meet human needs.

One of the strengths of Marx's critique of political economy is that it has the capacity to explain this tendency to hypostatize features of bourgeois society as resulting from the fetish forms inherent in capitalism. Noting the distinction between use value and exchange value, Bennett explains how "Marx defined a commodity as an article produced from the start for large-scale market exchange."[65] The problem with taking this definition of the commodity as a starting point, however, is that it does not capture the essence, and thus the historical specificity, of the commodity form. By focusing on the exchange-value moment of the commodity without treating it as the necessary appearance of value, Bennett draws the conclusion that the commodity form is an essential feature for any society, capitalist or otherwise, with a complex division of labor. If a commodity is simply a product of human labor that is transferred to another person via equal exchange, then there's no point in objecting to the commodity form unless one seeks to abolish the division of labor itself, which seems neither feasible nor desirable. Like the political economists critiqued by Marx, Bennett does not ask

> why labour is expressed in value, and why the measurement of labour by its duration is expressed in the magnitude of the value of the product. These formulas, which bear the unmistakable stamp of belonging to a social formation in which the process of production has mastery over man, instead of the opposite, appear as much a self-evident and nature-imposed necessity as productive labour itself.[66]

An emphasis on the category of value, however, reveals the centrality of the commodity form in capitalist society as well as the possibility of abolishing it. Bennett draws attention to important yet neglected sources of ethical motivation and inspiration in unlikely places such as the commodity fetish, but in the process of doing so she also unintentionally draws attention *away* from the possibility of moving beyond the commodity form. This possibility of overcoming second nature's domination over humanity could motivate and inspire a movement dedicated to a transformative approach to ecological politics that seeks to bring about the reorientation of production toward the inclusive goods advocated by Bennett herself.

Conclusion

"No theory today escapes the marketplace," not even Adorno's critical theory of nature.[67] But his theory does point beyond capitalism by showing how the fetish forms of bourgeois society prefigure the possibility of a postcapitalist future where the "natural law" of value and the alienated labor it presupposes cease to exist. Moreover, Adorno grounds the possibility in the tendency for the dynamic of capital to minimize the role of direct human labor in the production process through the introduction of scientific and technological innovations. While Vogel persuasively demonstrates the danger of romantic appeals to nature-in-itself and Bennett creatively reveals the ethical potential of commodity fetishism, both theorists overlook the possibilities disclosed by Adorno. At a time when some of the most visionary voices in environmentalism cannot imagine a world beyond wage labor even when indulging in a moment of utopian speculation,[68] when postenvironmentalists who "step back to rethink everything" call for actions to curb greenhouse gas emissions on the basis that responding to the challenge posed by global climate change has potential to create millions of jobs,[69] Adorno's analysis suggests that these approaches risk affirming "the spirit of a society in which the ideal of full employment is substituted for that of the abolition of labor."[70] Overcoming the opposition between jobs and the environment, from this perspective, embraces the positivity that negative dialectics avoids by refusing to affirm moments of false reconciliation.

Neither romantic nor blind to the emancipatory potential of commodity fetishism, Adorno's critical social theory of nature demonstrates how the *image* of nature can remind us of the possibility of pursuing ends other than the never-ending pursuit of surplus value. It is in the spirit of this aspect of his thought that we ought to understand Adorno's provocative claim that nature "does not yet exist."[71]

CHAPTER 7

From Nature to Matter

Jane Bennett

Vital Materiality

Shortly after Earth Day, 1975, and inspired by Henry Thoreau's *Walden*, E. F. Schumacher's *Small Is Beautiful*, Rachel Carson's *Silent Spring*, Murray Bookchin's *Post-Scarcity Anarchism*, and Garrett Hardin's "Tragedy of the Commons," I became an environmentalist.[1] I pursued that identity for thirty years or so. But now I'm considering becoming a materialist when I grow up. Not a *historical* materialist, but a more animistic or at least less anthropocentric kind of materialist, one for whom "materiality" includes more than the social and economic structures of humans. In this materialism, matter is not the brute stuff for our vital projects or the inorganic obverse of life but is itself a lively actor in the world. This is a materiality whose vitality infects and infuses our bodies, our tools, and our institutions even as it also disrupts, vies against, exceeds, and sometimes destroys them. This materiality is not inert, brute, raw, or capable only of the motion of bare repetition or mechanical reproduction.

I still vote green, and I still try to tread lightly on the Earth. I abhorred the Bush administration's overtly propollution policies and lament still the

Obama administration's more subtle endorsement of them. I reject the American equation of prosperity with wanton consumption of energy and of soon-to-be-landfill commodities and am, in that sense, an antimaterialistic materialist. Along with Thomas Princen, William Connolly, Wendell Berry, Val Plumwood, Wade Sikorski, Rom Coles, Melissa Orlie, and many others inside and outside of political theory, I believe that a central goal of politics today should be to create a more sustainable political economy of production and consumption. Perhaps also like them, I wonder if the category "environmentalism," with its suggestion that the nonhuman world is a background for action rather than an effect-producing assemblage of human and nonhuman actants, is our best conceptual bet. I find myself drifting instead toward a new(ish) or renewed "materialism," for both philosophical and pragmatic-political reasons. I'm thinking that a more ecologically sustainable American public culture might be encouraged by a discursive shift from "nature" to "materiality"—from the earth conceived as the passive environment within which human activity takes place to earth conceived as a swarming assemblage of active, vital materialities.

There is no doubt that the social movement of environmentalism, with its master term "nature," has raised a host of important political-philosophical questions. Some of these concern the preservation of pure nature or the wild untouched by humans, and others are premised on the idea that the unit of environmentalist concern can only be "second nature," i.e., a hybrid of nature and culture, outside and inside, *phusis* and *nomos*. These questions have included the following: Is capitalism/socialism/urbanization/economic development consistent with environmentalism? What conception of nature is embedded in different political cultures? How to move toward a greener economy/energy policy/transportation policy/food and agricultural policy? Is government regulation, market incentives, or a cultural shift in consumption patterns the best means toward the end of sustainability? How do issues of race, class, and gender intersect with and complicate questions of nature? How to foster environmental justice? Should we approach nature through the category of instrumental value or intrinsic value? Should we take the problem-centered path of Deweyan pragmatism or the metaphysical turn of Deep Ecology? Can animals and plants bear legal rights, or is the framework of rights too narrow to access what matters about flora and fauna?

All good questions, but the one that calls me most is not quite on the list: How better to represent and more attentively respond to the *force of things*? How, in other words, to become more sensitive to the affects and effects of lively nonhumans, such as animals, vegetables, minerals, artifacts, technologies, weather, and other things whose vitality we ignore at our peril? These materialities form powerful biocultural assemblages, for example, hurricanes-FEMA-global warming, or stem cells-scientific research-ensouled embryos, or worms-topsoil-garbage, or electricity-deregulation-fire-greed-blackout, or *e.coli*-abbatoirs-agribusiness.

Like the vital materialism I admire, an environmentalism of "second nature" also names as the locus of efficacy (and as its unit of analysis) an *assemblage* of humans and nonhumans. But the discourse of second nature tends still to give primacy to the human actors, presenting the nonhumans as but a function of human norms, words, perceptions, concepts, images, moods. The moments of independence, or recalcitrance, *or positive vitality* of nonhuman beings, things, or energies are elided in the rush to avoid the essentialization, romanticization, reification, or divinization of Nature. Still, the discourse of "second nature" forces us to ask: can the political will to forge less noxious modes of production and consumption endure the demise of the master term of environmentalism, that is, "nature"? I think that it can and that a politics of vital materiality might be a way forward.

What are the advantages or possible advantages of a politics of *materiality* over a politics of *nature*? First, if nature has derived much of its force from its status as an opposition term to culture, to all that bears the dirty imprint of humanity, materiality is a figure that applies more symmetrically to humans and nonhumans alike. *I* am material, the pigeons in the park are material, the viruses in my nose and on the doorknobs are material, doorknobs are material, as is the dust on the floor. To replace nature with the figure of materiality is to encourage an approach to political theorizing that *horizontalizes* the relations between humans, biota, and abiota and thus encourages attentiveness to the profound (although not necessarily moral) connectedness of all things. Such an approach blasphemes against an implicit moral imperative within political thought: thou shalt seek what is distinctive about humanity, thou shalt isolate a human nature that is worthy of dignity *because* it is qualitatively distinct from all other forms in nature. The figure of materiality, as a way to denote what the ancient Greeks called *phusis*, does not lend itself as readily to the picture of a world as a hierarchy or one that is naturally divided up into subjects existing across an abyss from objects. Or at least it does not do so once materiality is pulled away from matter conceived as the other to life, about which I'll have more to say later.

A second possible advantage of the figure of materiality over that of nature is that its history is less entangled with organicism. By organicism I mean a particular image of structure: the kind of collective that is, as Kant put it, "both cause and effect of itself."[2] The figure of nature has tended to conjure the image of a structure whose parts conjoin *in order to* maintain an enduring whole: organisms, with their tendency toward equilibrium, are groupings whose indigenous parts are never extraneous or perverse. In contrast, when various *materialities* form a working whole, their structure can be more readily imagined as one whose swervy elements do not all serve the same purpose or any bona fide purpose at all. If "nature" lends itself to the fantasy of a harmonious and purposive unity (or to an order of Creation in which every hair on my head is numbered), materiality can evoke an assemblage held together by ties that are more contingent, tense, mobile, or temporary.

But why invoke and deploy *any* ontological master concept—nature, second nature, *or* materiality? Why not, for example, take the route of pragmatism and focus on concrete problems as they arise, without the fancy metaphysical footwork? Because I want some term to mark the active presence, the amazing power, of nonhuman or not-quite-human things and forces, because I think it is ethically important to try to mark this "outside" even if, as Nietzsche believed, it is an ungraspable "monster of *energy*," a "play of forces and waves of forces, at the same time one and many."[3] Even if, in other words, earth is a mobile flow that only temporarily congeals into entities and thus is not really susceptible to any high-quality knowing on our part. I want some term to mark the *givenness* of this activity, of this effectivity or even agency whose ultimate source is *not* human (or divine) and that is not merely resistant to human will but is embedded in it as well as engaged in a life of its own. The term nature could be and has been used to mark this independent agency, but, in the wake of the constructive or linguistic turn at the end of the twentieth century, it has become too easily aligned with an outside construed as *of our own making* and thus, as Max Weber puts it, as something that is, at least, "in principle" calculable.[4]

So, what I think needs to be done is this impossible task: to give voice to an active, nonhuman materiality that participates, often antagonistically with humans, in force fields of agency, in assemblages that are agentic in the sense of capable of producing unheralded, potent effects. This materiality is stuff that itself becomes otherwise than it is—is as much wind as thing, impetus as entity, energy as matter. I'm after a materiality that is quasi-agentic but not subject-like, vital but not moral, having trajectories but not intentions. I wonder whether a world experienced as filled with this materiality would pose a stronger challenge than "nature" currently does to the destructive fantasies of mastery that infuse American consumption and production practices. The idea of a *vital* materiality is, I admit, hard to swallow, for I have deep attachments to the idea that matter is not life and to the notion that real agency is an exclusively human affair.

Second Thoughts and Nature's Swarm

But I need to take a step back. For it's not quite accurate to say, as I have, that the figure of "nature" cannot accommodate the idea of vital materiality. Nature is, after all, one of the most internally complex figures at play in Western thought; it always operates as a sticky web of images. So to invoke "nature" is automatically to call up a *swarm* of elements and affects, of thing-concepts, each of which helps to give form to the others. A. O. Lovejoy, the great historian of ideas, listed sixty-six senses of the term nature.[5] I'll focus on just three elements in the prolific and self-dirempting swarm of nature, the last of which opens the door to a vital materiality.

The first hornet in the swarm of nature is the Given: the figure of what is always already there, the found or stumbled upon rather than the made. This thereness preexists me and you and us and renders absurd the idea of (human or divine) creation *ex nihilo*. Political theorists are familiar with a variety of conceptualizations of the Given: Derrida inflected it as the Gift or the pure offering that always arrives in advance of thought; Heidegger spoke of a thrownness (or sometimes of the primordial); Jesus and some of his followers called it *logos;* Hobbes, Locke, and Rousseau imagined it as "the state of nature" or the original condition that precedes self-consciousness and culture. (The state of nature is also sometimes imagined as the default condition into which self-consciousness and culture tend to devolve.) The Homeric Greeks may have called it *dike*.

As you can see from that list, the hornet of the Given can appear as a protean and vague gift but also as an enduring essence more susceptible to our knowing. As the Given moves toward the latter, presencing less as an existential *condition* and more as an ontological *substance*, it morphs into a second hornet in the swarm. This could be described as nature qua Brute Matter, nature, that is, as a set of *blocks*—blocks both in the sense of *discrete entities* that can be combined in productive ways by humans (building blocks) and in the sense of *resistant bodies* that impede the movements of human bodies and wills (blockages).

A third hornet in the swarm is the perverse twin of this hulking and recalcitrant brute: it is nature as creative Life Force, nature as fecundity, Isis or Aphrodite, the "Spring" movement of Vivaldi's Four Seasons. The third hornet (nature as the restless power to conjure up new emergents) and the second hornet (nature as the stable substrate of brute matter) have what Merleau-Ponty called a chiasmatic relationship: they flow into and back from each other, endlessly.[6]

The difference between nature as brute matter and nature as protean creativity ("Life") is nicely captured by the distinction, key to Spinoza's *Ethics*, between *natura naturata* and *natura naturans*. *Natura naturata:* passive matter that has been organized into an eternal order of Creation. *Natura naturans* or naturing nature: the uncaused causality that ceaselessly generates new forms.[7] When the English romantics and the American transcendentalists sought to refine their senses, they did so in part to be able to better *detect* the creative life force of *natura naturans*.[8] Nature as fertility, or even as the wilder and more open-ended "generativity," was emphasized by Whitehead's process philosophy, according to which nature was "a continuous stream of occurrence."[9] Deleuze and Guattari, drawing upon Spinoza, romanticism, Whitehead, and others (including Nietzsche, Kafka, and Bergson), put this spin on *natura naturans:* "Nature is like an immense Abstract Machine," a "pure plane of immanence . . . upon which unformed elements and materials dance."[10]

Nature as free creativity seems also to have been a key part of the meaning of the ancient Greek *phusis* (foo'sis), of which the Latin *natura* is an equivalent. *Phusis* comes from the verb *phuo* (foo'-o), which probably meant "to puff" or "to blow," that is, to swell up, but the verb was used only in the implied sense of to germinate or sprout up, to bring forth, open out, or hatch. *Phusis* thus speaks of a process of morphing or change or deformation, that is to say, of the becoming-otherwise of things.

The point of my foray into the semantic and affective swarm that is "nature" is this: an active becoming, a creative not-quite-human force capable of producing the new, buzzes within it. Is this the vibrant matter of which I dream? It could be. Provided, of course, that this vital force is not imagined as something immaterial, as, for example, a spirit of Life that animates a naturally dull matter. It may be only a step from the creative agency of a "life spirit" to a materiality that is itself this creative agency. I'm not sure whether that is a small step or a giant leap. How important is the idea that matter is not itself life? Why has the matter/life binary been so persistent, so affectively charged, despite the fact that the line between life and matter, organic and inorganic, becomes every day more difficult to discern?

Matter Versus Life

What I will do next is consider these questions by engaging briefly with a tradition that posits the existence of a "vital force" in matter but that, unlike me, tenaciously insists that that force must be nonmaterial. This is a tradition of vitalism, in particular its late nineteenth-century version. I focus on two of its advocates, the philosopher of "creative evolution" Henri Bergson and his contemporary, the German embryologist Hans Driesch. Vitalism also has its twenty-first-century advocates, including George W. Bush and other evangelical defenders of "the culture of life."[11] My foray into vitalism is designed to explore the matter/life distinction and to understand better some of the reasons for its philosophical and psychological tenacity, a tenacity that functions as a block to the vital materialism I seek.

At the heart of the vitalist position is the idea that "life" is radically different from "matter," that there exists a life principle that animates matter without itself being of a material nature. In Bergson's and Driesch's time, this life force was said to provide the impetus for morphological changes in the embryo, but it was also thought to be responsible for the developmental processes of personality and history.

The nineteenth-century vitalists disagreed among themselves about just how to depict this (nonmaterial) vital force—Bergson's *élan vital* competed, for example, with Driesch's notion of *entelechy*. But on the question of "matter," they agreed both with each other and with the (mechanistic) materialists of their time: matter was unfree and deterministic (though "dynamic" in the sense of capable of undergoing regular, successive changes of state). The vitalists located "life" outside the realm of mechanistic matter, whereas the "materialists" of the day insisted that all bodies, however complex, minute, or subtle, were (ultimately) explicable in mechanical or "physicochemical" terms. Bergson and Driesch enjoyed great popularity in America—when Bergson lectured in Manhattan, it produced one of the first documented traffic jams. This was in large part because they were received as affirming moral freedom in the face of a modern science whose pragmatic success was threatening to confirm that the universe was a godless machine.

Driesch, today much less well-known than Bergson, was an independently wealthy German embryologist. He was one of the first non-Jews to be stripped of his professorship by the Nazis because he objected to their use of his idea of vital force to justify the German conquest of less "vital" peoples. Driesch was also a Kantian of sorts, and it will be useful, before we encounter his notion of vital force (*entelechy*), to have a sense of Kant's version, *Bildungstrieb*.

Kant articulated a particularly strong version of the claim that materiality is inert and passive: "we cannot even think of living matter as possible. (The concept of it involves a contradiction, since the essential character of matter is lifelessness, *inertia*.)"[12] But if there was an unbridgeable chasm between matter and life, how then to explain the peculiar *intimacy* of matter with life in the case of organisms? Kant solves the problem by invoking a special, nonmaterial "formative force" that is operative in organisms but not in other material forms such as crystals or machines. This *Bildungstrieb* animates matter and gives it a purpose, which is to move from an undifferentiated mass to an organized articulation of cooperating parts, the highest version of which is Man.

Approximately one hundred years later, Driesch will affirm Kant's claim that matter is in need of some supplement if it is to become active and organized. Driesch became famous for his experiments on cell division in the sea urchin, which demonstrated to him that life was qualitatively different from matter—inexplicable if conceived exclusively as a physicochemical mechanism. The goal of his laboratory work was not only to discover the *mechanics* of morphogenesis but also to learn what *animated* the process: "Why then occurs all that folding, and bending . . . ? There must be something that *drives them out*, so to say."[13] Driesch named that animating impetus not *Bildungstrieb* but *entelechy*, a term he borrowed loosely from Aristotle.[14]

In addition to *animating* matter, *entelechy* also *arranges* or artistically composes the bodies of organisms. In order to see how *entelechy* does this in a "nonmechanical" way, we need to take a closer look at morphogenesis, or the mode of becoming Driesch says is unique to organisms. "Morphogenesis" refers both to the process by which a blastocyst[15] moves from a less to a more differentiated form ("ontogenesis") and to the process by which a mature organism re-forms itself in response to damage or disease ("restitution"). While inorganic matter can of course *change*, only life can *morph*. A crystal formation, for example, can diminish or increase in mass, but it cannot become qualitatively more complex, and it cannot restore itself by replacing or repairing parts such that the "same" whole endures.

Neither can inorganic systems—mere matter—*learn from their experiences*, says Driesch, for that entails not only "the mere recollection of what has happened, but . . . also the ability to use *freely* in another field of occurring the elements of former happening for newly combined individualised specificities of the future which are *wholes*."[16] For Driesch, such free action, which is tailored specifically to the situation at hand, constitutes the "*directing*" action of *entelechy*.

In addition to animating, arranging, and directing wholes, the powers of *entelechy* also include *choosing* from among the various formative possibilities internal to the emergent organism. For Driesch, there are always more potential shapes and lines of development for a cell, organ, or an organism than become actual. In (what we would call) the stem cells of the sea urchin, for example, Driesch speaks of the "enormous number of possibilities of happening in the form of difference of 'potential'" in each cell. But, asks Driesch, if "something else *can* be formed than actually is formed, why then does there happen in each case just what happens and nothing else?"[17] Again he reasons that there *must* be some agent responsible for the singular specificity of the outcome, some agent guarding the entrance to actuality: *entelechy*.[18]

To be sure, Driesch insists, *entelechy* can only make use of "the possibilities of becoming" that are "physico-chemically prepared" and cannot, for example, make sulfuric acid if no hydrogen is present. But it can "*suspend* for as long a period as it wants any one of all the reactions which are *possible* with such compounds as are present, and which would happen without *entelechy*."[19] Here we see how Driesch strives to describe a life-matter relationship that is as close as it can possibly be while still retaining the qualitative distinction. Driesch stops just short of affirming a figure of vital materiality, a materiality that is itself the vital, animate, and agentic force.

What also intrigues me about *entelechy* is the way it is a figure of an *impersonal* form of agency. *Entelechy* is not the unique possession of each individual, not a unique soul, but rather an *immanent* vitality flowing across all living bodies. (This will make *entelechy*, unlike soul, resistant to the strongest or most punitive notions of personal moral responsibility.) *Entelechy* coordinates parts on behalf of a whole without following a rigid, pregiven plan; it answers events innovatively and perspicuously, deciding on the spot and in real time which of the many possible courses of development will in fact happen. But the agentic capacity of *entelechy* is not conceived as autonomy, as it is for Kant, for *entelechy* is constrained by the materiality it inhabits and by its own lack of extension in space. But despite this heteronomy, it has real efficacy: it animates, arranges, and directs the bodies of the living.

Driesch's invention of *entelechy* as a creative causality is propelled by his assumption that matter is stuff so passive and dull that it could not possibly have done the tricky work of organizing and maintaining morphing wholes. Sometimes this matter is infused with *entelechy* and becomes "life," and sometimes it isn't and coagulates into inorganic machines. Driesch thought he had to figure *entelechy* as immaterial because his notion of materiality was yoked to the notion of a mechanistic, deterministic machine. Back in 1926, Mikhail Bakhtin wrote an interesting rebuttal to Driesch, arguing that he failed to imagine the possibility of "a relentlessly self-constructing, developing machine [which] . . . builds itself not from pre-prepared parts, but from self-constructing ones." Such a machine, were it to be damaged, would indeed be capable of a self-repair prompted and guided by subtle physicochemical signals and thus would have no need for something like *entelechy*.[20]

Driesch's now more famous colleague Henri Bergson also offered a vitalism based upon the distinction between life and matter, though Bergson openly acknowledged that these categories freeze what are but "tendencies" of a cosmic flow.[21] Life names a certain propensity for "the utmost possible" activeness, a bias in favor of mobile and morphing forms. Matter names a certain leaning toward passivity, a tendency in favor of stable formations.

If *entelechy* has the power to "impel" organic self-repair and to "drive" physicochemical processes onward, Bergson's *élan vital* emphasizes this sparking, instigating quality: *élan vital* is "the tremendous internal push of life," "the primitive impetus of the whole," the "impulse which thrust life into the world, which made it divide into vegetables and animals, which shunted the animal on to suppleness of form, and which, at a certain moment, in the animal kingdom threatened with torpor, secured that, on some points at least, it should rouse itself up and move forward."[22]

Driesch's *entelechy* aimed to arrange and then maintain the organic whole. The specific means picked for this task vary because they are chosen in "individual correspondence" to the circumstances at hand. Bergson repeats Driesch's claim that the means deployed by vital force are contingent upon the specifics of their enactment, but this contingency is more radical for Bergson. The means available to *élan vital* do not preexist—not even as latent possibilities—the exact moment of their deployment. What is more, the aim of *élan vital* can not be *maintenance* of the whole because for Bergson any whole that would be maintained is not "given" but always in transition, on the way in or out. *Élan vital* aims, rather, to increase the *instability* of wholes, to "insert some *indetermination* into matter. Indeterminate, *i.e.* unforeseeable, are the forms it creates in the course of its evolution."[23] *Élan vital* causes any particular material form to "overflow its present."[24] Moreover,

> It would be futile to try to assign to life an end. . . . To speak of an end is to think of a pre-existing model which has only to be realized. It is to suppose, therefore, that all is given, and that the future can be read in the present. . . . Life, on the contrary . . . is undoubtedly creative, *i.e.* productive of effects in which it expands and transcends its own being.

> These effects were therefore not given in it in advance, and so it could not take them for ends.[25]

Conclusion

Bildungstrieb, *entelechy*, and *élan vital* are three figures of vital force conceived as supplements to a naturally passive or mechanical matter. *Entelechy* and *élan vital* are agentic in the sense of engaging in actions that are more than reflexes, instincts, or prefigured responses to stimuli. Though *entelechy* is less freely ranging in operation than *élan vital*, not quite the "ceaseless upspringing of something new, which has no sooner arisen to make the present than it has already fallen back into the past,"[26] both have the power to enliven the materiality they inhabit.

One can view these figures of vital force as attempts to acknowledge the presence, the reality, of an ontological vitality that does not quite get captured by the idea of matter as determinate, predictable, fixed, or fully calculable. I share the vitalists' concern to find a way to mark this force, though I am not a vitalist in the sense of one who affirms the existence of agents operating outside of a "physicochemical" sphere. I aspire instead, as I confessed at the start, to become a vital materialist—in the tradition of Lucretius, Nietzsche, Whitman, and Deleuze, insofar as each can be seen as advocates of an *immanent* or earthy vitalism. Driesch and Bergson share with me an ontological imaginary in which processes of becoming always vie with actual beings, but for them becoming includes a moment of transcendence in the form of entelechy or *élan*. They could not quite endorse a "materialism" adequate to the virtual complexity of life. But perhaps now we can.

Obstacles to this remain, of course. As soon as the vitality of materiality presents itself in public, as it did with Hurricane Katrina in 2005, or with the failure of electricity in the blackout of much of North America in 2003, or with the ability of a bird's song or a stone's texture to stop us dead in our tracks, it is immediately re-presented as a human effect, an effect of our actions, moods, ideologies, fantasies, power plays—as if humans really did have a monopoly on agency, as if agency was not always the effect of an assemblage of human and nonhuman actants.

It's true that there is no such thing as wholly *unmediated* access to the vital force, as the very notion of "second nature" notes. But it also seems to me to be a worthy, if quixotic, project to try to affirm—however badly and crudely—the vital force of material assemblages and to try to acknowledge it in our political analyses. Why? Because humans are *not* really masters of earth. Why? Because the figure of materiality as passive matter poses one of the many impediments to a more ecological, more sustainable way of living.

In 1848, Ralph Waldo Emerson wrote in his journal: "I have no longer any taste for these refinements you call life, but shall dive again into brute matter."[27] I too go diving there, and like Emerson, I find the matter not so brute at all. I am aware that the idea of a matter that is itself vital and lively is difficult to swallow. And not only because it threatens our identity as beings at the top of the hierarchy of nature; as beings who, while in nature, can also transcend it. My vital materialism also bears an uncanny resemblance to several discredited cultural formations, not only vitalism, but animism and the romantic quest for the thing-in-itself. The similarity resides at least in this: my aspirational identity too requires a particular kind of perceptual disposition, one awake to the force of things. I've learned a lot about how to induce in oneself this attentiveness from Emerson and Thoreau but also from the careful laboratory observations of Hans Driesch and from the Earth Day environmentalists like Schumacher and Carson whom I invoked at the start. Without proficiency in this careful kind of perceiving, earth will appear as if it consisted in human subjects who confront inanimate objects, in human minds that give form to passive matter.

Michel Foucault famously said that "There are times in life when the question of knowing if one can think differently than one thinks, and perceive differently than one sees, is absolutely necessary."[28] Our time—of global warming, mounting piles of garbage and toxic waste, accelerating rates of energy and other resource consumption—seems to me to warrant eccentric, experimental thinking, including the idea of a vital materiality.

NOTES

INTRODUCTION: POLITICS ON THE TERRAIN OF SECOND NATURE

Crina Archer, Laura Ephraim, and Lida Maxwell

1. A few important examples are Giorgio Agamben, *Homo Sacer: Sovereign Power and Bare Life*, trans. Daniel Heller-Roazen (Stanford, Calif.: Stanford University Press, 1998); Wendy Brown, *States of Injury: Power and Freedom in Late Modernity* (Princeton, N.J.: Princeton University Press, 1995); William Connolly, *Identity/Difference: Democratic Negotiations of Political Paradox* (Minneapolis: University of Minnesota Press, 1991), and *The Terms of Political Discourse*, 3rd ed. (Oxford: Blackwell, 1993); Bonnie Honig, *Political Theory and the Displacement of Politics* (Ithaca, N.Y.: Cornell University Press, 1993); Chantal Mouffe, *The Democratic Paradox* (New York: Verso, 2000); Richard Rorty, *Contingency, Irony, and Solidarity* (Cambridge: Cambridge University Press, 1989); and Linda Zerilli, *Signifying Woman: Culture and Chaos in Rousseau, Burke, and Mill* (Ithaca, N.Y.: Cornell University Press, 1993).

2. The growing consensus on the value of denaturalizing political categories even exerted a pull upon the renowned liberal philosopher John Rawls, who in *Political Liberalism* (New York: Columbia University Press, 1993) distanced himself from prior invocations of the autonomous self to invoke a conventional consensus instead as grounds for liberalism's legitimacy. His earlier *A Theory of Justice* (Cambridge, Mass.: Harvard University Press, 1971) was critiqued from many quarters for preserving an indefensible essentialized view of the autonomous self: to name a few influential examples, Susan Okin argued that the Rawlsian self was implicitly masculinist in *Justice, Gender, and the Family* (New York: Basic Books, 1991); Michael Sandel critiqued Rawls's ontological assumption of autonomy from a communitarian perspective in *Liberalism and the Limits of Justice* (Cambridge: Cambridge University Press, 1998); and Bonnie Honig critiqued Rawls's containment of the self's alterity (*Displacement*, esp. chap. 5, "Rawls and the Remainders of Politics," 126–161). For an even more thoroughgoing endeavor to set liberal political thought on an antifoundationalist ground, see Richard Flathman, *Willful Liberalism: Voluntarism and Individuality in Political Theory and Practice* (Ithaca, N.Y.: Cornell University Press, 1992).

3. Stephen White, *Sustaining Affirmation: The Strengths of Weak Ontology in Political Theory* (Princeton, N.J.: Princeton University Press, 2000), 4.

4. Diana Coole and Samantha Frost have referred to this "blurring" of nature and humanity in the introduction to their co-edited *New Materialisms: Ontology, Agency, and Politics* (Durham, N.C.: Duke University Press, 2010), 11.

5. See, e.g., Martha Nussbaum and Cass Sunstein, *Animal Rights: Current Debates and New Directions* (New York: Oxford University Press, 2004); and *Clones and Clones: Facts and Fantasies about Human Cloning* (New York: Norton, 1998).

6. See the various contributions to *Reinventing Nature? Responses to Postmodern Deconstruction*, ed. Michael E. Soulé and Gary Lease (Washington, D.C.: Island, 1995).

7. William Chaloupka, "Green Naturalism: The Politicization of Environmental Theory," *Political Theory* 31, no. 6 (2003): 871–882.

8. See William Cronon, ed., *Uncommon Ground: Rethinking the Human Place in Nature* (New York: Norton, 1995).

9. See, for example, Terry Hoy, *Toward a Naturalistic Political Theory: Aristotle, Hume, Dewey, Evolutionary Biology, and Deep Ecology* (Westport, Conn.: Praeger, 2000); Avner De-Shalit, *The Environment: Between Theory and Practice* (Oxford: Oxford University Press, 2000); and Andrew Dobson and Robyn Eckersley, eds., *Political Theory and the Ecological Challenge* (Cambridge: Cambridge University Press, 2006).

10. Chaloupka, "Green Naturalism," 872.

11. Richard Dagger, "Stopping Sprawl for the Good of All: The Case for Civic Environmentalism," *Journal of Social Philosophy* 34 (2003): 28–43, 29.

12. Ibid.; cf. Özgüç Orhan, "The Civic Environmental Approach," *The Good Society* 17 (2008): 38–43.

13. Terence Ball, "Democracy," in *Political Theory and the Ecological Challenge*, ed. Andrew Dobson and Robin Eckersley (Cambridge: Cambridge University Press, 2006), 144.

14. Ibid.

15. Ibid., 145.

16. John Dryzek, *Deliberative Democracy and Beyond* (Oxford: Oxford University Press, 2000), 146–147.

17. Bruno Latour, *The Politics of Nature: How to Bring the Sciences into Democracy*, trans. Catherine Porter (Cambridge, Mass.: Harvard University Press, 2004).

18. Robert Sessions succinctly sums up this aversion to human-centered value systems: "Deep ecologists trace most environmental destruction to the anthropocentric attitude that says (1) nonhuman nature has no value in itself,

(2) humans (and/or God, if theistic) create what value there is, and (3) humans have the right (some would say the obligation) to do as they please with and in the nonhuman world as long as they do not harm other humans' interests." Robert Sessions, "Deep Ecology vs. Ecofeminism: Healthy Differences or Incompatible Philosophies?," *Hypatia* 6, no. 1 (Spring 1991): 90–107, 91.

19. Bruno Latour and Steve Woolgar, *Laboratory Life: The Construction of Scientific Facts* (Princeton, N.J.: Princeton University Press, 1986); and Bruno Latour, *Science in Action: How to Follow Scientists and Engineers through Society* (Cambridge, Mass.: Harvard University Press, 1988).

20. Latour, *Politics of Nature*, 62–70.

21. Mark B. Brown, *Science in Democracy: Expertise, Institutions, and Representation* (Cambridge, Mass.: MIT Press, 2009).

22. In this vein, the tendency of deep ecologists to depict the nature it seeks to preserve and protect as essentially prediscursive and external to human cultural and political life has been challenged by some feminists as replicating the conceptual framework that long justified the oppression of women, to the extent that "both represent the nonrational or irrational radical other of 'man.'" Wendy Lee-Lampshire, "Anthropomorphism without Anthropocentrism: A Wittgensteinian Ecofeminist Alternative to Deep Ecology," *Ethics and the Environment* 1, no. 2 (Fall 1996): 91–102, 92. Lee-Lampshire's position in this article is resonant with the paradigm that we are here calling "second nature." She offers a Wittgensteinian approach to anthropomorphizing nonhuman objects as a way to "blur," rather than obliterate, the line between human/nonhuman, such that our efforts to think of nonhuman objects as "like us" work to unsettle our assumption that we know what "we" are "like."

23. On this point, see William Cronon's "The Trouble with Wilderness; or, Getting Back to the Wrong Nature," in *Uncommon Ground*, 69–90.

24. Ronald M. Green, *Babies by Design: The Ethics of Genetic Choice* (New Haven, Conn.: Yale University Press, 2007), 4, 10.

25. Ibid., 11, our emphasis. John Harris, another bioethicist, argues similarly that "reproductive cloning" should be understood as "part of reproductive liberty more generally" because it allows individuals—rather than the state—to control their reproductive lives. John Harris, *On Cloning* (New York: Routledge, 2004), 144.

26. Ray Kurzweil, *The Singularity Is Near: When Humans Transcend Biology* (New York: Penguin, 2005), 9.

27. Charles de Montesquieu, *The Persian Letters*, trans. C. J. Betts (New York: Penguin, 1993), 129–130.

28. Charles de Montesquieu, *The Spirit of the Laws*, trans. Anne Cohler, Basia Miller, and Harold Stone (Cambridge: Cambridge University Press, 1997), book 1, chap. 3.

29. Giambattista Vico, *On the Most Ancient Wisdom of the Italians Unearthed from the Origins of the Latin Language*, trans. L. M. Palmer (Ithaca, N.Y.: Cornell University Press, 1998), 93.

30. Vico's view of knowledge as enabled by human creativity is based upon his so-called *verum-factum* principle, that "the true is precisely what is made." Ibid., 46.

31. Giambattista Vico, *The New Science of Giambattista Vico: Unabridged Translation of the Third Edition (1744) with the addition of "Practic of the New Science,"* trans. Thomas Goddard Bergin and Max Harold Fisch (Ithaca, N.Y.: Cornell University Press, 1984), 377.

32. In Friedrich Nietzsche, *Untimely Meditations*, ed. Daniel Braezaele, trans. R. J. Hollingdale (Cambridge: Cambridge University Press, 1997), 57–124.

33. Ibid., 76.

34. Ibid., 76–77.

35. Many in political theory have come to Nietzsche's rethinking of nature through Heidegger's rethinking of technology. But this Heideggerian route into Nietzsche tends to mute the significance of "second nature" for political thinking today. Heidegger finds something similar to what Nietzsche calls "second nature" in the *techne* of antiquity—but not in the technologies of modernity. In the distant past, he thinks, human participation in "bringing forth" nature worked to reveal or occasion nature's life-sustaining forces. But today, Heidegger argues, our technologies only reveal our own, human purposes; by dominating nature, we deny it any significance except as a reserve for realizing our whims. Heidegger could be read as critiquing modern technology for *destroying* second nature, thereby making impossible the consonance between human and nonhuman forces that the ancients enjoyed. Read in this way, Heidegger sounds a valuable cautionary note about the undeniably destructive tendencies of modern technology while resisting nostalgia for the purity of first nature. In this sense, he stands to contribute to our second nature approach. However, insofar as Heidegger encourages a nostalgic attitude toward *second* nature, confining it to an unrecoverable past, he discourages explorations of modern technology that engage its capacity both to destroy and create second natures—the kind of explorations this volume contains and seeks to encourage. See Martin Heidegger's *The Question Concerning Technology and Other Essays*, trans. William Lovitt (New York: Harper & Row, 1977).

36. Judith Butler, *Gender Trouble: Feminism and the Subversion of Identity* (New York: Routledge, 1990); and *Bodies That Matter: On the Discursive Limits of "Sex"* (New York: Routledge, 1996).

37. Judith Butler, "Contingent Foundations: Feminism and the Question of Postmodernism," in *Feminists Theorize the Political*, ed. Judith Butler and Joan Scott (New York: Routledge, 1996), 3–21, 16.

38. Anne Fausto-Sterling, "The Five Sexes: Why Male and Female Are Not Enough," *The Sciences* (May/April 1993): 20–24.

39. Dorothy Roberts, "Race, Gender, and Genetic Technologies: A New Reproductive Dystopia?," *Signs* 34 (2009): 783–804.

40. For an excellent overview and analysis of the criticisms of Bt cotton in the local, national, and international spheres, see Vandana Shiva, Ashok Emani, and Afsar H. Jafri, "Globalisation and Threat to Seed Security: Case of Transgenic Cotton Trials in India," *Economic and Political Weekly* 34, no. 10/11 (March 1999): 601–613. As Shiva et al. emphasize, Monsanto holds an internationally recognized patent on Bt cotton seed, a legal situation that makes it a crime to store or share the seed or cross-pollinate it with other strains. Despite Monsanto's efforts to control use of its product, Bt cotton itself has proven difficult to contain, often contaminating neighboring fields and raising the specter of the eventual eradication of non-genetically-altered cotton in many areas of rural India. Additionally, there is increasing evidence in the scientific community that many plant diseases and crop pests are capable of rapid adaptation to genetically modified seeds, a situation that has led Monsanto to produce new (and patented) Bt cotton strains to keep up with adaptation.

41. This approach predominates in the much of the literature critical of the effects of global corporations in developing countries. See Shiva et al., "Globalisation and Threat"; also Robert L. Ostergard Jr., Matthew Tubin, and Jordan Altman, "Intellectual Property in the Biotechnology Industry," *Third World Quarterly* 22, no. 4 (August 2001): 643–656.

42. For a discussion of the innovative democratic features of the social movement that has grown in resistance to Monsanto's corporate products and policies in India, see Smitu Kothari, "Inclusive, Just, Plural, Dynamic: Building a 'Civil' Society in the Third World," *Development in Practice* 9, no. 3 (May 1999): 246–259.

43. Jill Didur encapsulates the limits of these two approaches succinctly, writing of genetically modified objects (GMOs) that "they are either desired *or* feared with little attention to some of the issues concerning the relationship between genetic information and its materiality and the context in which it is found. They are *either* a humanist dream as in Sloterdijk's view of genetic engineering *or*, ironically, a humanist nightmare, as in much of the activist discourse on GMOs." Jill Didur, "Re-Embodying Technoscientific Fantasies: Posthumanism, Genetically Modified Foods, and the Colonization of Life," *Cultural Critique* 53 (Winter 2003): 98–115, 111–112.

1. NECESSITY AND FORTUNE: MACHIAVELLI'S POLITICS OF NATURE
Yves Winter

1. Machiavelli's works are cited according to the following translations unless otherwise indicated. Niccolò Machiavelli, *The Prince*, trans. Harvey C. Mansfield, 2nd ed. (Chicago: University of Chicago Press, 1998), abbreviated as P; *Discourses on Livy*, trans. Harvey C. Mansfield and Nathan Tarcov (Chicago: University of Chicago Press, 1996), abbreviated as D; *Art of War*, trans. Christopher Lynch (Chicago: University of Chicago Press, 2003), abbreviated as AW; *Florentine Histories*, trans. Laura F. Banfield and Harvey C. Mansfield (Princeton, N.J.: Princeton University Press, 1988), for which I use FH; *Chief Works, and Others*, trans. Allan H. Gilbert, 3 vols. (Durham, N.C.: Duke University Press, 1989), abbreviated as CW. For Italian references or my own translations (where indicated), I have relied mostly on the following edition: Niccolò Machiavelli, *Tutte le opere storiche, politiche e letterarie*, ed. Alessandro Capata (Rome: Newton, 1998).

2. See, for instance, Carl Schmitt, *The Concept of the Political*, trans. George Schwab (Chicago: University of Chicago Press, 1996), 58–68; Peter E. Bondanella and Mark Musa, "An Essay on Machiavelli," in *The Portable Machiavelli* (New York: Penguin, 1979), 26–27.

3. Wendy Brown and Russell Price have insisted on the significance of *ambizione* in Machiavelli's thought. But whereas Brown makes a case for *ambizione* as a constitutive element of Machiavelli's anthropology, Price argues that Machiavelli ascribes it primarily to the *grandi*. Wendy Brown, "Renaissance Italy: Machiavelli," in *Feminist Interpretations of Niccolò Machiavelli*, ed. Maria J. Falco (University Park: Pennsylvania State University Press, 2004), 124–127; Russell Price, "*Ambizione* in Machiavelli's Thought," *History of Political Thought* 3, no. 3 (1982): 401.

4. Harvey C. Mansfield and Nathan Tarcov, "Introduction," in *Discourses on Livy*, by Niccolò Machiavelli (Chicago: University of Chicago Press, 1996), xl.

5. P D, 4; X, 44; D I.P, 5; I.29; 65; I.57, 114; I.58, 117; III.21, 263.

6. Whether Machiavelli indeed propounded an anthropology is controversial. Brown makes a strong case for an anthropological basis of Machiavelli's writing on the basis of the concept of *ambizione*. Lefort argues against the idea that Machiavelli's political theory derives from a notion of human nature and instead suggests that it derives from a logic of class conflict. Münkler emphasizes the hypothetical character of Machiavelli's pessimistic view of human nature. Brown, "Renaissance Italy: Machiavelli," 119–129; Claude Lefort, *Le travail de l'œuvre Machiavel* (Paris: Gallimard, 1986), 722; Herfried Münkler, *Machiavelli. Die Begründung des politischen*

Denkens der Neuzeit aus der Krise der Republik Florenz (Frankfurt a.M.: Fischer, 2004), 269.

7. P VII, 30; XVII, 68; XXIII, 95; XXVI, 100; D I.16, 44; III.22, 266; III.29, 277; III.39, 299.

8. D I.33, 72; I.37, 78; III.27, 275; P XIX, 76.

9. P III, 8; III, 14; D III.6, 234.

10. P XVIII, 70; XXV, 99; D I.40, 86; I.41, 90; I.42, 90.

11. The quotation is from the fragment "Del modo di trattare i popoli della Valdichiana ribellati," *Tutte le opere*, 381. Gilbert's *Chief Works and Others* unfortunately only translates an abridged version of this text.

12. Cicero, *De Oratore*, II, 9, 36; *De Inventione*, I, 50.

13. Max Horkheimer, "Anfänge der bürgerlichen Geschichtsphilosophie," in *Gesammelte Schriften* (Frankfurt a.M.: Fischer, 1987), 2:181–182.

14. Polybius, *Histories*, trans. W. R. Paton, Loeb Classical Library (Cambridge, Mass.: Harvard University Press, 1923), 3:289.

15. The extent to which Machiavelli's concept of history is modeled on the repetition of the same is disputed. Those who emphasize Machiavelli's modernity and his break with the culture of classical antiquity tend to highlight the theme of the new, the new prince, the new modes and orders Machiavelli claims to discover, the "untrodden" path, on which he sees himself (D I.P, 5). Thus Gramsci underscores Machiavelli's call for a new prince in the final chapter of *The Prince* while disregarding the problem of historical repetition entirely. Garin, meanwhile, has drawn attention to how closely Machiavelli's thought mirrors the cyclical model propounded by Polybius. Vatter attempts to merge the idea of historical repetition with the Gramscian emphasis on revolutionary time. Eugenio Garin, *Machiavel entre politique et histoire* (Paris: Éditions Allia, 2006), 26; Antonio Gramsci, "The Modern Prince. Essay on the Science of Politics in the Modern Age," in *The Modern Prince and Other Writings* (New York: International Publishers, 1957); Miguel E. Vatter, *Between Form and Event: Machiavelli's Theory of Political Freedom* (Dordrecht: Kluwer Academic Publishers, 2000), 133–215.

16. This, as Gramsci notes, is the meaning of the final chapter of *The Prince*. Gramsci, "The Modern Prince."

17. Münkler, *Machiavelli*, 247.

18. Letter to Vettori, August 26, 1513 (CW, 923).

19. "Tercets on Fortune," CW 747.

20. See Yves Winter, "Plebeian Politics: Machiavelli and the Ciompi Uprising," *Political Theory* 40, no. 6 (2012).

21. Machiavelli reinforces this claim in D I.3, 15, where he says that men work well only through necessity, and later, he even claims, "necessity produces *virtù*" (D II.12, 153). Mansfield points to this "crescendo," where

"necessity goes from being a support of virtue, to a condition of virtue, to a producer of virtue, and finally to a virtue itself." Harvey C. Mansfield, *Machiavelli's Virtue* (Chicago: University of Chicago Press, 1996), 15.

22. One of Machiavelli's favorite examples in this context is Venice, where necessity forced the inhabitants to "live in the waters" and to figure out "how they could live decently when they had no use of the land; and going in their ships throughout the world, they filled their city with a variety of merchandise." FH, I.29, 41.

23. Brown, "Renaissance Italy: Machiavelli," 142.

24. Pliny, *Natural History*, trans. H. Rackham, vol. 1, Loeb Classical Library (Cambridge, Mass.: Harvard University Press, 1938), VIII, 1–5.

25. "The Golden Ass," VIII (CW, 772). The theme of the human coming into the world naked and without protection is drawn from Cicero's *De natura deorum*, II, 47.

26. Jill Kraye, "Moral Philosophy," in *The Cambridge History of Renaissance Philosophy*, ed. Charles B. Schmitt, et al. (Cambridge: Cambridge University Press, 1988), 308.

27. Ibid., 310ff.

28. Aristotle, *Physics*, ed. Jonathan Barnes, trans. R. P. Hardie and R. K. Gaye, *The Complete Works: The Revised Oxford Translation* (Princeton, N.J.: Princeton University Press, 1984), II, 196b112, cf. also 197a191–198, b133–137.

29. Robert Orr, "The Time Motif in Machiavelli," *Political Studies* 17, no. 2 (1969): 153; Hanna F. Pitkin, *Fortune Is a Woman: Gender and Politics in the Thought of Niccolò Machiavelli* (Chicago: University of Chicago Press, 1999), 138–139.

30. Orr, "The Time Motif in Machiavelli," 153. See also Pitkin, *Fortune Is a Woman*, 138–139; Alan H. Nelson, "Mechanical Wheels of Fortune, 1100–1547," *Journal of the Warburg and Courtauld Institutes* 43 (1980): 227–233.

31. Brown, "Renaissance Italy: Machiavelli," 137.

32. "Tercets on Fortune," CW 745–749.

33. Leo Strauss, *Thoughts on Machiavelli* (Chicago: University of Chicago Press, 1958), 214.

34. Brown, "Renaissance Italy: Machiavelli," 128.

35. Maurice Merleau-Ponty, "Note sur Machiavel," in *Signes* (Paris: Gallimard, 1960), 276.

36. The theme of the changing times and the need for actors to change with these times is also present in many of Machiavelli's letters: "Thus because times and affairs in general and individually change often, and men do not change their imaginings and their procedures, it happens that a man

at one time has good fortune and at another time bad." Letter to Piero Soderini, January 1512 (CW, 897).

37. Vatter goes as far as to argue that *fortuna* "provides the conceptual schema for modern revolutionary action. . . . Instead of making action correspond to the times, action is assigned the task of changing the times." Vatter, *Between Form and Event*, 134.

38. Pitkin, *Fortune Is a Woman*, 169.

39. Titus Livy, *History of Rome*, trans. B. O. Foster et al., Loeb Classical Library (Cambridge, Mass.: Harvard University Press, 1919–1959), 2:30.

40. Victoria Kahn, *Machiavellian Rhetoric: From the Counter-Revolution to Milton* (Princeton, N.J.: Princeton University Press, 1994), 57. The juxtaposition of a "realm of representation" to a "realm of necessity" is somewhat misleading, for representation and necessity, as I will show below, cannot be pried apart.

41. See Sheldon Wolin, *Politics and Vision*, expanded ed. (Princeton, N.J.: Princeton University Press, 2004), 190–191.

42. Merleau-Ponty, "Note sur Machiavel," 273.

43. Pitkin, *Fortune Is a Woman*, 144.

44. Ibid., 151.

45. Orr, "The Time Motif in Machiavelli," 155–157.

46. Martin Heidegger, "The Question Concerning Technology," in *Basic Writings*, ed. David Farrell Krell (New York: HarperCollins, 1993).

47. This objectification of nature finds its aesthetic counterpart in a new representation of landscape and space that emerges in the Italian Renaissance and that can be diagnosed in fourteenth-century writers like Petrarca and in painters like Giotto and that spreads throughout Europe in the fifteenth century. Karlheinz Stierle, "Die Entdeckung der Landschaft in Literatur und Malerei der italienischen Renaissance," in *Vom Wandel des neuzeitlichen Naturbegriffes*, ed. Heinz-Dieter Weber (Konstanz: Universitätsverlag Konstanz, 1989), 40.

2. BURNING THE DEAD AND THE WAYS OF NATURE

Thomas Laqueur

1. Robert Hertz, "A Contribution to the Study of the Collective Representation of Death," in *Death and the Right Hand*, trans. Rodney Needham and Claudia Needham (1907; repr. Aberdeen: Cohen and West, 1960), 36–37.

2. See István Rév, "The Necronym," in *Retroactive Justice: Prehistory of Post-Communism* (Stanford, Calif.: Stanford University Press, 2005), 52–93.

3. Herodotus, *The History*, trans. David Grene (Chicago: University of Chicago Press, 1987), 228 (3.38).

4. George M. A. Wortherspoon, *Cremation, Ancient and Modern: The History and Utility of Fire-Funeral* (London: Sunday Lecture Society, 1886), 12, *passim.*

5. This is the definition given by Edmund Parkes, MD, FRS, in his widely circulated and much reprinted *Manual of Practical Hygiene: Prepared Especially for the Use of Medical Service on the Army* (London: John Churchill and Sons, 1864). There were editions of this book in 1866, 1869, and 1873; these would have been the ones quoted approvingly by the early advocates of cremation. Parkes makes the case that the *Report of the Royal Commission* of 1857 that investigated the public health debacle of the Crimean War changed the role of the army doctor and, by implication, of doctors generally. They were no longer to be concerned just with the care of the sick but also with preserving the health of the living.

6. Sir Henry Thompson, *Modern Cremation: Its History and Practice to the Present Date*, 4th ed. (Waterloo Place: Smith, Elder, 1901).

7. Ibid., vii. My emphasis.

8. This is the point of the excellent revealing collection of essays covering almost three millennia by Lorraine Daston and Fernando Vidal, eds., *The Moral Authority of Nature* (Chicago: University of Chicago Press, 2004).

9. Thompson, *Modern Cremation.*

10. Ibid., 21. Thompson and others got these figures for gas from the calculations of Sir Lionel Playfair, who when he first produced them had no interest in cremation but was aligned then with burial reformers. Hon. and Rev. W. H. Lyttelton, *Scripture Revelation of the Life of Man after Death* (London: Dolby, Isbisher, 1875), xxii–xxiii.

11. William Eassie, *Healthy Homes: A Handbook to the History, Defects, and Remedies of Drainage, Ventilation, Warming, and Kindred Subjects* (London: Simpkins, Marshall and Co., 1872), vii. *Sanitary Arrangements for Use of Officers of Health, Architects, Builders, and Householders* (London: Smith Elder, 1874), 2, 12; for the mundane but important details of the project, see 85–86 on the evils of cesspits or 60 for the perfect arrangement of the seat and trap of the water closet.

12. William Eassie, *Cremation of the Dead: Its History and Bearings upon Public Health* (London: Smith, Elder & Company, 1875).

13. Parkes, *Manual*, 99.

14. Ibid., 154.

15. Ibid., 394.

16. Ibid., 395.

17. Edward J. Bermingham, *The Disposal of the Dead: A Plea for Cremation* (New York: Bermingham and Co., 1881), 75, 48; William Holden, *Cremation*

versus Burial: An Appeal to Reason against Prejudice (Hull and York: A. Brown and Son, 1891), 20–21.

18. Zachary Cope, *The Versatile Victorian: Being a Life of Sir Henry Thompson, 1820–1904* (London: Harvey and Blythe, 1951), 124.

19. Thompson's letter on the subject of dust collection is in the *Times of London* (January 1, 1904) and is reprinted in ibid., 125. *The Academy*, 238.

20. Cope, *The Versatile Victorian.*

21. J. Cuthbert Welch, *Cremation the Best Mode of Sepulture, Read Before the Reading Literary and Scientific Society, April 9th, 1889* (Reading: Turner Brothers, Steam Printers, 1889), 11.

22. Catherine Gallagher, *The Body Economic: Life, Death, and Sensation in Political Economy and the Victorian Novel* (Princeton, N.J.: Princeton University Press, 2006).

23. L. S. Mercier, *Corps Législative*, Conseil des Cinq-Cents. *Sur les sépulcres privées* (Paris: 18 Frimaire, Year V-1796). Quoted in Michel Ragon, *The Space of Death: A Study of Funerary Architecture, Decoration, and Urbanism*, trans. A. Sheridan (Charlottesville: University Press of Virginia, 1983), 283–284.

24. Eassie, *Cremation of the Dead*, 2.

25. Teresa Lewis, *Cremation* (London: Thomas Scott, n.d. [c. 1880]), 6, 10.

26. Abraham Emrys-Jones, *Disposal of the Dead: Present System of Burial—Earth to Earth—Objections to and Advantages of Cremation*, Health Lectures, series 11, no. 5 (Manchester and Salford Sanitary Association, 1888), 77.

27. Rev. H. R. Haweis, *Ashes to Ashes: A Cremation Prelude* (London: Daldy, Isbister, & Co., 1875), 105; see 258–260 for the full mathematical justification of these bizarre calculations.

28. Giambattista Vico, *The New Science of Giambattista Vico: Unabridged Translation of the Third Edition (1744) with the Addition of "Practic of the New Science,"* trans. Thomas Goddard Bergin and Max Harold Fisch (Ithaca, N.Y.: Cornell University Press, 1984).

29. Nicole Loraux, *Born of the Earth: Myth and Politics in Athens*, trans. Selina Stewart (Ithaca, N.Y.: Cornell University Press, 2000).

30. Garry Wills, *Lincoln at Gettysburg: The Words That Remade America* (New York: Touchstone, 1992).

3. CORPSES FOR KILOWATTS? MOURNING, JUSTICE, BURIAL, AND THE ENDS OF HUMANISM

Bonnie Honig

1. This essay draws on parts of an earlier one called "The Other Is Dead" (*Triquarterly Review*). That essay began my work on Sophocles' *Anti-*

gone, which five years later became a book, *Antigone, Interrupted* (Cambridge: Cambridge University Press, 2013). The essay that appears here was completely rewritten after the book's completion and radically revises the earlier article's argument, while positioning it in relation to some recently published work on Dickinson. This new paper bears the traces of a conversation with Viv Soni, whom I thank. For comments on the paper, I am indebted to Laura Ephraim, Davide Panagia, and especially Lida Maxwell.

2. "The facility plans to sell the electricity to local power companies. Some might find this concept creepy. Others might be pleased to learn that the process 'makes cremation much greener by utilizing its by-products,' in the words of cremation engineer Steve Looker, owner and chief executive officer of the Florida-based company B&L Cremation Systems, which is unaffiliated with the Durham enterprise" (December 13, 2011). http://www.lifeslittlemysteries.com/corpses-crematorium-electricity-2214/.

3. For a less sovereigntist version of green burial, see Sarah Taylor's *Eternally Green: American Religion and the Ecology of Death* (Berkeley: University of California Press, forthcoming).

4. On this, see Anne-Lise François: "The rush to lay claim and assign an owner to uncounted time [is] typical of the anxiety over waste in a secular age. The call on individuals to establish rather than merely assume their claims to truth and power can render limitless their sense of responsibility for missed potential." *Open Secrets: The Literature of Uncounted Experience* (Stanford, Calif.: Stanford University Press, 2007), 213.

5. Ibid., 171.

6. Similarly admiring of nonhappening (though from decidedly different perspectives) are the several readings of Melville's "Bartleby" issued in recent years by Deleuze, Agamben, and Rancière.

7. The various forms of chastened and pluralized agency noted here need not be seen as alternatives. Deleuze's vitalism, for example, partners well with his admiration for Bartleby.

8. Richard Flathman, *Willful Liberalism: Voluntarism and Individuality in Political Theory and Practice* (Ithaca, N.Y.: Cornell University Press, 1992).

9. On Butler's shift from reiterating to sovereignty to lamenting it, see Ackerman and Honig, "Un-Chosen: Judith Butler's Jewish Modernity" (forthcoming); and Honig, "Feminist Theory and the Turn to Antigone," in *Antigone, Interrupted.*

10. Another example is one I explore elsewhere: the embrace by the food politics group, Slow Food, of globalization on behalf of more ecological food production practices. See my *Emergency Politics* (Princeton, N.J.: Princeton University Press, 2009). On the importance of service and exposure to politics, see Bonnie Honig, "The Politics of Ethos. Stephen White: *The Ethos of*

a Late-Modern Citizen," *European Journal of Political Theory* 10, no. 3 (2011): 422–429.

11. Somehow the postmortem perspective impresses on us something we might also see in life were our vision sharper: the disappearance of non-working life (and death!) or rather its alteration into something else. Leisure, now often called "down time," is referred to these days as an opportunity to "recharge our batteries." This now ubiquitous phrase both robotizes the human and naturalizes it, identifying human agency with battery energy and collapsing the human into the force of labor that Hannah Arendt saw as marking the victory of nature over freedom. In the world of labor, productivity takes the place of the human-defining artifice of inaugural promising that, from an economic perspective, makes no sense, though in this, precisely, inheres its capacity to make sense of the common world, as Arendt argued in *The Human Condition* (Chicago: University of Chicago Press, 1958). As Davide Panagia reminds me, another iteration of this problem is at the center of *The Matrix*, where machines use human bodies to generate the energy needed to replace that of the mortal sun.

12. On the alternative symbolic possibly to be glimpsed by encounter with the Real, see James R. Martel, *Textual Conspiracies* (Ann Arbor: University of Michigan Press, 2011, chap. 4, esp. 143–149).

13. I discuss the example of AIDS activism and the politics of burial at greater length in *Antigone, Interrupted.*

14. Jean Comaroff, "Beyond Bare Life: AIDS, Biopolitics, and the Neoliberal Order," *Public Culture* 19, no. 1 (2007): 197–219.

15. Anne-Lise François, *Open Secrets*, 157.

16. *Sophie's Choice*, dir. Alan Pakula (1982). Sophocles, *The Three Theban Plays: Antigone, Oedipus the King, and Oedipus at Colonus* (New York: Viking, 1982).

17. Jacques Derrida, *The Work of Mourning*, ed. Pascale-Anne Brault and Michael Naas (Chicago: University of Chicago Press, 2001).

18. Sometimes, the dead body serves as a prod to justice, albeit not as corpus delecti. This is the case when justice is not sought for the dead by way of the dead, as when, in Sophocles' *Antigone*, Creon decrees that Polynices' body will be left unburied as a lesson to all about the fate of traitors to the polis.

19. On mourning practice as key to the Iranian Revolution, see my "What Foucault Saw at the Revolution," *Political Theory* 36, no. 2 (April 2008): 301–312. On the ethical and political aspects of Cindy Sheehan's mourning practice and Argentina's mothers of the Plaza, see my "Antigone's Two Laws," *New Literary History* 41, no. 1 (2010): 1–33.

20. The film *The Three Burials of Melquiades Estrada* explores the questions posed here about the instrumentality and dignity of the dead and of

service to them. The film does so in order also to explore the full development of male-to-male devotion in the context of its prohibition, however, enabling the romance only postmortem. That said, the scenes where Tommy Lee Jones cares for and preserves the corpse of his beloved friend are moving and insightful explorations of the practice of after-death care. These are also bound up with vengeance and justice in a way that instructively troubles the distinction Laqueur tries to make.

21. Upon hearing that Nathan has threatened to kill her and Stingo, Sophie says, "I don't care that I'll die. I'm afraid that he'll die without me" (as her children did).

22. For Anne-Lise François, though, Dickinson's work is not per se devoted to mourning nor grief.

23. Literature is François's example of aneconomic worth, exemplified, once again, by Dickinson, whom François describes as writing "without commitment to any one set of readerly expectations, only confronting readers with a negation as unequivocal and weightless as an earlier affirmation" (*Open Secrets*, 157).

24. Ibid., 151.

25. Ibid., 157.

26. It is also the case that her ideal is not only modest (chastened, undefined, and unoccasioned); it is surely also grandiose (self-chastening, refusing, demurring).

27. But connections are established also between Stingo and Wolfe, one of which is Stingo's production of a *lot* of pages. Notably, an anonymous reviewer in *Scribner's* compared Wolfe to Walt Whitman.

28. One might think that Nathan's personal quest to bring the Nazis to justice is a symptom of his madness; he is not a lawyer, not a politician, not a vigilante. He is not in any position to really do this work. But one could just as well infer that the film's point is that he who pursues justice for the Holocaust—or chooses to do so—must be mad or will surely be driven mad by the impossible quest.

29. On the conjoining of wedding and burial rites in Ancient Greece, see Olga Taxidou, *Tragedy, Modernity, and Mourning* (Edinburgh: University of Edinburgh, 2004); and Rush Rehm, *Marriage to Death* (Princeton, N.J.: Princeton University Press, 1994).

30. We might see his elegy as a speech *act* of course, but it does not rise to the level of labor. It is, in any case, undecidable. From François's perspective, it is too much; from mine, here—too little.

31. In the trio of terms "butchered," "betrayed," and "martyred," we may hear Aristotle's three kinds of friendship, each with its own (an)economy, each postulating, we might say extending Aristotle, its own unique kind of

death: use (butchery), pleasure (betrayal), and virtue (martyrdom). What is key here is that Stingo's list does not distinguish these traits, as if some of the dead are one sort and others another. Instead, the implication is that the categories are contaminated by one another, such that some of the dead are undecidably martyred, betrayed, and butchered. On the implications of Aristotle's three kinds of friendship for politics and mourning, see Derrida, *The Politics of Friendship*. In a way, my alternative to François, calling for the recombination of the three kinds of mourning, is similar to Derrida's treatment of Aristotle here. On Derrida on this topic and on the fecundity of this particular site of undecidability for political theory, see chapter 3 of my *Democracy and the Foreigner* (Princeton, N.J.: Princeton University Press, 2001).

32. Bertram Wyatt-Brown, "William Styron's *Sophie's Choice:* Poland, the South, and the Tragedy of Suicide," *Southern Literary Journal* 34, no. 1 (2001): 56–67.

33. On the fantastic nature of such futures and their undesirable political impact, see James Martel, *Textual Conspiracies*.

34. Preferring Melville to Whitman because of the latter's nationalism, see Franny Nudleman's *John Brown's Body: Slavery, Violence, and the Culture of War* (Chapel Hill: University of North Carolina Press, 2004).

35. In "Crossing Brooklyn Ferry," Whitman says, "Just as you are refreshed by the gladness of the river and the bright flow, I was refreshed." Walt Whitman, *Leaves of Grass*, ed. Jerome Loving (Oxford: Oxford University Press, 1990).

36. As I read it in *Antigone, Interrupted*, the play stages in their variety many kinds of death and death service. Polynices' is only one of several deaths that call for some sort of contested ritual response. Thus the focus is on the conflict between different mourning practices in the emerging democratic polis and also on the production of the play's timelessness over time.

37. Is Creon not impotent? His first act of would-be power is to issue an edict that though announced is at first not heard by everyone—Ismene is not aware of it until Antigone tells her—is then grumbled about by the people, and is finally disobeyed, not once but twice. Antigone, who melancholically mourns her irreplaceable brother but calls children replaceable while knowing she will never have any of her own, mirrors Sophie but also inverts her.

38. On the significance of Antigone's call for vengeance, see my *Antigone, Interrupted*.

39. *Sophie's Choice* takes the Civil War as its context as well. The question of the (im)possibility of closure after the Holocaust is in a way posed by contrast with the same question, which was once posed about the U.S. Civil War. This is one subtle implication, it seems to me, of the film's references to Dickinson and Whitman.

40. This is a pollution not subject to Durham-style recycling, we might think. But in the end, Oedipus is put to use when his corpse, buried but unlocated outside Athens, founds a hero cult that protects the city.

41. Sophocles, *Antigone*, 35.

42. Ibid., 174.

43. Ibid., 225–226.

44. Ibid., 233; cf. 325.

45. See G. W. F. Hegel, *The Phenomenology of Spirit*, trans. A. V. Miller (Oxford: Oxford University Press, 1979); also Bernard Williams, *Shame and Necessity* (Berkeley: University of California Press, 1994).

46. Dishonoring the dead is prohibited by conventional rules of warfare, themselves increasingly attenuated in this period and immediately after. Since violations of these rules were by this time not uncommon and were soon to become even more common, during the Peloponnesian Wars, it may have been Sophocles' intent to call attention to this issue as well. On the increasing violation of rules of war after the Peloponnesian Wars and the ensuing controversies, see Jill Frank, "Wages of War: Judgment in Plato's *Republic*," *Political Theory* 4, no. 35 (August 2007): 443–467.

47. Indeed, as Jill Frank points out in a comment on Nonet's *Antigone*, Tiresias will later say that Creon was a good ruler (994). Frank nicely observes that this suggests Ismene was not cowardly but astute when, early in the play, she chose to wait rather than to challenge Creon's edict. At the beginning of the play, it is not yet clear that Creon's edict is unjust nor that he is a tyrant. He isn't, yet. See Frank, "The *Antigone's* Law," *Law, Culture, and the Humanities* 2, no. 3 (October 2006): 336–340.

48. Michelle Gellrich, *Tragedy and Theory* (Princeton, N.J.: Princeton University Press, 1988).

49. The dead Polynices is left to die like an animal because he is a traitor, but he is not left outside the city, like a true traitor; he is rather inside its bounds. Simon Goldhill points out that "the tensions of the play are emphasized by having Polynices' body left on the land of the city." *Reading Greek Tragedy* (London: Cambridge University Press, 1986), 89 n. 18.

50. See Steven Johnston's *The Truth about Patriotism* (Durham, N.C.: Duke University Press, 2008).

51. Although not all cultures seek to interrupt nature's processes in the same way. In Judaism and Islam, embalming is forbidden because it slows the processes of decomposition. For others, embalming is valued for that very reason, as in ancient Egypt and Homeric Greece. Notably, Thebes, the mythic Greek city, had been the capital of Egypt thousands of years earlier, marking a point of contact in mythic and theatrical terms for a historical supposition (ventured as well by Vernant): that the Greeks may well have been

familiar with Egyptian practices of embalming. The reference to oils and unguents as ingredients of physical restoration in Homer certainly suggests it.

52. Jean-Pierre Vernant, *Mortals and Immortals: Collected Essays*, ed. Froma I. Zeitlin (Princeton, N.J.: Princeton University Press, 1991), 74; Achilles' disfigurement of Hektor is discussed on p. 70 (citing *Iliad*, 22, 401–403). The idea that decomposition begins in life (with aging) and is a source of anxiety (as it obviously is in our culture and as it surely was in Homeric Greece, a fact to which Priam, Hektor's father, is all too alert) suggests that, in concerns about the decomposition of the dead, there is a certain displacement.

53. Emphasis added. Ken Picard, "Dead Wrong: Are Vermonters Getting Stiffed on the Facts about Home Funerals?" in *Seven Days* (January 31, 2007), http://www.sevendaysvt.com/features/2007/dead-wrong.html. Beth Knox says, "It's amazing the amnesia we have as a society. . . . In every room I lecture in there's someone who says, 'We cared for my great aunt that way,' or whatever. In two generations, this information has been lost to us."

54. *Crossings* also describes itself as "A home funeral and green burial resource center" (Crossings.net). See also Rachel S. Cox, "A Movement to Bring Grief Back Home: Many Bereaved Opting to Bypass Funeral Industry," *Washington Post* (June 5, 2005); Vince Darcangelo, "Taking Care of Our Own: Beth Knox Educates the Public on Home Death-Care Options," *Boulder Weekly*, http://archive.boulderweekly.com/110603/buzzlead.html. See also *Caring for the Dead: Your Final Act of Love* (Hinesburg, Vt.: Upper Access Books, 1987), a state-by-state compendium of laws governing the handling of the dead without an undertaker, authored by Lisa Carlson, founder of the Funeral Ethics Organization, Hinesburg, Vt. On the power of the undertakers' lobby and state interests in the matter, see Judith Chevalier and Fiona M. Scott Morton, "State Casket Sales and Restrictions: A Pointless Undertaking?" NBER Working Paper no. W12012 (February 2006), http://ssrn.com/abstract=881246.

55. Whitman, *Leaves of Grass.*

56. On this point, I am indebted to George Kateb.

57. On this, see Judith Shklar's discussion of work and its dignity in *American Citizenship: The Quest for Inclusion* (Cambridge, Mass.: Harvard University Press, 1991).

58. The notion of corpus delecti originates, ironically, he says, in the Nazis' exposure of Russian crimes at Katyn, and which refers to the law and science whereby the body of the crime, the corpus delecti, the dead body, "can be made to speak the truth by providing evidence about how it came to die." See Thomas Laqueur, "The Dead Body and Human Rights," in *The Body*, eds. Sean Sweeney and Ian Hodder (Cambridge: Cambridge University Press, 2002).

59. Ibid., 92.

60. For more on this and related topics, see Nancy Wood, *Vectors of Memory: Legacies of Trauma in Postwar Europe* (Oxford: Berg Publishers, 1999) and Katherine Verdery, *The Political Lives of Dead Bodies: Reburial and Post-socialist Change* (New York: Columbia University Press, 1999).

61. Anne-Lise François, *Open Secrets*, 171.

4. THE "UNNATURAL GROWTH OF THE NATURAL": RECONSIDERING NATURE AND ARTIFICE IN THE CONTEXT OF BIOTECHNOLOGY

Ashley Biser

1. Leon Kass, "The Wisdom of Repugnance," in *The Ethics of Human Cloning*, by Leon Kass and James Wilson (Washington, D.C.: AEI Press, 1998), 19.

2. Francis Fukuyama, *Our Posthuman Future: Consequences of the Biotechnology Revolution* (New York: Farrar, Straus and Giroux, 2002), 6. Indeed, it is the continuing development of science and technology that have forced Fukuyama to rethink the "end of history" thesis for which he is best known. In Fukuyama's words: "As the more perceptive critics of the concept of the 'end of history' have pointed out, there can be no end of history without an end of modern natural science and technology" (15).

3. A note on the choice of thinkers with whom I engage: Habermas and Fukuyama are two of the few political theorists who have specifically addressed questions surrounding the ethics of genetic technologies. Kass is a bioethicist by trade—a particularly prominent one, who chaired George W. Bush's Council on Bioethics. His work is frequently cited, and Fukuyama makes explicit reference to his thinking. For my purposes, each thinker functions as a relatively mainstream example of their respective spheres of influence: professional bioethics and policy making (Kass), political science writ large (Fukuyama), and political theory (Habermas).

4. Jürgen Habermas, *The Future of Human Nature*, trans. William Rehg, Max Pensky, and Hella Beister (Cambridge: Polity Press, 2003), 23.

5. Kass, "The Wisdom of Repugnance," 8.

6. Fukuyama, *Our Posthuman Future*, 7.

7. Fukuyama's overarching goals in *Our Posthuman Future* are threefold. First, he wishes to introduce his readers to recent research in neuroscience, pharmacology, and genetics, to suggest that this research (and the technologies it enables) carries with it disturbing potentialities. Second, he offers a philosophic argument in favor of a stable conception of human nature that is informed by recent biological research. However, he warns his readers that "those not inclined to more theoretical discussions of politics may choose to

skip over some of the chapters here" (16). The final, and in his opinion more important, section of the book entails a discussion of exactly how biotechnology ought to be (and is) regulated. In this section, he admonishes his readers to "act!" with regard to biotechnology and prevent "a posthuman future and the potential moral chasm that such a future opens before us" (17).

8. See, for example, Sarah Franklin and Celia Roberts, *Born and Made: An Ethnography of Preimplantation Genetic Diagnosis* (Princeton, N.J.: Princeton University Press, 2006). This dualism is also sometimes cast in terms of the distinction between chance and choice. See Alan Buchanan et al., *From Chance to Choice: Genetics and Justice* (New York: Cambridge University Press, 2000); Michael Sandel, "The Case Against Perfection," *Atlantic Monthly* (April 2004): 50–62. In each case, thinking proceeds by distinguishing a domain over which we have little control from one that includes the product of human action. Kass, Fukuyama, and Habermas, the thinkers with whom this essay is concerned, not only represent the best-known exemplars of this trend (see note 3) but also articulate the issue most clearly.

9. Reprogenetics refers to an emerging field that combines assisted reproductive and genetic technologies.

10. The question of whether nature has ever been something separate from ourselves is a topic far too complex for me to address here (and depends entirely on the standpoint from which it is taken up). Whether or not the distinction between nature and artifice has ever corresponded to empirical reality is one that recent works such as Bruno Latour's *Politics of Nature* have subjected to critical inquiry. For a more thorough discussion of the political implications of this constructed distinction, see Bruno Latour, *Politics of Nature* (Cambridge, Mass.: Harvard University Press, 2004); Donna Haraway, *Modest Witness@Second Millennium. FemaleMan© Meets OncoMouse™: Feminism and Technoscience* (New York: Routledge, 1997). For my purposes, I am less interested in the empirical basis of the distinction than in its effects on our thinking. I only ask what the blurring of this distinction does to our ability to think ethically in the manner suggested by Arendt.

11. Hannah Arendt, "On Hannah Arendt," in *Hannah Arendt: The Recovery of the Public World*, ed. Melvyn Hill (New York: St Martin's Press, 1979), 336. Arendt uses the banister metaphor to help articulate how we think in a context in which the "safe guiding lines" of tradition are no longer meaningful.

12. Habermas, *The Future of Human Nature*, 23.

13. Ibid., vii.

14. Kass, "The Wisdom of Repugnance," 12. In the terminology of "begetting," Kass belies his Christian roots. Because Kass comes out of a far more conservative (and far less secular) background than the other thinkers

mentioned here, his worries are of a somewhat different ilk. In addition to the concern over instrumentalization and the distinction between the begotten and the made, he worries about the breakdown in traditional marriage as instigated by feminists and gay rights advocates (7). His worries about cloning and artificial insemination are based at least in part on the fact that they are forms of asexual reproduction—which enable the "manufacture" of children without the experience of the deep "profundity of sex" between a man and a woman (24).

15. He laments that bioethicists must now "risk charges of giving offense to those adults who are living in 'new family forms' or to those children who, even without the benefit of assisted reproduction, have acquired either three or four parents or one or none at all." Ibid., 26, 7.

16. When natural and conventional practices conflict, the latter become "unnatural" and should inspire gut feelings of "repugnance" (ibid., 19). This attempt at hierarchical ordering is, according to theorists like Donna Haraway, intrinsic to the nature/artifice (or what she terms nature/culture) distinction. Donna Haraway, "A Manifesto for Cyborgs: Science, Technology, and Socialist Feminism in the 1980s," *Socialist Review* 80 (1985): 65–108, 167. For her, the dismantling of these oppositions is thus part of an emancipatory project.

17. Fukuyama, *Our Posthuman Future*, 13.

18. Ibid., 15. For instance, Fukuyama suggests that a better understanding of human nature might help explain the persistence of "capitalist liberal democratic institutions" because it would presumably show that the assumptions embedded in these institutions conform more closely to human nature than do alternative attempts at social organization (106). He connects biotechnology to socialism and other forms of "engineering" that represent "techniques for pounding the square peg of human nature into the round hole of social planning" (15).

19. Ibid., 147.

20. I should note that my claims regarding Habermas are restricted to his work in *The Future of Human Nature*. In placing the text of such a distinguished political theorist alongside those who certainly do not share either his political views or theoretical sophistication, I intend only to underscore the ubiquity of the nature/artifice dualism in discussions of reprogenetics.

21. Habermas, *The Future of Human Nature*, 87. His primary concern about genetic technologies is that he believes that the knowledge of oneself as externally designed—that is, the knowledge of oneself as the product of parents' choices about the characteristics they want their child to display—will interfere with the self-understandings of both the resulting child and his/her contemporaries.

22. Ibid., 72, 59.

23. Ibid., 41. I should note that Habermas's concerns about genetic technologies are exacerbated by the context in which he writes, namely a German state that is (rightly) extremely cautious about any research that calls to mind the eugenic practices of the National Socialists. As he recognizes, debates over genetic technologies have a far different tone in Europe than in the United States—despite this country's own experience with eugenic theories and practices (75).

24. Indeed, Habermas argues for a very different kind of "moralizing human nature" than that engaged in by thinkers like Kass and Fukuyama (ibid., 24). Unlike more conservative thinkers, Habermas calls for regulation in the interest of expanding the range of opportunities available to future children—not curtailing them.

25. Ibid., 40.

26. Ibid., 23. The extent to which Habermas's, or Fukuyama's and Kass's, understanding of genetic technologies rests on a false sense of genetic determinism—that is, the idea that we are controlled by our genes—is a topic for another day. I should, however, note that he makes extensive use of the terminology of genetic "programming"—a concept that has been greatly undermined by more recent research into gene interactions and of which thinkers like Evelyn Fox Keller are extremely critical. Evelyn Fox Keller, *The Century of the Gene* (Cambridge, Mass.: Harvard University Press, 2000).

27. Habermas, *The Future of Human Nature*, 25.

28. Ibid., 125.

29. Ibid., 54, 127.

30. Ibid., 67.

31. I should be clear that I am not suggesting we should simply accept reprogenetic technologies in an uncritical manner. All three thinkers suggest that the bioethics profession has become extremely adept at providing this kind of retrospective justification for controversial technologies. Serving on commissions and advisory boards, "the ethicists have for the most part been content, after some 'values clarification' and wringing of hands, to pronounce their blessings upon the inevitable" (Kass, "The Wisdom of Repugnance," 10). In an insightful comment, Ulrich Beck suggests that technoscience thus proceeds via a "policy of the *fait accompli.*" Ulrich Beck, *Risk Society: Towards a New Modernity*, trans. Mark Ritter (Newbury Park, Calif.: Sage, 1992), 207. For this reason we should be wary of the assertion that a technology no longer requires critical engagement simply because it has become commonplace. What I am suggesting here, however, is that this kind of defensive posture is unproductive and that there are more useful ways to approach reprogenetics.

32. This isn't simply a matter of scientific research outpacing critique. Instead, I wish to suggest that the particular dualism upon which Kass, Fukuyama, and Habermas base their critique makes their task more difficult. Because their argument suggests that ethical thinking is already threatened, new technologies only serve to exacerbate the threat to the nature/artifice distinction. This leaves the reader wondering whether it is already too late to mount a critique of reprogenetics or, alternately, whether these concerns have been overstated. Neither response is particularly conducive to public engagement with the ethical dilemmas posed by these technologies—indeed, both would seem to beg the question of "why bother?"

33. See the essay "Tradition and the Modern Age" for Arendt's discussion of precisely how and why tradition no longer functions to guide thinking. Hannah Arendt, in *Between Past and Future: Eight Exercises in Political Thought* (New York: Viking, 1968), 17–40.

34. Hannah Arendt, "Personal Responsibility under Dictatorship," in *Responsibility and Judgment*, ed. Jerome Kohn (New York: Schocken, 2003), 27.

35. Arendt, "On Hannah Arendt," 336.

36. Hannah Arendt, "Understanding and Politics," in *Essays in Understanding: 1930–1954*, ed. J. Kohn (New York: Harcourt Brace, 1994), 310. Also Hannah Arendt, *The Origins of Totalitarianism* (New York: Harcourt Brace & Company, 1948), viii; hereafter *OT.*

37. Arendt, "Personal Responsibility under Dictatorship," 37.

38. Although Arendt admits that thinking is not itself a political activity, she is nonetheless attuned to its potential political effects. In calling for a move toward political rather than philosophical questions, I draw upon her overarching efforts (in *The Human Condition* and elsewhere) to recognize the importance of politics and the need to "think what we are doing." Hannah Arendt, *The Human Condition* (Chicago: University of Chicago Press, 1958), 5; hereafter *HC.*

39. Kimberly Curtis, "Hannah Arendt, Feminist Theorizing, and the Debate over New Reproductive Technologies," *Polity* (Winter 1995): 159–187, 185.

40. Hannah Arendt, *The Life of the Mind* (New York: Harcourt Brace & Company, 1971), 25, 32. Hereafter *LM.*

41. Indeed, Arendt is often understandably criticized for the rigidity of her concepts, their historical inaccuracy, and their inapplicability to modernity.

42. Haraway, "A Manifesto for Cyborgs," 66. In her essay "Toward an Agonistic Feminism: Hannah Arendt and the Politics of Identity," Bonnie Honig says that "Arendt herself would undoubtedly have been hostile to this [Honig's] radicalization of her work but I believe that . . . it is very much in

keeping with her politics." Bonnie Honig, in *Feminist Interpretations of Hannah Arendt*, ed. Bonnie Honig (University Park: Pennsylvania State University Press, 1995), 137. I have attempted to craft this paper along similar lines. I should be clear, then, that this is not an argument about Arendt's intentions or her own conception of modern technoscience. Instead, it is an argument in favor of a way of *interpreting* her work—using it as the material out of which we might craft something new.

43. I would argue that the latter comportment makes public discussions of genetic technologies easier because it aligns more closely with the mode of inquiry of many scientists. Whereas the defensive posture puts critics at odds with their subject of inquiry, the latter comportment enables a critique of genetics more akin to literary criticism—in which the critique is motivated by a love of the object of inquiry (literature) that is shared by both critics and practitioners (authors). As Don Ihde argues, modeling critiques of science and technology after literary criticism might enable a far different relationship between science and its skeptics. See Don Ihde, "Why Not Science Critics?" *International Studies in Philosophy* (1997).

44. Arendt, "Understanding and Politics," 310. The attempt to articulate the resources Arendt might offer for a contemporary critique of reprogenetics has been made by others, most notably Kimberly Curtis in her thought-provoking essay "Hannah Arendt, Feminist Theorizing, and the Debate over New Reproductive Technologies." Maren Klawiter offers another critique of in vitro fertilization, surrogate motherhood, and genetic engineering from an Arendtian perspective. Klawiter uses Heidegger to critique these technologies and turns to Arendt only at the end of her piece to suggest that the rejection of earthbound existence Arendt chronicles should be read as "modern society's rejection of woman and . . . reproduction." See Maren Klawiter, "Using Arendt and Heidegger to Consider Feminist Thinking on Women and Reproductive/Infertility Technologies," *Hypatia* (Fall 1990): 65–89, 77. Because this interpretation raises the complicated question of Arendt's relationship to feminism writ large, I will leave aside Klawiter's critique, at least for the moment, and focus on Curtis's, which seems to constitute a far more defensible reading of Arendt.

45. *Physis* and *nomos* are usually translated as "nature" and "convention." Whether Habermas's and Fukuyama's are accurate interpretations of Aristotle is not the point here. However, I will suggest that Arendt, in her insistence on "natural processes," underscores the fact that *physis* is not a static concept but a state of activity.

46. Kass, "The Wisdom of Repugnance," 24.

47. In *The Attack of the Blob*, Hanna Pitkin argues that Arendt's understanding of nature undergoes a full-scale transformation between the writing

of Varnhagen's biography. See Hannah Arendt, *Rahel Varnhagen: The Life of a Jewess*, ed. Liliane Weissberg, trans. Richard and Clara Winston (Baltimore, Md.: Johns Hopkins University Press, 1997), hereafter *RV;* and *The Human Condition.* In keeping with the chronological structuring of her book and its focus on the concept of the social, Pitkin suggests that Arendt shifts from articulating nature as something opposed to society to understanding it as part and parcel of the social. Hanna Pitkin, *The Attack of the Blob: Hannah Arendt's Concept of the Social* (Chicago: University of Chicago Press, 1998), 76. I would suggest that this earlier understanding of nature does not disappear altogether but is instead overlaid with other conceptions.

48. As Curtis notes, this experience of the majesty of nature contributes to "a very fundamental sense of belonging to the earth." Curtis, "Hannah Arendt," 183.

49. We can read these various conceptions as simply incoherent—yet more evidence of Arendt's impossibly paradoxical understanding of the human condition. Or (perhaps and) we can recognize that these inconsistencies are themselves reflective of the multidimensionality of the concept—the fact that it changes shape depending on the perspective from which one engages it.

50. See also Hannah Arendt, "What Is Freedom?" in *Between Past and Future: Eight Exercises in Political Thought* (New York: Viking, 1968), 144. Hereafter *WF.*

51. Mary Dietz provides a useful overview of "feminist receptions" of Arendt's work and this oft-cited criticism on the part of thinkers like Adrienne Rich and Mary O'Brian. See Mary Dietz, "Feminist Receptions of Hannah Arendt," in *Feminist Interpretations of Hannah Arendt*, ed. Bonnie Honig (University Park: Pennsylvania State University Press, 1995).

52. Note that in these artificially natural processes of human history, nature and artifice are always already intersecting.

53. There are many affinities between Arendt's discussion of the pitfalls of historiography and her critique of technoscience (c.f., Hannah Arendt, "The Concept of History," in *Between Past and Future: Eight Exercises in Political Thought* [New York: Viking, 1968]), but I cannot address them fully in the space I have here. In another paper, "From Telescope to PCR: Arendt on How We Use Our Tools," I argue that we can extract from her mode of historiography a way of thinking technoscience that resists the pull of process.

54. That one of Arendt's more extensive discussions of natural processes can be found in the essay "What Is Freedom?," which is prefaced with a concern not about totalitarianism but modern science, shows that for Arendt the questions of politics, freedom, science, and technology are all intertwined. Bringing these concerns about freedom to questions of reprogenetics

is partially what I mean when I advocate a political comportment toward this phenomenon.

55. Natural processes are also involved in action (especially with regard to modern technoscience). More on this later.

56. For her, the problem with conceptions of human nature is threefold. First, the very idea of a human nature implies that this nature is immutable—incapable of being changed. Given her experience with totalitarianism, Arendt argues that this is a false hope. Above all, her works suggest "we can, with a frightening degree of ease, adjust ourselves to ignoble conditions." Curtis, "Hannah Arendt," 176. Second, Arendt believes that, even if something like a human nature did exist, it would be unknowable to any but a god—someone or something that is itself not human (*HC*, 10). Third, and most important for our purposes, the idea of human nature can interfere with our ability to understand events and phenomena. In *The Origins of Totalitarianism*, Arendt argues that the assumption that human beings act on the basis of rational interests blinded observers to the significance of totalitarian propaganda (*OT*, 347). Because observers assumed that both Hitler and the masses would act on this basis, they were unprepared to confront "the lack of self-interest of masses who are quite prepared to sacrifice themselves" (*OT*, 348). This "anti-utilitarian" behavior thus "introduced into politics an element of unheard-of unpredictability" (*OT*, 347). While these observations may seem far removed from her discussion of human nature in *The Human Condition*, they offer a prime example of how preconceived categories imposed onto a phenomenon function to obscure what is really happening. Moreover, Arendt's discussion of human nature highlights that it is often the *attribution* of naturalness, not its factuality, that is the target of Arendt's critique.

57. Automation, the third of Arendt's stages, is rapidly coming to an end, she suggests, with the advent of the atom bomb, and modern technoscience represents both the culmination and the overcoming of this last stage (*HC*, 149).

58. Habermas, *The Future of Human Nature*, 72.

59. Arendt uses this phrase in the context of her discussion of the social—that sphere in which the matters of the household (*oikos*) become public. Nonetheless, it suggests that "*animal laborans* is the accomplice of a nature that threatens the man-made world, not with natural decay, but with an unnatural growth." Linda Zerilli, "The Arendtian Body," in *Feminist Interpretations of Hannah Arendt*, ed. Bonnie Honig (University Park: Pennsylvania State University Press, 1995), 176.

60. Pitkin, *The Attack of the Blob*, 74.

61. Fukuyama, *Our Posthuman Future*, 119.

62. Curtis, "Hannah Arendt," 179.

63. Habermas, *The Future of Human Nature*, 62.

64. Curtis, "Hannah Arendt," 160.

65. Take, for example, Habermas's insistence on the "authorship" of one's own life story. Whereas Arendt recognizes that stories are told by others about an individual's words and deeds and refuses the terminology of "authorship" (*HC*, 186, 184), Habermas places considerable importance on the ability of an individual to construct his/her *own* life history. He sees this ability as central to the development of personal identity (Habermas, *The Future of Human Nature*, 59).

66. This interpretation is obviously complicated by Habermas's insistence on the need for debate and discussion surrounding reprogenetics. Because he wants these questions to be subject to the decision-making processes of a liberal constitutional state, he cannot tell his readers how to think and act (as Kass and Fukuyama do) but only encourage them to do so.

67. Curtis, "Hannah Arendt," 160.

68. Ibid., 172.

69. Curtis articulates this difference in the following manner. For her, birth control, sterilization, and abortion function to protect us from nature's compulsion—"giv[ing] women respite from life's tyranny in favor of a less biology-driven existence" ("Hannah Arendt," 178). In vitro fertilization, artificial insemination, surrogate motherhood, and genetic engineering, on the other hand, import natural processes into the human artifice, thereby constituting technoscientific actions. In this way, they intensify the "tyranny of natural processes" to which women are subject (179). I should be clear that Curtis's attempt to enable a feminist critique of new reproductive technologies that does not inhibit a woman's right to an abortion is an important one. All too often the debates surrounding abortion and reproductive technologies are aligned in ways that are detrimental to both. Habermas provides a convincing critique of the attempts to elide the differences between abortion and genetic technologies in *The Future of Human Nature*, 23–29.

70. Curtis, "Hannah Arendt," 159, 178.

71. Although Arendt does assert that *homo faber*'s activities, from the perspective of nature, are just as destructive those of *animal laborans.* "From the viewpoint of nature, it is work rather than labor that is destructive, since the work processes take matter out of nature's hands without giving it back to her in the swift course of the natural metabolism of the living body" (*HC*, 100).

72. In this sense, the human artifice is inherently "frail" (*HC*, 188)—requiring protection from both labor and action. This interpretation might suggest that Arendt sees the human artifice as a static entity that is continually assaulted by both labor's processes and action's unpredictability. As I will

argue later, I think this is a problematic and unproductive interpretation. Because the world is built through the manipulation of natural things and is constituted by speech and action, it is always already intertwined with both labor and action. This latter interpretation suggests that the boundary separating nature from artifice is inherently porous.

73. For her, Arendt's work "reveals a vision of what it means to live a fully human life in which our experiences of nature's necessity and our distinctively human capabilities exist in a difficult tension, a tension Arendt regards as a necessary precondition for human freedom and self-determination" (Curtis, "Hannah Arendt," 172). Absent this tension, we are unable to recognize ourselves as "subject to" necessity. "What we lose, then, is not necessity, but the bearings by which we are able to distinguish between freedom and necessity" (ibid., 185).

74. Interestingly, Habermas makes a similar move in his discussion of Arendt. Praising her emphasis on the importance of natality, Habermas argues that birth represents a beginning we cannot control (*The Future of Human Nature*, 58). It thereby functions as both a "divide" and a "bridge" between nature and culture that he sees as necessary to the adult's ability to distinguish his own self-determined actions from those imposed by necessity (59). "It is only by referring to this difference between nature and culture, between beginnings not at our disposal, and the plasticity of historical practices that the acting subject may proceed to the self-ascriptions without which he could not perceive himself as the initiator of his actions and aspirations" (ibid.). Although he is right to see natality as a crucial contribution of Arendt's thinking to work on reprogenetics, this insistence on the divide represented by birth highlights the extent to which he remains mired in the nature/artifice dualism. If we understand Arendt as beginning with the premise of interconnection, the idea of a birth as a "divide" or a "bridge" (ibid.) is incoherent because there are no two things to be bridged. Just as Curtis's focus on natality distracts from the far more interesting question about how reprogenetics affects our conceptions of plurality, so too does Habermas's.

75. E.g., Hannah Arendt, "Truth and Politics," in *Between Past and Future: Eight Exercises in Political Thought* (New York: Viking, 1968).

76. Curtis, "Hannah Arendt," 187. Importantly, Curtis never enlists the state in what remains an effort to "fully theorize" the challenges posed by new reproductive technologies (ibid.). She has far too great an understanding of the "myriad of unjust patriarchal legal, political, and social practices" sanctioned by state regulation to make this move (ibid.). In this sense, hers lacks the more empirical attempt at shoring up this barrier we located in Kass, Fukuyama, and Habermas's works.

77. Ibid., 176.

78. Reprogenetic technologies have yet to acquire the kind of widespread acceptance (and understanding) that characterizes these first three technologies.

79. Curtis, "Hannah Arendt," 161.

80. Note that this question assumes none of the defensiveness that characterizes inquiries about the status of the nature/artifice distinction. It has no predetermined answer and does not require a stance on whether human nature is ever a useful conceptual construct.

81. Indeed, totalitarianism represents a monstrous failure on the part of both thinkers and the masses to engage in this crucial activity.

82. See also *HC*, 137, 167, 173, 182, 191; *LM*, 170, 178, 201; "Truth in Politics," 257, *passim*. I explore these stabilizing forces and the activity of taking our bearings elsewhere.

83. What is important to recognize, however, is that conceptual constructs like the nature/artifice dualism can only ever offer "isolated islands of certainty in an ocean of uncertainty" (*HC*, 244). Precisely because of the unpredictability of action, "guideposts" are never fixed. They are neither immune to change nor safe from destruction. For Arendt, the realm of human affairs is inherently "frail," and orienting ourselves within it can be an arduous and confusing task (*HC*, 188).

84. The extent to which Arendt's understanding of the difference between the world and the earth is premised on Heidegger's thinking is a question to which I cannot do justice here. However, it is interesting to note, as Dana Villa does, that a Heideggerian understanding of the world places even more importance on the relationships between human beings. Dana Villa, *Arendt and Heidegger: The Fate of the Political* (Princeton, N.J.: Princeton University Press, 1996), 122.

85. In her discussions of totalitarianism, Arendt suggests that it was this phenomena's ability to isolate individuals—thereby disrupting this web of interrelationships—that made it so fundamentally disorienting (*OT*, 474).

86. As Curtis recognizes, this distinction has been used to legitimize a great many practices and prejudices of which we may wish to rid ourselves (Curtis, "Hannah Arendt," 187). In her "Cyborg Manifesto," Donna Haraway celebrates the demise of distinctions like nature and artifice for precisely this reason. In her work she, too, suggests that technologies like pacemakers and insulin pumps, which appropriate and regulate the so-called natural activities of the body, challenge our ability to distinguish between the "natural and artificial . . . self-developing and externally-designed" (69). But her attitude toward the blurring of this distinction is one of appreciation rather than apprehension. There is an element of pride in her proclamation that "by the late twentieth century, our time, a mythic time, we are all chimeras, theorized

and fabricated hybrids of machine and organism; in short, we are cyborgs" (167). Although these examples fail to grasp Arendt's understanding of "producing" nature, Haraway nonetheless offers a good reason for why we might not wish to hold on so tenaciously to the nature/artifice dualism. Because dualisms like nature and artifice carry with them a hierarchical ordering whereby one side is accorded epistemic precedence over the other, Haraway connects their dismantling to an emancipatory project.

87. Arendt's conception of plurality seems particularly well suited to discussions of reprogenetics, given that the human genome itself rests on a similar duality—it is both what is common to all humans (as opposed to other species) and what differentiates each individual from every other. It is this latter quality of the genome—its uniqueness to every human being—that enables the widespread use of DNA for identification purposes.

88. Habermas, *The Future of Human Nature*, 52.

89. Ibid., 62.

90. In particular, I remain unconvinced that the relationship between parent and child is the most useful one for thinking about the political implications of reprogenetics. Because this relationship is always asymmetrical, it seems an odd one to use as the basis for a critique of how reprogenetics affects "interaction" in "an intersubjectively shared lifeworld" (Habermas, *The Future of Human Nature*, 34).

91. Cf. note 73 for a discussion of Habermas's use of Arendt's conception of natality. Given space constraints, I cannot go into greater detail as to how reprogenetics might alter conceptions of natality other than to say that these concerns are intricately linked to the condition of plurality and the concern for freedom. "Seen from the viewpoint of the automatic processes which seem to determine the course of the world, [action] looks like a miracle. In the language of natural science, it is the 'infinite improbability which occurs regularly'" (*HC*, 246). Natality is for Arendt a way of naming the miraculous—the fact that each new person by virtue of their distinctiveness is capable of beginning something new (*HC*, 247). Whether reprogenetics, by attempting to control this beginning, affects our conceptions of natality is therefore a question for another day, but the attempt to control the unpredictable should not go unnoticed.

92. It is also possible to understand genetic variation in terms of diversity—whereby differences are treated merely as differences, absent a hierarchical ordering. This is how many scientists would describe the term. Precisely because reprogenetic technologies have the potential to redefine conceptions of disease and disability (see Ruth Hubbard and Elijah Wald, *Exploding the Gene Myth: How Genetic Information Is Produced and Manipulated by Scientists, Physicians, Employers, Insurance Companies, Educators, and Law Enforcers* [Boston:

Beacon, 1999], 58), they are ripe for debate, and this phenomenon appears differently depending on the perspective from which it is engaged.

93. See Eric Parens and Adrienne Asch, eds. *Prenatal Testing and Disability Rights* (Washington, D.C.: Georgetown University Press, 2000).

94. Jacqueline Stevens, "Racial Meanings and Scientific Methods: Changing Policies for NIH-Sponsored Publications Reporting Human Variation," *Journal of Health Politics, Policy, and Law* 28, no. 6 (December 2003): 1033–1087.

95. Fukuyama, *Our Posthuman Future*, 10; Curtis, "Hannah Arendt," 180.

96. Hubbard and Wald, *Exploding the Gene Myth*, 58.

97. Discussions of asymptomatic and presymptomatic individuals—those who do not manifest any phenotypic symptoms but are nonetheless known to have the genetic sequences associated with diseases like Huntington's—underscore the fact that molecular differences have become increasingly important to conceptions of disease.

98. Hannah Arendt, "The Conquest of Space and the Stature of Man," in *Between Past and Future: Eight Exercises in Political Thought* (New York: Viking, 1968), 270. Arendt's mistrust of scientific language is based on its use of mathematics. For her, mathematics is a "non-spatial symbolic language" (*HC*, 265) that "overrules the testimony . . . of the senses" (*HC*, 267). It is based in abbreviations and symbol and "contains statements that can in no way be translated back into speech" (*HC*, 4).

99. Curtis, "Hannah Arendt," 179.

100. It is precisely because the "relevance of speech is at stake" that Arendt insists that technoscience is "a political question of the first order and therefore can hardly be left to the decision of professional scientists or professional politicians" (*HC*, 3).

5. POTENTIALITIES OF SECOND NATURE: AGAMBEN ON HUMAN RIGHTS

Ayten Gündoğdu

1. See, among others, Seyla Benhabib, *The Rights of Others: Aliens, Residents, and Citizens* (Cambridge: Cambridge University Press, 2004); Saskia Sassen, "The Repositioning of Citizenship: Emergent Subjects and Spaces for Politics," *Berkeley Journal of Sociology* 46 (2002): 4–26; and Yasemin Soysal, *Limits of Citizenship: Migrants and Postnational Membership in Europe* (Chicago: University of Chicago Press, 1994).

2. Perry Anderson, "*Force and Consent*," *New Left Review* 17 (September–October 2002): 5–30.

3. Wendy Brown, "'The Most We Can Hope For . . .': Human Rights and the Politics of Fatalism," *South Atlantic Quarterly* 103, no. 2/3 (Spring/Summer 2004): 451–463.

4. David Kennedy, "The International Human Rights Movement: Part of the Problem?" *Harvard Human Rights Journal* 15 (2002): 101–125, 103.

5. See the introduction to this volume.

6. Miriam Ticktin, "Where Ethics and Politics Meet: The Violence of Humanitarianism in France," *American Ethnologist* 33, no.1 (February 2006): 33–49; see also Miriam Ticktin, *Casualties of Care: Immigration and the Politics of Humanitarianism in France* (Berkeley: University of California Press, 2011).

7. In fact, Ticktin's theoretical framework draws on Agamben's work significantly. For another Agamben-inspired analysis of the problematical effects of a humanitarianism centered on suffering bodies, see Didier Fassin, "Compassion and Repression: The Moral Economy of Immigration Policies in France," *Cultural Anthropology* 20, no. 3 (August 2005): 362–387.

8. Giorgio Agamben, *Homo Sacer: Sovereign Power and Bare Life*, trans. Daniel Heller-Roazen (Stanford, Calif.: University of Stanford Press, 1998). Hereafter *HS*.

9. Ticktin, "Where Ethics and Politics Meet," 42.

10. Michel Foucault, *The History of Sexuality, Volume 1: An Introduction*, trans. Robert Hurley (New York: Vintage, 1988), 143; *"Society Must Be Defended:" Lectures at the Collége de France*, trans. David Macey (New York: Picador, 2003), 241.

11. Agamben's appropriation of Foucault's "biopower" in these terms has been criticized particularly for its dehistoricization and overgeneralization; see Peter Fitzpatrick, "These Mad Abandon'd Times," *Economy and Society* 30, no. 2 (May 2001): 255–270; and Katia Genel, "The Question of Biopower: Foucault and Agamben," *Rethinking Marxism* 18, no. 1 (January 2006): 43–62.

12. See Carl Schmitt, *Political Theology: Four Chapters on the Concept of Sovereignty*, trans. George Schwab (Chicago: University of Chicago Press, 2005), 5.

13. For an analysis of Benjamin's concept, see Anton Schütz, "Thinking the Law with and against Luhmann, Legendre, Agamben," *Law and Critique* 11 (2000): 107–136, 122–126. For a critique of Agamben's appropriation of Benjamin without attending to the implications of his historical materialism, see Jean-Philippe Deranty, "Agamben's Challenge to Normative Theories of Modern Rights," *borderlands e-journal* 3, no. 1 (2004).

14. For a careful analysis showing the problems of reading *bios/zoē* as a dichotomous conceptual pair defining not only Aristotle's work but also the Greek polis, see James Gordon Finlayson, "'Bare Life' and Politics in Agamben's Reading of Aristotle," *Review of Politics*, 72, no. 1 (Winter 2010): 97–126.

15. For a further analysis, see particularly Andrew Norris, "Introduction: Giorgio Agamben and the Politics of the Living Dead," in *Politics, Metaphysics, and Death: Essays on Giorgio Agamben's* Homo Sacer, ed. Andrew Norris (Durham, N.C.: Duke University Press, 2005), 1–30.

16. Agamben analyzes this process of separation, isolation, and inclusive exclusion in terms of the workings of an "anthropological machine" in Giorgio Agamben, *The Open: Man and Animal*, trans. Kevin Attell (Stanford, Calif.: Stanford University Press, 2004).

17. See also Giorgio Agamben, *Means without Ends: Notes on Politics*, trans. Vincenzo Binetti and Cesare Casarino (Minneapolis: University of Minnesota Press, 2000), 20. Hereafter *MWE*.

18. Several times in *Homo Sacer*, Agamben reminds his readers that "bare life" is not natural life; bare life is produced only when the politicization of natural life leaves certain categories of living beings at the threshold of natural and political and exposes them to violence at this "no-man's land between the home and the city" (see *HS*, 90). By using phrases such as "bare natural life," particularly in the section on the inauguration of modern biopolitics with rights declarations, Agamben blurs his own distinction. Instead of reading this conceptual confusion as an inconsistency on the part of the author, it might be possible to think of it as a manifestation of how modern biopolitics blurs conventional distinctions by an unprecedented politicization of life.

19. For Arendt's critical analysis of the "rights of man," see, in particular, Hannah Arendt, *The Origins of Totalitarianism* (New York: Harcourt, [1951] 1973), 290–302; *On Revolution* (London: Penguin, [1963] 1990), 107–109, 148–149; and "'The Rights of Man': What Are They?" *Modern Review* 3, no. 1 (1949): 25–37.

20. See Arendt, *The Origins of Totalitarianism*, 296–297. I discuss Arendt's approach to human rights elsewhere; see Ayten Gündoğdu, "'Perplexities of the Rights of Man': Arendt on the Aporias of Human Rights," *European Journal of Political Theory* 11, no. 1 (January 2012): 4–24.

21. See Arendt, *The Origins of Totalitarianism*, 267–290.

22. Brown, "The Most We Can Hope For," 454.

23. Jacques Rancière, "Who Is the Subject of the Rights of Man?" *South Atlantic Quarterly* 103, no. 2/3 (Spring/Summer 2004): 297–310, 307.

24. Foucault, *Society Must Be Defended*, 248.

25. Judith Butler, *Precarious Life: The Powers of Mourning and Violence* (London: Verso, 2004), 89, 91.

26. See also Giorgio Agamben, *State of Exception*, trans. Kevin Attell (Chicago: University of Chicago Press, 2005), 88. Hereafter *SE*.

27. Deranty also uses the term "counternarrative" in his analysis of Agamben, though without fully exploring its methodological implications; see Deranty, "Agamben's Challenge to Normative Theories of Modern Rights."

28. Giorgio Agamben, *The Signature of All Things: On Method*, trans. Luca D'Isanto and Kevin Attell (New York: Zone, 2009), 9.

29. See in particular Philippe Mesnard, "The Political Philosophy of Giorgio Agamben: A Critical Examination," trans. Cyrille Guiat, *Totalitarian Movements and Political Religions* 5, no. 1 (Summer 2004): 139–157; Mark Mazower, "Foucault, Agamben: Theory and the Nazis," *boundary 2* 35, no. 1 (Spring 2008): 23–34. For a careful analysis (and defense) of Agamben's approach to history, see in particular Leland de la Durantaye, *Giorgio Agamben: A Critical Introduction* (Stanford, Calif.: Stanford University Press, 2009), chap. 6.

30. There is now a burgeoning secondary literature on Agamben's work, and it is impossible to provide here a comprehensive list of all of his critics—let alone present their criticisms in all their complexity. Many critics, however, have resorted to conceptual resources of alternative theoretical traditions to contest Agamben: There are, for instance, several Foucaultian accounts that criticize Agamben's use and abuse of "biopower"; see, among others, Fitzpatrick, "These mad abandon'd times"; Genel, "The Question of Biopower"; and Paul Patton, "Agamben and Foucault on Biopower and Biopolitics," in *Giorgio Agamben: Sovereignty and Life*, ed. Matthew Calarco and Steven DeCaroli (Stanford, Calif.: Stanford University Press, 2007), 203–218. Furthermore, Agamben's account of "potentiality" and "power" has been subjected to critical scrutiny by Antonio Negri, who draws on Spinoza. See Antonio Negri, "Giorgio Agamben: The Discreet Taste of the Dialectic," in *Giorgio Agamben: Sovereignty and Life*, 109–125; and Cesare Casarino and Antonio Negri, "It's a Powerful Life: A Conversation on Contemporary Philosophy," *Cultural Critique* 57 (Spring 2004): 151–183. Agamben's analysis of "sovereignty" has also been criticized from different theoretical perspectives: William Connolly counters Agamben's account of sovereignty by turning to thinkers such as Tocqueville and Gilles Deleuze. See William Connolly, "The Complexities of Sovereignty," in *Giorgio Agamben: Sovereignty and Life*, 23–42. In a similar vein, Andreas Kalyvas criticizes Agamben's failure to analyze the "multiple forms and rich democratic potentials of sovereign politics" and offers an alternative account of political power by drawing on Plato's "weaving" metaphors. See Andreas Kalyvas, "The Sovereign Weaver: Beyond the Camp," in *Politics, Metaphysics, and Death: Essays on Giorgio Agamben's* Homo Sacer, 107–134, 118. My critique shares with these analysts, particularly with Connolly and Kalyvas, a commitment to an analysis of sovereign

power that emphasizes its heterogeneous, contingent, and unforeseeable potentials. I also suggest that the political effects of human rights cannot be captured within the singular logic attributed by Agamben to biopolitical sovereignty. However, I propose to offer this critique not by turning to different theoretical traditions but by reading Agamben against Agamben. In other words, I am interested in putting into use some of the tensions and paradoxes in Agamben's own account of sovereign power.

31. See Jean-Luc Nancy, *The Birth to Presence*, trans. B. Holmes et al. (Stanford, Calif.: Stanford University Press, 1993), 43–44; Benjamin S. Pryor, "Law in Abandon: Jean-Luc Nancy and the Critical Study of Law," *Law and Critique* 15, no. 3 (January 2004): 259–285; and Igor Stramignoni, "When Law Stands Still: Land Contracts in English Law and Law's 'Abandonment' of Everyday Life," *Law and Critique* 12, no. 2 (May 2001): 105–134.

32. For an analysis criticizing Agamben's poststatist move and insisting instead on the state, see Paul Passavant, "The Contradictory State of Giorgio Agamben," *Political Theory* 35, no. 2 (April 2007): 147–174. For an elaboration of Agamben's response to such institutionalist strategies, see Nasser Hussain and Melissa Ptacek, "Thresholds: Sovereignty and the Sacred," *Law and Society Review* 34, no. 2 (2000): 495–515, 511–512.

33. Of particular interest are Agamben's critical reflections on Derrida's reading of Kafka's "Before the Law" (*HS*, 49–62). See also the essays in Giorgio Agamben, *Potentialities*, ed. Daniel Heller-Roazen (Stanford, Calif.: Stanford University Press, 1999); hereafter *P.* See especially "The Messiah and the Sovereign: The Problem of Law in Walter Benjamin" (*P*, 160–174) and "*Pardes:* The Writing of Potentiality" (*P*, 205–219). For a detailed analysis of the differences between Agamben and Derrida on these issues, see Catherine Mills, *The Philosophy of Agamben* (Montréal: McGill-Queen's University Press, 2002), 121–122; and "Agamben's Messianic Politics: Biopolitics, Abandonment and Happy Life," *Contretemps* 5 (2004): 42–62; Adam Thurschwell, "Specters of Nietzsche: Potential Futures for the Concept of the Political in Agamben and Derrida," *Cardozo Law Review* 24, no. 3 (March 2003): 1193–1259.

34. William Connolly has also criticized Agamben for imposing a stringent "logic," constituted of "ironclad paradoxes," on sovereignty; see Connolly, "The Complexities of Sovereignty," 30. Although I do agree with the main arguments of Connolly's critique, I also want to add that the imposition of this "logic" is indeed in tension with some of the premises of Agamben's own theory.

35. Max Horkheimer and Theodor W. Adorno, *Dialectic of Enlightenment: Philosophical Fragments*, ed. Gunzelin Schmid Noerr, trans. Edmund Jephcott (Stanford, Calif.: Stanford University Press, 2002), 8.

36. Aristotle, *The Metaphysics*, trans. Hugh Lawson-Tancred (London: Penguin, 1998), 259.

37. David E. Johnson, "As *If* the Time Were Now: Deconstructing Agamben," *South Atlantic Quarterly* 106, no. 2 (Spring 2007): 265–290, 285.

38. Jessica Whyte, "'I Would Prefer Not To': Giorgio Agamben, Bartleby, and the Potentiality of the Law," *Law and Critique* 20, no. 3 (November 2009): 309–324, 315.

39. See, among others, Leland de la Durantaye, "Agamben's Potential," *Diacritics* 30, no. 2 (Summer 2000): 3–24; Bruno Gullì, "The Ontology and Politics of Exception: Reflections on the Work of Giorgio Agamben," in *Giorgio Agamben: Sovereignty and Life*, 219–242; Whyte, "I Would Prefer Not To."

40. De la Durantaye, *Giorgio Agamben*, 245.

41. For analyses of *sans-papiers*, see, among others, Mireillo Rosello, "Representing Illegal Immigrants in France: From *Clandestins* to *L'affaire des Sans-papiers de Saint-Bernard*," *Journal of European Studies* 28, no. 1–2 (March 1998): 137–151; and Vincenzo Ruggiero, "The Fight to Reappear," *Social Justice* 27, no. 2 (Summer 2000): 45–60.

42. Cissé v. France, *Human Rights Case Digest* 13, no. 3–4 (2002): 311–313, 312.

43. Ruggiero, "The Fight to Reappear," 53.

44. Madjiguène Cissé, "The *Sans-Papiers:* A Woman Draws the First Lessons," in *We Are Everywhere: The Irresistible Rise of Global Anticapitalism*, ed. Notes from Nowhere (London: Verso, 2003), 43.

45. See ibid., 40.

46. For an insightful analysis of the unpredictable and plural temporalities of rights, see Bonnie Honig, *Emergency Politics: Paradox, Law, Democracy* (Princeton, N.J.: Princeton University Press, 2009), 55–56.

47. For an analysis of the indeterminacy of rights declarations, see especially Jacques Derrida, "Declarations of Independence," *New Political Science* 15 (1986): 7–15; and Bonnie Honig, "Declarations of Independence: Arendt and Derrida on the Problem of Founding a Republic," *American Political Science Review* 85, no. 1 (March 1991): 97–113.

48. For other analyses pointing out how rights declarations can be reappropriated in ways contesting their given formulations, see, among others, Étienne Balibar, "What Is a Politics of the Rights of Man?" in *Masses, Classes, Ideas: Studies on Politics and Philosophy before and after Marx* (New York: Routledge, 1994), 205–225; Jacques Rancière, *Dis-agreement: Politics and Philosophy* (Minneapolis: University of Minnesota Press, 1999; 2004); and Joan Wallach Scott, *Only Paradoxes to Offer: French Feminists and the Rights of Man* (Cambridge, Mass.: Harvard University Press, 1996).

49. For a critique of this fatalistic pragmatism in the case of human rights, see Brown, "The Most We Can Hope For." The target of Brown's criticism is Michael Ignatieff's minimalist defense of a politics of human rights in *Human Rights as Politics and Idolatry*, ed. Amy Gutmann (Princeton, N.J.: Princeton University Press, 2001).

6. THE UTOPIAN CONTENT OF REIFICATION: ADORNO'S CRITICAL SOCIAL THEORY OF NATURE
Christopher Buck

1. Axel Honneth, *The Critique of Power: Reflective Stages in a Critical Social Theory* (Cambridge, Mass.: MIT Press, 1991), xix. While Honneth is referring to the German reception of Adorno, his comment holds true for the secondary literature on Adorno in English as well. See Romand Coles, "Ecotones and Ecological Ethics: Adorno and Lopez," in *The Nature of Things: Language, Politics, and the Environment*, ed. J. Bennett and W. Chaloupka (Minneapolis: University of Minnesota Press, 1993), 226–249; and chap. 5 of Andrew Biro, *Denaturalizing Ecological Politics: Alienation from Nature from Rousseau to the Frankfurt School and Beyond* (Toronto: University of Toronto Press, 2005), 117–159.

2. Theodor W. Adorno, "On Subject and Object," in *Critical Models: Interventions and Catchwords* (New York: Columbia University Press, 1998), 245–258, 247.

3. Honneth, *The Critique of Power*, xxi.

4. A noteworthy exception is the ecosocialism of the Green Party activist Joel Kovel, who shares the concern that "few today even bother to think about the kinds of society that could replace the present with one of ecological rationality, and most of that speculation is within a green paradigm limited by an insufficient appreciation of the regime of capital and of the depths needed for real change." See Joel Kovel, *The Enemy of Nature: The End of Capitalism or the End of the World?* (London: Zed, 2002), 222–223.

5. Adorno's indebtedness to Marxian value theory has been obscured in E. B. Ashton's English translation of *Negative Dialectics*, which renders the German term *Ware* as "merchandise" instead of "commodity" and *Tausch* as "barter" rather than "exchange" (as in exchange value). Fredric Jameson suggests that these mistakes "might lead a paranoid to believe that this translation aimed precisely at producing a post- and non-Marxist Adorno 'for our time.'" See Fredric Jameson, *Late Marxism: Adorno, or the Persistence of the Dialectic* (London: Verso, 1990), x.

6. Steven Vogel, *Against Nature: The Concept of Nature in Critical Theory* (Albany, N.Y.: SUNY Press, 1996).

7. Jane Bennett, "The Force of Things: Steps toward an Ecology of Matter," *Political Theory* 32, no. 3 (June 2004): 347–372.

8. Jane Bennett, *The Enchantment of Modern Life: Attachments, Crossings, and Ethics* (Princeton, N.J.: Princeton University Press, 2001).

9. Bennett, "The Force of Things," 358.

10. An affinity exists between the motivations behind my reconstruction of Adorno's critical social theory of nature and Nikolas Kompridis' project of developing a "vision of critical theory that, in recognition of the various ways in which conditions of modernity obscure or foreclose our possibilities, conceives itself as a possibility-disclosing practice." See Nikolas Kompridis, *Critique and Disclosure: Critical Theory between Past and Future* (Cambridge, Mass.: MIT Press, 2006), xi.

11. Theodor W. Adorno, *Negative Dialectics* (New York: Continuum, 1973), xix.

12. Ibid., 6.

13. Ibid., 146. Translation amended.

14. Karl Marx, *Capital* (New York: Penguin, 1990), 1:126.

15. In various contexts, Bennett endorses the commercial art associated with all three of these commodities insofar as it grants nonhuman entities the power to act. See *The Enchantment of Modern Life*, 111–112; and "The Force of Things," 347, 356.

16. Marx, *Capital*, 1:127.

17. Ibid., 128.

18. For an earlier treatment of this concept, see Theodor W. Adorno, "The Idea of Natural-History," in *Things beyond Resemblance: Collected Essays on Theodor W. Adorno*, ed. Robert Hullot-Kentor (New York: Columbia University Press, 2006), 252–269.

19. Adorno, *Negative Dialectics*, 354–355. Translation amended.

20. Ibid, 355.

21. Theodor W. Adorno, *Minima Moralia* (London: Verso Press, 1978), 43–44.

22. Adorno, *Negative Dialectics*, 146–147. Translation amended, emphasis mine.

23. Ibid., 147. Translation amended.

24. Theodor W. Adorno, *Aesthetic Theory* (Minneapolis: University of Minnesota Press, 1998), 12.

25. Ibid., 33.

26. Ibid., 65.

27. Ibid., 69.

28. Ibid., 46. A better translation of *Mangel* would be "want," which would correspond to passages in *Negative Dialectics* where Adorno notes the

"absurdity that real want [*Mangel*] is continuing in a society whose state of production no longer admits the plea that there are not enough goods to go around" and where he envisions a world in which "the productive forces are freed to the point where men will no longer be engulfed in a practice that want [*Mangel*] exacts from them." *Negative Dialectics*, 121, 244. Thanks to Peter Fenves for highlighting the awkwardness of the phrase "abolition of scarcity."

29. Vogel, *Against Nature*, 5.
30. Ibid., 3.
31. Ibid., 82.
32. Ibid., 83.
33. Ibid., 88.
34. Ibid., 87.
35. For a more empirically oriented defense of an argument similar to the one I am attributing to Adorno, see Andre Gorz, *Reclaiming Work: Beyond the Wage-Based Society* (Cambridge: Polity Press, 1999).
36. Vogel, *Against Nature*, 93.
37. Ibid., 193.
38. Ibid., 89.
39. Ibid., 94.
40. Adorno, *Aesthetic Theory*, 12.
41. Vogel, *Against Nature*, 95.
42. My critique of Vogel's philosophy of practice parallels and is indebted to Moishe Postone's critique of what he refers to as "traditional Marxism," which treats labor as the standpoint rather than the object of its critique of capitalism: "The result is a critique of . . . the lack of social recognition given to the unique significance of direct human labor as an element of production—rather than a critique of that labor and an analysis of the historical possibility that it be abolished." See Moishe Postone, *Time, Labor, and Social Domination: A Reinterpretation of Marx's Critical Theory* (Cambridge: Cambridge University Press, 1993), 70.
43. Steven Vogel, "Nature, Practice, Construction: Response to Critics," *Capitalism, Nature, Socialism* 9, no. 3 (September 1998): 35–40, 39.
44. Karl Marx, "For a Ruthless Criticism of Everything Existing" (letter to A. Ruge), in *The Marx-Engels Reader*, ed. Robert C. Tucker (New York: Norton, 1978), 12–15, 13.
45. Max Horkheimer and Theodor W. Adorno, *Dialectic of Enlightenment: Philosophical Fragments* (Stanford, Calif.: Stanford University Press, 2002), 191.
46. Jane Bennett, *The Enchantment of Modern Life*, 10.
47. Bennett, "The Force of Things," 349.

48. Ibid., 357.
49. Ibid., 365.
50. Ibid., 364.
51. Ibid., 362.
52. Adorno, *Negative Dialectics*, 197.
53. Bennett, *The Enchantment of Modern Life*, 19. Bennett then expresses reservations about "the pursuit of pure freedom" by turning to Kafka's tale of Rotpeter, the ape-man who found a way out of his cage (which is not to be confused with freedom) by acting human: "If freedom is the transcendence of power and external to a system of constraints, Rotpeter desires it not, for such isolation spells death." Ibid., 20.
54. Ibid., 89.
55. Ibid., 113.
56. Karl Marx, *Capital*, 1:164–165.
57. Bennett, *The Enchantment of Modern Life*, 113.
58. Ibid., 118.
59. Ibid., 121.
60. Ibid., 114.
61. Ibid., 113. Emphasis mine.
62. Ibid., 114.
63. Marx, *Capital*, 1:167–168.
64. Ibid., 1:153–154.
65. Bennett, *The Enchantment of Modern Life*, 116.
66. Marx, *Capital*, 1:174–175.
67. Adorno, *Negative Dialectics*, 4.
68. See Paul Hawken, Amory Lovins, and L. Hunter Lovins, *Natural Capitalism: Creating the Next Industrial Revolution* (Boston: Little, Brown and Company, 1999), 1.
69. Michael Shellenberger and Ted Nordhaus, "The Death of Environmentalism: Global Warming Politics in a Post-Environmental World," 7, 29–30. http://www.thebreakthrough.org/PDF/Death_of_Environmentalism.pdf.
70. Adorno, *Aesthetic Theory*, 319.
71. Ibid., 74.

7. FROM NATURE TO MATTER
Jane Bennett

1. Many of the themes in this essay, which was first given at the "Second Nature" conference at Northwestern University in 2007, have been developed in Jane Bennett, *Vibrant Matter: A Political Ecology of Things* (Durham, N.C.: Duke University Press, 2010). Rachel Carson, *Silent Spring* (Boston:

Houghton Mifflin, 1962); Garrett Hardin, "The Tragedy of the Commons," *Science* 162, no. 3859 (December 1968): 1244–1248; E. F. Schumacher, *Small Is Beautiful: Economics as If People Mattered* (New York: Harper Perennial, 2010); Henry David Thoreau, *Walden and Resistance to Civil Government*, ed. William Rossi (New York: Norton, 1992).

2. Immanuel Kant, *Critique of Judgment*, trans. Werner S. Pluhar (Indianapolis, Ind.: Hackett, 1987), #372, 251.

3. Friedrich Nietzsche, *The Will to Power* (New York: Random House, 1987), #1067, 550. Nietzsche's category of "Life" includes both organic and inorganic materialities.

4. Max Weber, "Science as a Vocation," in *From Max Weber: Essays in Sociology*, ed. H. H. Gerth and C. Wright Mills (Oxford: Oxford University Press, 1981), 139.

5. See the appendix of A. O. Lovejoy and G. Boas, *Primitivism and Related Ideas in Antiquity* (Baltimore, Md.: Johns Hopkins University Press, 1935); and A. O. Lovejoy, "Nature as Aesthetic Norm," in *Essays in the History of Ideas* (Baltimore, Md.: Johns Hopkins University Press, 1948), 69–78.

6. See Maurice Merleau-Ponty, *The Visible and the Invisible*, trans. Alfonso Lingis (Evanston, Ill.: Northwestern University Press, 1968). The history of political-theological-scientific thought in the West is full of battles over just what *kind* of "arrangement" nature is: Is the order of things fixed from the start or still evolving? Is there a telos to its evolution, or is its movement open-ended? Is the regularity and/or progress of nature a function of physicochemical laws or of divine will? Or, as Kant insists, regardless of the truth of things-in-themselves, must we humans, as a condition of our very thought, *conceive* of nature as a purposive order?

7. Spinoza, Part I (prop XXIX, Scholium) of *The Ethics:* "by 'Natura naturans' we must understand . . . the attributes of substance that express eternal and infinite essence; or . . . God in so far as he is considered a free cause. By 'Natura naturata' I understand all that follows from the necessity of God's nature, that is . . . all the modes of God's attributes in so far as they are considered as things . . ." See Baruch Spinoza, *Ethics, Treatise on the Emendation of the Intellect, and Selected Letters*, trans. Samuel Shirley, ed. Seymour Feldman (Indianapolis, Ind.: Hackett, 1992), 52.

8. This universal creativity requires a special sensibility to detect because, as Samuel Coleridge noted, process is "suspended and, as it were, quenched in the product [i.e., *natura naturata*.]" "On the Prometheus of Aeschylus," in *The Complete Works of Samuel Coleridge*, ed. James Marsh (London: Harper & Brothers, 1858), 354.

9. The sense of nature as a creative *process* was emphasized by Whitehead in his 1919 lectures at Trinity College: "when we seek definitely to express

the relations of events which arise from their spatio-temporal structure, we approximate to simplicity by progressively diminishing the extent . . . of the events considered. . . . We finally reach the idea of an event so restricted . . . as to be without extension in space or extension in time. Such an event is a mere spatial point-flash of instantaneous duration. I call such an ideal event an 'event-particle.' You must not think of the world as ultimately built up of event-particles. That is to put the cart before the horse. The world we know is a continuous stream of occurrence." See Alfred North Whitehead, *The Concept of Nature: Tarrner Lectures Delivered in Trinity College, November 1919* (Cambridge: Cambridge University Press, 1920), 172.

10. Gilles Deleuze and Felix Guattari, *A Thousand Plateaus: Capitalism and Schizophrenia*, trans. Brian Massumi (Minneapolis: University of Minnesota Press, 1987), 255.

11. I focus here on the vitalism of Bergson and Driesch, examining the latter-day vitalism of "the culture of life" in chapter 6 of *Vibrant Matter*.

12. Kant, *Critique of Judgment*, #394, 276.

13. Hans Driesch, *The Science and Philosophy of the Organism: The Gifford Lectures Delivered before the University of Aberdeen in the Year 1907* (London: Adam and Charles Black, 1908), 50, my emphasis. On this point, Driesch echoes Kant's claim that in judging *organized* beings, "we must always presuppose some original organization that itself *uses* mechanism" (*Critique of Judgment*, section 80, #418, 304, my emphasis).

14. Driesch retained the idea of a self-moving and self-altering power but rejected its peculiarly Aristotelian teleology. He does not elaborate on his differences with Aristotle and says only that he will retain Aristotle's idea that "there is at work a something in life phenomena 'which bears the end in itself.'" Driesch, *The Science and Philosophy of the Organism*, 144.

15. A blastocyst is the developmental stage of a fertilized egg when it has changed from a solid mass of cells into a hollow ball of cells around a fluid-filled cavity.

16. Driesch, *The Science and Philosophy of the Organism*, 79.

17. Hans Driesch, *The Problem of Individuality* (New York: Macmillan & Co., 1914), 38. In the vocabulary of today, it might be said that the stem cells have not yet been channeled into their respective "fate paths."

18. "According to our hypothesis . . . in each of the *n* cells the *same* great number of possibilities of becoming is physico-chemically prepared, but checked, so to say, by entelechy. Development of the system now depends, according to our assumption, upon the fact that entelechy *relaxes its suspensory power* and thus . . . in cell *a* one thing is allowed to occur, in cell *b* another, and in cell *c* something else; but what now actually occurs in *a* might also have occurred in *b* or *c*; for *each one* out of an enormous number of pos-

sibilities *may* occur in each cell. Thus, by the regulatory *relaxing* action of entelechy in a system in which an enormous variety of possible events had been suspended by it, it may happen that an *equal distribution* of *possibilities* is transformed into an *unequal distribution* of *actual effects*." Ibid., 39.

19. Driesch, *The Science and Philosophy of the Organism*, 180.

20. Mikhail Bakhtin, "Contemporary Vitalism," in *The Crisis in Modernism: Bergson and the Vitalist Controversy*, ed. Frederick Burwick and Paul Douglass (Cambridge: Cambridge University Press, 1992), 95–96. Bakhtin names this alternative machine image "modern dialectical materialism," in contrast to Driesch's "naive-mechanist point of view with its fixed and immovable machines" (96).

21. "*All reality is . . . tendency, if we agree to call tendency a nascent change of direction.*" See Henri Bergson, *The Creative Mind: An Introduction to Metaphysics*, trans. Mabelle Andison (New York: Citadel, 1974), 188.

22. Henri Bergson, *Creative Evolution* (Mineola, N.Y.: Dover, 1998), 132.

23. Ibid., 126. Also: "at the root of life there is an effort to engraft on to the necessity of physical forces the largest possible amount of *indetermination*" (114).

24. Ibid., 103.

25. Ibid., 51–52. Deleuze says that for Bergson "there is no 'goal,' because these directions . . . are themselves created 'along with' the act that runs through them." Gilles Deleuze, *Bergsonism*, trans. Hugh Tomlinson and Barbara Habberjam (New York: Zone, 1990), 106. Driesch offers a qualified endorsement of Bergson on this point, writing in a note in the second volume of the Gifford Lectures that "Bergson denies 'finalisme radical,' the term being understood, as far as I can see, in the sense of a general plan of the universe in every detail. At the end of this book we shall do the same. But Bergson also objects to 'finalite' as a principle of life; he puts his 'élan vital' in its place—granting that it resemble 'finalism' more than mechanism. . . . [This is because] Bergson only analyses phylogeny; in ontogeny *le tout est donne*—and *yet* there is 'vitalism.'" Driesch, *The Science and Philosophy of the Organism*, 313.

26. Bergson, *Creative Evolution*, 47.

27. Ralph Waldo Emerson, *Journals and Miscellaneous Notebooks: 1847–1848* (Cambridge, Mass.: Belknap, 1960), 10:335.

28. Michel Foucault, *The History of Sexuality, vol. 2: The Use of Pleasure*, trans. Robert Hurley (New York: Vintage, 1990), 8.

CRINA ARCHER is a Ph.D. candidate in Political Science at Northwestern University. She is completing a dissertation project that examines temporality in democratic political thought, with a focus on temporal representations of revolutionary change. She is coauthor of *Obstacles to Ethical Decision Making: Mental Models, Milgram, and the Problem of Obedience* (Cambridge University Press, 2013).

JANE BENNETT is Professor of Political Science at Johns Hopkins University and the editor of the journal *Political Theory*. Her recent books are *Vibrant Matter: A Political Ecology of Things* (Duke University Press, 2010) and *The Enchantment of Modern Life* (Princeton University Press, 2001).

ASHLEY BISER is Assistant Professor in the Politics and Government Department at Ohio Wesleyan University. She earned her Ph.D. in political science from the University of Minnesota. Her work focuses on the complex intersections between science, technology, and politics in the works of Hannah Arendt and Martin Heidegger.

CHRISTOPHER BUCK is Assistant Professor of Political Theory in the Department of Government at St. Lawrence University in Canton, N.Y. His current research focuses on how critical theory's method of immanent critique can disclose possibilities for ecological and social transformations during times of economic crisis.

LAURA EPHRAIM is Assistant Professor of Political Science at Williams College. Her research considers intersections between political theory, the history of science, and technofuturism.

AYTEN GÜNDOĞDU is Assistant Professor of Political Science at Barnard College–Columbia University. Her current research centers on human rights, immigration, and the political thought of Hannah Arendt. She has work published and forthcoming in *Contemporary Political Theory*, *European Journal of Political Theory*, and *Law, Culture, and the Humanities*.

Bonnie Honig is Sarah Rebecca Roland Professor of Political Science at Northwestern University and senior research professor at the American Bar Foundation in Chicago. She is the prizewinning author of *Political Theory and the Displacement of Politics* (Cornell University Press, 1993), *Democracy and the Foreigner* (Princeton University Press, 2001), *Emergency Politics: Paradox, Law, Democracy* (Princeton University Press, 2009), and *Antigone, Interrupted* (Cambridge University Press, 2013). She has edited or coedited *Feminist Interpretations of Hannah Arendt* (Penn State University Press, 1995), *Skepticism, Individuality and Freedom: The Reluctant Liberalism of Richard Flathman* (University of Minnesota Press, 2002), and the *Oxford Handbook of Political Thought* (Oxford University Press, 2006), and her work has been translated into Swedish, Spanish, Italian, French, Greek, and Japanese. She is currently working on a new project called *Public Things*, for the Thinking Out Loud series in Sydney, Australia.

Thomas Laqueur is Helen Fawcett Professor of History at the University of California, Berkeley. His current book project, *The Work of the Dead* (forthcoming), examines the relationship between death and modernity. His previous books include *Solitary Sex: A Cultural History of Masturbation* (Zone Books, 2003) and *Making Sex: Body and Gender from the Greeks to Freud* (Harvard University Press, 1990).

Lida Maxwell is Assistant Professor of Political Science at Trinity College. Her research interests include contemporary democratic theory, the history of political thought, and law and politics. She is currently working on a book about political trials. Her book project, *Public Trials*, explores the legal and political dilemmas that arise from the intersections between law and politics in several eighteenth-, nineteenth-, and twentieth-century political trials, as well as the implications of these dilemmas for contemporary political theory and practice.

Yves Winter is Assistant Professor of Political Science at the University of Minnesota. His research focuses on theories of violence, and he is currently working on a book manuscript on violence in the political thought of Niccolò Machiavelli.

INDEX